SKI JOY

THE STORY OF WINTER SPORTS

HARRY STONE

authorHOUSE®

AuthorHouse™ UK Ltd.
500 Avebury Boulevard
Central Milton Keynes, MK9 2BE
www.authorhouse.co.uk
Phone: 08001974150

Published by AuthorHouse 05/07/2012

ISBN: 978-1-4389-0116-9 (sc)

This book is printed on acid-free paper.

ACKNOWLEDGEMENTS

I would like particularly to acknowledge with thanks the help of: Elisabeth Hussey, Jo Evans and Judy Hillman for their advice; for the permission to include quotations given me by the family of Kenneth Foster, Peter Lunn and Mrs.James Riddell and the estates of Noël Coward and Paul Gallico; for the provision and permission to use photographs given me by the Ski Club of Great Britain, Sir Roger Gibbs and the St.Moritz (Cresta) Tobogganing Club, Count Maxmilian Lamberg, The Kandahar Review, The International Ski-ing History Association, The Swiss Tourist Office, The St.Anton Ski Museum and the Information Offices of Courchevel, Kitzbühel, St.Anton, St. Moritz, Zermatt, and Photograph Hugo of Val d'Isére.

CONTENTS

Chapter I Eccentric Pioneers 1860 - 1900   1

Conan Doyle and other indomitable British eccentrics - Commandeering the mountaineers' freezing hotels - Whymper's disaster on the Matterhorn - Grindelwald and the awesome North Face - Victorian lady water colourists - Village parochialism and Zermatt hostility - TB curing on Arosa balconies - Badrutt promotes St.Moritz - His guests skate and curl and adopt the luges used by the locals - An irksome journey and indifferent food - Bandy, ice hockey and cricket on skates - Primitive ski technique - Uncomfortable and inadequate clothing borrowed from the shooting moors.

Chapter II Society Decorum 1900 - 1914   23

Construction of the mountain railways brings society to St.Moritz - The development of luxury hotels and a special etiquette - Small chapels for worthy parsons - Mr. Burberry's invention gives women tailored skirts - English skiers introduce the Norwegian ski-ing style - Learning by the book and through the clubs - Ski elaborations: jumping and ski-joring - Curling, ice hockey and ski bikes - Bobs and skeletons split the lugers - English and Continental skaters; a matter of space - Gymkhanas, afternoon tea and diversions during the tedious evenings.

Chapter III The Boisterous Young Things 1921 - 1939   42

Aftermath of the Great War - Snobs and Sir Henry Lunn's travel agency - Commandeered mountain railways, funiculars and sobering experiences with cable cars - Emergence of the piste - The irrepressible racers at Mürren and Wengen - Racing becomes international and timing becomes faster - The start of ski schools and Schneider's Arlberg Crouch - Skis acquire metal edges and heel clamp bindings - Schneider, St.Anton's film star - Seiler's lavish launch party -Kitzbühel, a distinguished history - The Prince of Wales, accompanied by an unrecognised Mrs. Simpson, puts Kitzbühel on the map - Ladies start wearing ski trousers - The early Winter Olympics and Sonja Henie revolutionizes ice skating - Ski jumpers leap further through bending forwards - Aprés ski capers and moonlit parties - Skating and ski clothes discover fashion - A winter branch of the Olympics - Continental skating leads the English a dance - Ice hockey and ski jumping - Shadow of the Anschluss.

Chapter IV Happy Days Again 1947 - 1965   80

Wartime incidents and St.Anton's unorthodox resistance movement - Sentiment at the Oslo Olympics - A royal race broadens the field - Queen Juliana at St.Anton, the British Royals at Klosters and the Spanish at Courchevel - The small travel agents appear - Currency allowance and deceits turn the British into bores - The Combined Services Club - Night revellers leave their hotels - The White Rose Club of romance and the Krazy Kangaroo - Aprés ski dives - Grossly extravagant parties - Bands play simple songs - The British revive the Cresta and Bob - Continental skating sets the pace - French rotation revolutionizes ski technique - Short skis cause bumps - Metal skis, plastic boots and a change in fashion - The ski-lift revolution.

Chapter V The Midas Touch 1966 - 1987 97

Ski lifts form chains and circles - Piste culture, markers and blood curdling wagons - Social effect of ski lifts on ski schools and picnic lunches - Main resorts remain indifferent to scandalous queuing - Cornelius Starr and wealthy cable car owners - The aristocracy buy their chalets and ordinary Frenchmen follow suit - The birth and development of custom made resorts - Runs sculpted from the mountain and perfect piste maintenance - Mountain resort architecture, access roads and altiports - The razzmatazz marketing of new resorts and ski champions as promoters - Skiwear becomes chic - Plastic skis and safety bindings - Prizes and commercial values - Commercialism turns into nationalism - Changes in ski technique - Ski manufacturers finance racing teams and introduce advertising

Chapter VI Television Rules 118

Television seizes control - Skating leaves the villages for the cities - Ski jumping seeks the spectacular with ski-flying - Masses swarm onto the slopes - Inter-valley lift links, cable car and trams - Coupons, abonnements and plastic cards - Crowding encourages idiosyncratic types of ski-ing, freestyle, flying kilometre and hang gliding - Snow boarding and its ski inheritance - Off piste, avalanche disasters and control - Snow cannon, major construction work and the Green influence - The flooding of Tignes - Zermatt has a typhoid scandal - Disruption of the village economy, collapse of the summer trade and hotel staffng problems, - Chalet agencies and apartment rental's - British and lowland labour causes upheavals in local employment - Land prices dispossess local people - The future of ski-ing.

Bibliography 137

Index 139

CHAPTER 1
ECCENTRIC PIONEERS
1860 - 1900

The pioneer skiers were certainly eccentric; they also had to prove impervious to the jeers of their neighbours. The townspeople of Glarus made such fun of Christopher Iselin he actually resorted to ski-ing at night. Perhaps it was this experimentation, literally in the dark, that enabled him eventually to become Swiss ski champion. Then there is the early twentieth century account in Richard Seligman's diary: "News that ski runners are about keep a whole village from church and set the village trooping to the nearest slopes to see and jeer at our clumsy gambols".

Dr. Alexander Spengler, with a practice in Davos, was another intrepid pioneer. He had first put on skis in 1870. They had been passed on to him by a patient. The reason was clear. The skis had come from Norway without any instructions. Fortunately they were not like some pairs being produced in Scandinavia at around this time; one a short, skin covered "pusher" and the other a disconcerting nine and a half feet long. So the doctor must have also had courage when the village boys took to aping him using barrel staves. How amazed they would all have been to learn that his exploits would in time be commemorated with a statue in the park.

Spengler even persuaded a fellow doctor, a German called Otto Herwig, to join him. In 1883 Herwig successfully made the trip on skis over to Arosa. And there he stayed - for the rest of his life. He brought the village a great deal more than the first pair of skis. He realised the area was ideally situated for patients suffering from tuberculosis and this introduced a new and highly lucrative local economy.

The English, of course, were also experimenting with Alpine ski-ing. Gerald Fox arrived at Grindelwald in 1891 and set about giving lessons. His credentials may have been curious but so were his methods. He hired a local lad with a shovel. In much the same way as replacing divots in a golf course, he had the lad fill in the holes his pupils made when they fell in the snow. Fox had another strange habit. He would put on his skis while still in his bedroom. After clattering along the passage, he would skim down the stairs and out through the door.

Throughout the late 'eighties, first in Davos and later at St.Moritz, Colonel Napier, son of the hero General of Magdalena, was also ski-ing. He did so with considerable dignity for he always had his valet in attendance. The valet was Norwegian so he may well have been acting as a - no doubt very deferential - ski instructor. It was rumoured he was even on skis when he brought the Colonel's breakfast tray down to the chalet.

Also around about this time there was another dignified figure on skis. It was the pastor ski-ing the slopes around Lech. As a man of God he had quite a number of his flock prepared to follow his lead. So many, in fact, that by 1902 there was a thriving Arlberg Ski Club.

Sir Arthur Conan Doyle, creator of the Sherlock Holmes stories, also crossed the Furka Pass from Davos to Arosa, with two local brothers as guides. Their ski-ing was evidently highly unorthodox. For the steeper parts they tied their skis together and tobogganed down the slopes. In writing about his exploits, Conan Doyle concluded: "My tailor tells me that Harris tweed cannot wear out. This is a mere theory, and will not stand a thorough scientific test. He will find samples of his wares on view from the Furka Pass to Arosa". None the less their progress was most satisfactory. They were expected to reach the village sometime during the afternoon. Instead they arrived while the villagers were still in church. As they ate their lunch they gleefully watched the assembling villagers unwittingly robbed of their anticipated pleasure of jeering at their antics.

Conan Doyle wrote about his adventure in "The Strand" magazine in 1894. It was the first popular account of ski-ing. Readers realised it was something anyone could do.

But the whole attitude towards ski-ing had changed with the publication of Nansen's book "Over Greenland by Ski" in 1890. It was an age when explorers such as Stanley at the Victoria Falls and Scott of the Antarctic were acclaimed as the personification of world exploration. Nansen made it clear, even in the title, how dependent he had been on his skis. Conan Doyle was to experience this change himself. While Nansen's book had evidently made no mark in Arosa, the people of Davos proved more ski-minded . Only a year after his Arosa experience he climbed the Jakobshorn peak above Davos. He walked the first part up to the tree line. He put on his skis only for the final section. Again he was watched by an entire village but this time he was accorded a very dfferent reception. There was no suggestion of ridicule. As he reached the summit the flags all over Davos were dipped in salute. Indeed his feat was accorded more lasting recognition with a plaque in the village park.

Professor Oscar Schuster achieved an even more enduring effect when he conquered the Monte Rosa. This was partly due to shrewdness. He celebrated his success by giving pairs of skis to 12 of the local guides and more skis to be shared among the village children. As a result the villagers were using skis as a matter of course even though Zermatt remained largely closed to winter visitors right up until the mid 'thirties.

At this time Ski-ing in the alps was little different from the traditional style in Scandinavia. It was "transport-derived" being primarily the best means for going to market or delivering the post. There was, of course, some recreational ski-ing.

The usual way of keeping control while ski running on these modest slopes was to stop by turning uphill. The first recognised turn was the telemark. It was introduced by skiers from Telemark in 1860 as a way of finishing the outrun after a jump. Used on the open slope, it allowed the skier to lean inwards naturally. The skier had to go right down on one knee as though dropping a profound curtsy. Then the tip of the inside ski was held against the binding of the outer. The turn bears no comparison with the sloppy heel-raising shuffle that has more recently come to be practised on the piste.

Then in 1895 a German, Mathias Zardski, promoted the use of the single lilienfeld pole as the point for turning, though, he emphasised, it should not be lent upon. This produced the S or stem turn which could be made several times in smooth succession without stopping. But most importantly it could be made on those much steeper slopes that are to be found in the Alps. As a consequence, the very next year the first central European downhill race was held in Germany.

All this did not really come to the attention of the English until 1901 when two powerful and tall gentlemen arrived at Davos. They were devotees of Zardski and were seen making "swings and turns to right and to left just like skaters on the ice. We realised all at once that we knew nothing about ski running. We thought they must be Norwegians but discovered that they were Englishmen, brothers named Richardson."

In contrast, downhill ski-ing had been established in the United States as far back as 1874 during the gold rush. When the seams in the valleys ran out, the prospectors had moved higher, right up into the snow region. Skis were introduced by the Scandinavian immigrants, particularly the Norwegians. Almost immediately the wild, impetuous, anything goes character of the prospectors ensured that this convenient way of moving around was turned into competition. Racing, along with jumping, emerged as a major attraction. Though it must be admitted the accompanying drinking and gambling provided equal attraction. Technique was sadly missing. While initially there were gschmozzle starts, the wild, daredevil nature of the participants soon made it advisable to have no more than four or six competitors starting at the same time. They were straight schusses and winning times were, to say the least, impressive. At La Porte, 1,400 ft were covered in 21 seconds. On the Howland "flat", 1,135 ft were covered in 20 seconds.

There was little choice as to whereabouts the British could ski in the Alps. They had to go to wherever there were hotels. Most of these had been built for mountaineers. Nor was there much choice over suitable slopes. Fortunately the two needs usually coincided. There was Chamonix at the foot of Mont Blanc and Grindelwald under the awesome north face of the Eiger. Alternatively the hotels could have been built for health reasons. Besides Arosa and Leysin providing cures for tuberculosis, St.Moritz was a spa. Or maybe the hotels were built for artists attracted by the sheer beauty of the scenery, notably at Zermatt, dominated by the majestic tricorn of the Matterhorn.

There was one grave shortcoming. These hotels had been built for summer visitors. The possibility of snow drifts, icicles and blizzards had not been taken into account. Admittedly the bedrooms in The Bear at Grindelwald did have stoves, but there was no central heating in the public rooms. As one chronicler rather plaintively bemoaned: " With 90 guests there is neither pleasure nor warmth in sitting in the sixth row of chairs before the only fire in the big hall".

In 1854 the only hostelry in Zermatt was the Hotel Cervie. However closer enquiry elicited that this was not really a hotel at all, merely three rooms in the doctor's house. The pastor evidently had an eye for business. He told his brother about the village's potential.

Sir Arthur Conan Doyle, nearest camera, and friends cause merriment among the local lads

3

Alexander Seiler duly arrived and promptly bought the doctor's house. He developed it into something like a proper hotel and renamed it the Monte Rosa. Today it has over 200 beds and has been so enlarged that the bureau and the smoking room are the only original parts still surviving.

It was from the Monte Rosa in 1865 that Edward Whymper, one of the most famous of all mountaineers, set out to make the first ascent of the Matterhorn. Ironically, as things turned out, the locals had a superstition that anyone who reached the top would never come down alive. This made it difficult to find anyone ready to act as guide. In a note declining to join the expedition, one of the leading scions of the Biner family wrote with logic that cannot be faulted:

"Dear Sir, I love you well, I know you are strong and sure of foot and I would like to go with you everywhere. But my mother, if we should slip and fall, it would be sad for me and sad for her".

Whymper had already made several attempts. Now he was aware that strong teams from other countries were making plans. This would probably be his last chance. Then suddenly he learnt that even this opportunity was in jeopardy. An Italian team had already set out from the south side. Whymper did not dare delay further. He gathered his team of highly experienced mountaineers. There was however one flaw. They had not climbed together before and the urgency prevented them from getting to know one another properly. However it was not considered a vital factor.

They triumphed. They beat the Italians and were the first to reach the top.

It was on the return journey that one of the party slipped and pulled down three others. The rest of the party braced themselves to take the strain. The rope, old and little thicker than a clothes line, broke.

Those killed included Lord Francis Douglas and Charles Hudson, a clergyman who lies buried under the altar in the little English church. It was, in fact, Hudson rather than Whymper who had mapped out the way of ascent and, had he returned, would have had much of the credit.

The tragedy made headlines in newspapers all over the world. Hundreds of artists impressions of the incident appeared along with dire warnings of the risks of mountaineering. Soon, inevitably, there were rumours of ugly dealings. At that time the German press was every bit as imaginative as the British is today. It was suggested that Whymper had cut the rope to save himself. Typically the journalists had not sought expert opinion. They entirely failed to appreciate that under such circumstances no one would have had time to produce a knife, let alone saw through the rope.

Seiler's keen business sense did not desert him. He realised that Whymper's presence would always create interest. So he allowed him, whenever he wished, to stay at the hotel free. The only stipulation was that he should pay his bar bills. Nevertheless for the rest of his life a now deeply morose Whymper resented having to pay for his drinks.

Even today the spirit of Whymper pervades Zermatt almost as completely as does the Matterhorn. There is a large statue of him in the main street and details of his expedition occupy a considerable section of the local museum.

It is the sheer north face of the Eiger, looming high and with the Jungfrau forming an even higher backdrop, that has made Grindelwald a major attraction for mountaineers. The 2,000 ft. wall seems very close and impressive, especially on a moonlit night. In early days, the locals ascribed the frequent rock falls to dwarfs seeking revenge because the villagers had refused their demands for food. Quite low down, there appears to be a large, lone and peculiarly bright greeny-yellow star. It is, in fact, the window in the station of the railway up to the Jungfraujoch. As at Zermatt, there is a gravestone in the English church that tells of a similar mountaineering disaster that overtook Julius Elliot, William Penhall and Peter Kaufmann.

The local guides have also experienced tragedy. In 1902 the brothers Robert and Henri Fearon failed to return from an expedition. Eventually their blackened bodies were discovered with their ice picks beside them. The handle on one had split. This provided the vital clue to the mystery. They must have been struck by lightning. This theory was strangely corroborated. One of the brothers had a camera. When the film was developed, a picture taken the previous evening had a slash of pure white across it where the lightning had penetrated.

Even in these early days, the north wall was proving a fatal attraction. Indeed so many climbers came to grief on it, the authorities instituted fines for anyone scaling it without permission. And those who did not climb watched progress through telescopes set up in the main street.

A macabre variation was when an Italian, Stefano Longhi had made a fatal slip. His corpse was left dangling on the end of the rope as it was considered too dangerous to recover it. But after 18 months, it became evident that the cold was preserving the body. Also there arose the macabre situation whereby visitors were paying 20 centimes a time for a telescopic view of it swinging in the wind. Altogether it was not conversant with a healthy tourist industry. So the Swiss organised a retrieval party of 23 men backed by Hermann Geiger with his ski equipped light aircraft. Fritz Jaun, as the most experienced guide, was lowered on the end of a 1,350 ft. rope. More and more was paid out and there was only 50 ft. left when he came level with the body. After securing the corpse, the two were raised almost face to face in a fearful minuet as they spun on the rope end. On regaining solid ground, progress was further hampered as the body was still frozen rigid. It was impossible to winch it more than two inches before it would snag on rock. Eventually, after getting it to the aircraft, the frozen limbs had to be forced in order to fit into the tiny cabin. It was returned to Longhi's relatives without any charge. Asked why he had risked his life, Jaun replied "Even the dead can be lonely".

Grindelwald is also unusual in having a glacier so close to the village it seems at times to be nudging into village life itself.

The 20m. glen or tongue of ice creeps to and fro by as much as 40 cm. a day. The total range is three km. so that when it is extended, it actually rounds a corner of the village. This occurred in 1815 and ladies, too delicate to walk, made it the subject for an excursion in their carriages. It reached down into the village again in 1910 and the children played at "angels descending" by sliding down the seracs or lumps of ice.

Another ice curiosity is the village skating rink. It is supposed to be in the shape of Lake Geneva. This would place Madame Molter's teashop as a highly appropriate substitute for the Nestle food factory.

The glacier which occasionally intrudes right into Grindelwald. Painting circa 1860

First seen from the Männlichen slopes, Grindelwald looks as though some giant has sprinkled chalets over the whole valley floor - rather carelessly, actually, for they spill up the mountain edges. The Bear is a comparatively small hotel and, since there are no large buildings, finding the centre is almost a matter of geometry.

The Bear Hotel was built in 1498 and for most of its time has remained in the Bosch family. In 1892 it was consumed by a scourge even worse than avalanches - fire. It broke out one hot, lazy summer's afternoon. The time could not have been worse. Many of the menfolk were up in the foothills, some making hay and others acting as guides for mountaineering visitors. Fanned by the warm foehn blowing up from Italy, the flames spread rapidly consuming up to 60 houses to the west. By nightfall a large part of the village was a charred ruin.

One of the hotels, however, was situated well out of the way on top of the Faulhorn. It depended almost entirely on one night stays by a clientele desirous of watching the sun rise over the Dom. To witness this sight called for considerable stamina. The expedition would begin the evening before with a five hour climb. Ladies usually made their way up the narrow winding track on some emaciated mule – with particular sympathy for the mule carrying the manageress of the Faulhorn for she was very fat. It is also reported the good lady smelt even stronger than the mule.

The guests were called from their beds literally before the crack of dawn. However their pains were well rewarded by a splendid and awesome sight. It has been described, admittedly in rather florid terms, by Daniel P. Rhodes:

"First there is a light, as it may be the beating back of silvery rays from the east; then, slowly, insensibly, there grows around this the perfection of form in an infinity of colour. Low in the skies, green - a faint, distant green - fades in an age of gold. All is bright with hope - nay brilliant with achievement; this light is beautiful and clear and the world's work may be done by it. Brief, though, its supremacy. Soon the imperial crimson overwhelms it and peak after peak is struck by the shafts of this new material radiance, only a few remaining in darkness - a dazzling and unheard of spectacle. Again there is a warning, a doubtful interval - at last, from out of which all things come slowly into the pure white light of gathering day."

The Victorian ladies also used to mountaineer. Normally encumbered with all the requirements of decorum they adopted a realistic approach - or rather departure. Once out of sight, they had no compunction over taking off their heavy tweed skirts, and handing them to the guides to carry.

But most of the ladies were inveterate and, indeed, indomitable sightseers. They made up the other major sector of the Swiss summer tourist trade. They would make their way on mules, sedan chair or on foot. They were usually armed with a parasol, an easel and a box of watercolours. Typical was Miss Durrand at Grindelwald. She had originally come out as a companion but had somehow stayed on for the next 50 years. It was not romance for she remained a spinster and gave devoted service to the English church. She also proved surprisingly tough. She celebrated her 70th birthday by climbing the Wetterhorn. Not that it was really climbing for she had two guides and while one pulled from the front the other pushed from behind. Nonetheless, altogether they made it successfully to the top.

The artistic value which these ladies attributed to the Alps was unequivocally confirmed in 1884 when the great Ruskin himself visited Zermatt. With all the infuriating self satisfaction of a sedentary critic he turned his withering comments on those scaling the Matterhorn. "The Alps themselves, which your own poets used to love so reverently, you look upon as soaped poles in a bear garden which you set yourselves to climb and slide down again with shrieks of delight". Considering he was writing when mountaineering was in its infancy, one wonders what he would have said about the hordes of skiers there today.

Seiler, astute as ever, noticed how well worn was the path winding 1,700 ft. up to the Riffelalp, a favourite point from which to see the Matterhorn. He had a lot of courage to accept the state of the path as surety for building another hotel. This he did.

He further raised the stakes by lavishing on it every luxury.

There were two dining rooms. One was the more exclusive so that it was immediately labelled, in the uncompromising class consciousness of the age, the House of Lords. The other was, of course, the House of Commons. He also built a sun lounge running the entire front of the building. But the real marvel was the hotel's success. The approach was by the Gornergrat mountain railway. But the bourgeoisie, ever ready to thwart him, refused permission to make a path from the station. The ever resourceful Seiler found the law said nothing against laying a railway line. So his hotel guests ended their journey along a spur line and with a flourish right up to the hotel door. Seiler also developed his own telegraph system. Whenever someone at Zermatt wanted a room at the Riffelalp, a sheet was spread on the roof of the Monte Rosa.

Although the villagers despised him as a newcomer, they did not hesitate to emulate him when his enterprises were proving profitable. Indeed the precise way they copied his ventures was nothing short of plagiarism. First they built the Zermatterhof, setting it challengingly across the road from the Monte Rosa. And now that the Riffelalp was evidently prospering, they set about building a rival hotel one shoulder of the mountain higher on the Riffelberg.

Even today, these Zermatt families form a bourgeoisie or group fanatical in their claims to superiority. Traditionally their interests were centred on sharing among themselves the grazing rights and fuel wood hewn from the forests. They should not offcially wield any influence in the democratically elected village commune or council. At Zermatt the bourgeois members managed, in practice, to get control of both and became a veritable Mafia. They would not even consider anyone wishing to join them if their ancestors had not been an inhabitant when the village had became "closed" in 1618. The Julens, the Perrens, the Biners and 18 other families, their aunts and their cousins and their cousins cousins altogether

The village as the ancestors of all true Zermattians knew it.

account for 1,400 people. Some bear a grudge against others to the extent some of the families have not exchanged pleasantries over the past 200 years. One thing, however, can be counted on to bring them into some sort of unity. This is the determination to keep the 2,200 other villagers as outsiders. They include not only the Seilers but all who may have lived in Zermatt a mere three or four generations.

So it was no surprise that when Seiler applied to join the burgeoisie he was rebuffed, even though some of the bourgeois were his employees. To be fair, beyond sheer priggishness, they were not happy that Seiler had 16 children. It did not take much to calculate that in due course the share of communal natural resources would be spread that much more thinly. But Seiler was not to be put off. First he appealed to the Commune. Then he applied to the Canton. Finally he applied to the Swiss Parliament itself. And still the locals refused to accept him. In the end the Commune had to be suspended by the Canton. They sent in a governor backed by 80 troops. And so Seiler duly acquired his burgership - 18 years after his initial application. Even today the bourgeois still contemptuously refer to his descendents as Paper Burghers.

Nor did the passing years make the old families any less vindictive. The manageress of the Hotel Tennerhof, next door to the Zermatterhof, also applied to become a member. She had excellent qualifications. Admittedly her family had not lived in Zermatt 300 years. They had, though, been there for seven generations. Her father was one of the most experienced and respected guides. He had climbed the Matterhorn over 200 times. But it was to no avail. Her application was contemptuously "put on file". When she persisted the Bourgeousie, with true autocracy, granted themselves permission to add a swimming pool to their Zermatterhof. They planned it so that it blocked the view from all but the top floor windows of her hotel.

Up until 1860 the mainspring of Swiss tourism remained mountaineers and sightseers. Then there came a momentous change. Visitors began arriving in the winter. To start with they were the patients of Doctors Herwig and Spengler. Soon, though, other doctors were proclaiming that high altitude was a benefit, even a cure, for tuberculosis.

Indeed when Dr. Herwig had started his clinic at Arosa, he had left behind him at Davos a village already largely given over to "curing".

Up till then, Egypt had been the only place that offered any benefit for sufferers. But the climate there did not remain benign for more than three months of the year. In the Swiss resorts however the "lunger" season started at the end of October and lasted right through till the middle of March.

The turpentine aroma from the all pervading Christmas trees was also presumed to be a balm. So whenever possible hotels would promote themselves as being "set amid pines".

Even today those resorts that were given over to "curing" can be easily recognised through the architecture. Buildings which might at first sight be taken as hotels are distinctive with their deep balconies. These were sanatoriums where the patients could be wheeled out into the cold air still in their beds. Many of these sanatoriums had the ground and lower floors built as a hotel. They were for those whose health had not yet fallen into too serious a decline. The floors above abruptly became a sanatorium, with chambermaids and floor waiters replaced by nurses and doctors in white coats.

Noël Coward in his autobiography written in the 'thirties, gives a vivid description of the peculiar social life forced upon guests in this environment:

"It was a strange life, gay in the evenings when everyone made an effort to dress, dine in the restaurant and dance afterwards in the bar. During the days, of course, everybody had cures and treatment to undergo, and the whole hotel seemed dead and empty. At night, however, it regularly awoke. The gambling machine in the bar tinkled merrily, the band played and there was the sound of corks popping and noisy conversation in many languages. Only very occasionally would someone slip away from the fun to flit upstairs, coughing almost furtively, into a stained handkerchief. Those evenings, with their noise and music and gaiety were slightly macabre, but somehow not depressing. It was as though they were unrelated to ordinary existence - a few detached hours of pleasure, floating between life and death, untouchable by the sadness of either. The knowledge that practically everybody present, themselves included, would probably be dead within a year or so was, I suppose, tucked away behind the laughter of most of the people there, but it was in no way apparent. There seemed to be no strain in the air, no eager snatching at flying moments. Perhaps the disease itself carried with it a compensating illusion that ultimate cure was certain, that all the slow tedium intricate process of dying was nothing more than an interlude of small discomfort."

Socially TB was not a subject on which one dwelt. It was associated with dirt and poverty and it was frighteningly infectious. For long Klosters suffered, even though it did not have any sanatoriums. Sufficient that it was situated on the leeward side of Davos. It mattered not that it was several kilometres further down the valley.

Arosa was claimed, at least by those living in Arosa, and by Dr. Herwig in particular, as being infinitely superior. Situated at 6,200 ft. above sea level, it has an 800 ft. edge over Davos and is all of 1,700 ft. higher than Leysin and Montana.

The offcial Arosa guide was proclaiming every imaginable reassurance for the would-be visitor. It was an idyllic situation, of course, for those with respiratory difficulties. "…..and the tortuous nature of the ground does not give opportunity for the wind to get up any strength... for bronchial tubes become very sensitive to wind." As though such questionable claims were not in themselves sufficient, they bordered on the alarmist. "When there is no wind …….. little heat is carried away from the body and hence there is not the danger from chills and colds, with their horrible consequence of bad relapse."

All this was indeed confirmed by a visitor writing to the local newspaper. He compared Arosa favourably to Davos. " There is an oppressive monotony about the latter which the charming varied outline of the hills around Arosa must ever present village pride".

Arosa was quick to appreciate the commercial advantages and made no secret of the services it had to offer. It was quite prepared to acknowledge all the precautions necessary for a "curing" resort. The offcial guide carried such forthright advertisements as "Dr. Schaeuble, dispensing chemist, laboratory for analysing sputum and urine. All kinds of English prescriptions made up". The Hotel Seehof reassured all potential guests that they had "good drainage" adding that it was "an English sanitary system".

By 1914 Arosa had six sanatoriums. There was one specifically for children while the Villa Gentiana was essentially for the British being run by an English doctor. He charged 14 shillings a day for a room with private bath and inclusive of all medical attendance. The ordinary hotels and pensions also accepted patients, with the exception of The Grand which loftily declared "No consumptive cases taken".

Only a year or two separated the arrival of the first TB patients and the first tourists bent on amusing themselves frolicking in the sun and snow. Indeed the date can be ascribed precisely to an afternoon in the autumn of 1864. Johannes Badrutt was the manager of one of the larger hotels in the summer spa of St.Moritz. Although he was the son of a humble muliteer he had a

The joys of travelling in 1900. The customs hall at Boulogne

shrewd business mind. He calculated he could double the income from the capital he had invested in his Kulm Hotel if only he could persuade people to come out in the winter. Like all good businessmen, he was also a good salesman. He was talking to the last few remaining guests that summer. He waxed quite lyrical over the beauties of winter, how in the Engadine the snow remains crisp and sparkling while above there is a blue sky and hot sun. While no doubt polite, there was no mistaking his guests remained sceptical. But Badrutt also knew how to make sure of his quarry. He offered them a remarkable proposition cunningly baited as a bet which his guests were bound to win. If they, together with as many friends as they liked, should return as his guests early in January, he promised that if they did not find it just as he described, they could stay at his expense for as long as they wished.

It was not, in fact, such a reckless offer. If the weather proved bad they would not have wanted to stay long. More to the point, Badrutt had calculated their bar bills alone would cover the cost.

The party duly came back and no sooner had their sleighs turned into the Julier Pass than they were dazzled by the sunshine and realised that Badrutt was right.

Badrutt had evidently selected his guests wisely. Besides running up hefty bar bills, they were in the right set in society and indeed their party included Lord Shaftesbury. Within two years there were 300 people staying during the winter season. Indeed, right up until the outbreak of the First World War three quarters of winter visitors at his Kulm Hotel were British. In contrast, Davos could boast only two visitors. But the demand was there and when, in 1875, the Hotel Belvedere announced it was opening in the winter it was almost immediately booked up for the entire season.

The luxury of a sleeper on the Engadine Express

The journey out to Switzerland may have been leisurely but it was decidedly irksome. Most people caught the train leaving Victoria at 7.40 in the morning. Without effective stabilisers, the boats pitched and rolled their way across the channel. Even in moderate swells, the saloons would be full of people looking decidedly queasy.

Right up until the First World War customs procedures at Boulogne were minimal and no one bothered over passports. Nor was there any need for travellers cheques. Ordinary cheques could be cashed just as easily as in London. The usual rate for tipping was one franc per week. For long stays, one franc a month was considered adequate.

The train arrived in Paris at 6.0 pm. And it was necessary to change trains. Before the days of the Engadine Express, it was also necessary to get out at Chur where there was the choice of closed or open carriages drawn by one or two horses. It was suggested, especially to the more delicate, that "most people find a sudden coming up to the height too great a strain on their lung and heart to complete the journey in a day". An overnight stop was therefore recommended at a village around the snow line, such as St.Peters on the way to Arosa. Those who decided to carry on would be puzzled as their driver would suddenly stop, dismount and "start rummaging around in a pile of snow at the side of the road. In due course he would uncover an antediluvian sledge, like a giant soap box on runners which at some long distant date had been embellished with a coat of paint." The passengers, along with the luggage and horses, would transfer to this vehicle. The driver, having barely bothered push the other vehicle to one side, would continue taking them on their way.

The food at the hotels was, at best, indifferent. An early visitor to St.Moritz wrote: "The meat is bad and the soup invariably requires a certain amount of Lieberg's Extract to make it worth eating. For three months the only vegetable that we had was potato"

Indolent visitors hired the locals as luge mules

Nor, if G. Scott Lindsay is to be believed, were things any better at Zermatt. Even in 1908 he was the only visitor that winter. Hardly surprising, really, for his diet comprised goats meat, goats milk and goats cheese "since when I have never been able to look a goat in the face, much less eat one."

Little wonder that the managers were able to count on their bar bills for profit.

The custom among mountaineers of eating at one long table was retained by winter sportsmen. Both Badrutt and Seiler, along with their families, sat at the top of the table. There was keen competition to sit near them. Progress up the board was partly through social standing and partly by the length of time one had already stayed at the hotel. The hotelier would give the signal when the meal was to be served and when everyone could get up at the end. Standards must have rapidly improved for among the waiters at the Monte Rosa was a youth called Caesar Ritz.

Johannes Badrutt was a hotelier in the old fashioned sense and took a personal interest in the welfare of his guests. He would, for instance, go with them to the shop to make sure they were not overcharged for the hire of a luge. Seiler, at Zermatt, took wholehearted interest in the achievements of his guests. He would personally see the climbers off at 5.30 in the morning. He would be there to welcome and congratulate or commiserate with them on their return.

Visitors were always made welcome at Grindelwald. This was largely due to the black-bearded Father Strasser. He had quickly recognised the potential prosperity the visitors could bring his impoverished parishioners. So he urged his flock to help make their stay pleasant and be friendly and even join in their recreations. But the welcome could vary considerably from village to village. For instance while it was always warm at Montana, the villagers of nearby Crans were notorious for being at least surly and often positively hostile.

These early visitors began taking an interest in the luges the locals used for carrying supplies across the snow. It was not long before they were using them for their own amusement. "The height of our ambition" wrote John Symonds, a consumptive staying at Davos, "was to get up enough speed to reach a certain telegraph post which stood where the Victoria Hotel now stands". Another procedure was to tow the luge to the top of the pass and sit on it for a picnic lunch. After resting a while, there was the clear ride all the way home, using "pegs" to punt along the flat bits. Later the more indolent took to hiring a villager as a mule cum chauffeur. He would have to pull the luge up the slope and sit in front and steer on the way down. The simplest way to brake was by digging in the heels. At one point there was a fashion for strapping skate blades underneath the boot. Another favoured brake was an iron bar. The spike would be pressed down manually to act as a drag.

The roads were used as ready made runs. Indeed, whereas today the new arrival might ask about the snow conditions, at that time the usual inquiry was after the condition of the roads.

In 1883 John Symonds founded the Davos Toboggan Club. With admirable foresight, he insisted that membership should be open to all nationalities. He saw it as an ideal opportunity for encouraging visitors to mix with the native villagers. And with considerable success for when the Club held its first race it was billed as an International Event. Justification for the claim rested on entrants reputedly coming from five countries. Certainly the runner-up was an Australian who had come over specially from St.Moritz. But proof that Club policy was already effective could be found in the winner who was the conductor of the Post Bus.

Two years later St. Moritz challenged a return match. The St. Moritz team were confident - too confident as things turned out. Knowing the run, they shot down at speeds beyond their capabilities which meant they also shot off at various corners. The Davos visitors, however, proceeded with caution and won all first three places.

Racing was also conducted on the road from Arosa down to Ruti. This provided two excitements in the form of S bends. The first corner was where the road doubles back on itself and was always good for a number of spills. The other was just before the winning post and could usually be relied upon to shake out any undeserving novices who had somehow managed to stay the course.

Spectators were strongly advised to stand on the inside of the curve where they would not be in danger should a competitor tear off at an uncontrolled tangent. The winning post was usually the bridge just before the village. A reasonable speed was between 40 and 50 mph. This was calculated through a complicated system with pre-set watches. It meant competitors had to start precisely on the minute.

Speed skating as developed on the Fenns. Initially it rivalled highly conventional English figure skating in popularity

14

There was, however, a drawback to using roads as racetracks. They were the sole means of access to the village. Consequently intrepid lugers could easily find themselves face to face with the fourgons or carts bringing supplies up from Chur. The more wily performers at Arosa would ask their hotelier to telephone the pub at Ruti an hour before they set off and instruct the landlord to offer free wine to all up coming drivers. What with the imbibing and exchange of gossip, they could be relied upon to linger sufficiently for the road to remain clear. On race days the committee undertook this responsibility. But it meant that events had to start early in order to finish before the Post Bus was on the way. It would, of course, have been unethical to offer such bribery to the driver of an official vehicle.

The hazards were even greater for those luging at night. Not only the sleigh drivers but all the locals had a habit at dusk of abandoning their carts wherever they might happen to be. Often they were slewed right across the road.

Skating was another amusement much enjoyed among the pioneer winter visitors. Speed skating in Britain had mainly been practised in the Fenns. The rough ice and tie-on blades meant it was almost entirely straight racing. Similar competitions were organised in the Swiss resorts and attracted widespread support. On the eve of the 1908 championships at Davos, it was snowing and the teams had to turn out and sweep the ice. However, by night time the fall had become so heavy it was evident they were losing the battle. Eventually an SOS was sent out to the hotels: "Will all Englishmen please come out and help". So Nelson-like an appeal could not go unheeded and literally dozens turned out and the next day the championships were held just as scheduled.

The National Skating Association had been started by a journalist, J.D.Digby, who wanted to clean up the bribery that was becoming excessive in Fenn racing. One example was when a skater challenged the claim by a director of the Great Eastern Railway that the train was the fastest way a man could move. A race was arranged along a stretch where the tracks ran beside the River Ouse. The skater was quite a way behind and approaching a bridge where the railway crossed the river, when he found the fireman had scattered ashes and clinker in his way. The ashes were still hot. Having successfully overcome this hazard he was duly rewarded by encountering a following wind. It allowed him not only to catch up but overtake the engine and win.

Within a year of the Association being founded in 1887, groups of pioneer figure skaters scattered throughout the country were applying to join.

English figure skating had recently been formalised by H.E.Vandervell. It had only become possible since he had the idea of screwing the blade onto the boot thus providing much more control. Nor are the blades so simple as they look. If they were just a bar of metal it would be almost impossible to move at all. They have, in fact, two edges through being hollow ground. The skater switches from one to the other simply by changing weight. But the blade is additionally very slightly curved from front to back.

These niceties combined with the fact the skater is very fast moving makes it extremely difficult to judge competitions. Indeed this is why judges often find it necessary to go down on hands and knees to study the tracings properly before awarding marks.

With these advances, Vandervell devised a system based on skating a circle. It could be two circles in the form of 8 or even two sections of a circle to form a 3. He was soon elaborating them with other long, swooping figures such as counters, brackets and rockers. When performed properly it all looked very impressive; everyone dressed in frock coats and hard hats and with a stiff bearing which required the spare leg and arm to be kept rigidly to the side.

Group skating was also popular. A caller stood on the bank directing what everyone was to do next. The figures could be repeated or varied, every three forming a "paragraph", by shouting such instructions as "twice back and forward, turn and inside, inwards turn off, meet."

Learners and those not particularly adept followed a simpler formation and kept in line behind the leader who called the figures. This way it was also fairly easy to cheat by surreptitiously putting down the other foot.

The Association's committee came in for a big shock with the first international figure skating championship in 1902. It had not crossed their minds that a woman could participate in anything so athletic as was required for the freestyle part of the programme. So there was consternation when the entrants included a Miss. Madge Syers. Not only did she come second but, had it not been for blatant male chauvinism, she would almost certainly have won. As soon as possible the committee drew up new rules banning ladies. They had three reasons made with all the lucidity of male logic. The first was that dresses prevented judges from seeing the feet. Second, and far more pertinent, was that a judge might be "attached" to the entrant. And, if all this was not considered more than sufficent, there remained the unarguable point that it is difficult to compare a woman with a man.

With the separation of the women's events, Madge Syers went on to win the World ice figure events in 1906 and 1907.

None of this prejudice dismayed Madge Syers in the least.. When it was announced that the 1908 Olympic Games would include a skating event held on one of the London artificial rinks, she entered her name, took part and won the Ladies Gold Medal.

Although the English style did not require so much ice as speed skating, it none the less needed a prodigious area. This was of no particular concern since it was evolved on lakes, notably in Regent's Park and the Serpentine. It had consequently assumed the luxury of vast space. But in the Swiss resorts, the lakes remain frozen throughout the winter so that numerous snow falls severely roughen and ruin the surface.

Indeed the pioneer TB skaters at Arosa usually started in November on the small lakes above Inner Arosa. But if there were early snow falls, there could still be good ice on the Unter or the Ober See, the lake at the bottom end of the village and which local credence held to be of immeasurable depth. At one time there had been efforts to provide an official rink there but somehow it never seemed clear of the last snowfall.

So serious figure skaters demanded the rinks should be made artificially. Initially at St.Moritz the visitors persuaded the authorities to install a sluice that diverted a stream to flow over the ice and provide a smooth surface. But in most resorts it is a matter of beating down snow to form the base. A smooth surface is then laboriously built up through sweeping followed by spraying. The men wore boards on their feet and guests would become used to waking up to the clop clop of wood on the ice.

At most resorts the provision of rinks was left to individual hotel managers such as Herr. Bosch offering 70,000 sq ft. at the Bear at Grindelwald and the 90,000 sq ft. provided by Herr Metzenthin at the Grand at Morgins.

At St.Moritz it was again Badrutt who provided the first proper ice rink. Here the prominent local exponent of skating was also the hotel's medical practitioner, Dr.Holland. Rather strangely, he had also secured the diplomatic post of Minister in charge of the British Legation at St. Moritz. He was thus able to practise his skating, diplomatic and medical skills all at the same time. He formed the St.Moritz Skating Association in 1902 and managed to have the most prestigious competition named after himself. Not that everyone was impressed. More than one visitor, according to reports, preferred the services of the local Swiss doctor - even though he was bordering on the senile.

The Davos Skating Club preceded St.Moritz by eight years. It was such an immediate success it was soon able to furnish its own rink of an immense 210,000 sq. ft. with a pavilion reaching the full length one side, conveniently acting as a wind shield. Here buffet luncheons were served daily.

Curling was another sport widely practised on the ice rinks. Davos was again to the fore with its curling club founded in 1888, six years ahead of St.Moritz.

Curling has been played in Scotland over the past 400 years. Development, it must be admitted, has been protracted. The first stones, some romantics claim they were preceded by cow pats, were selected for being well rounded from the streams. One of the earliest certain "louffers" dates from 1511. Today they are hewn from indigenous or volcanic rock but not granite. This is because the crystals of the different minerals must interlock to an intense degree if it is to remain largely impervious to the shock when repeatedly slammed down on the ice. Initially the rock was quarried in Ailsa Craig - in Scotland, of course. Now it is usually hewn in Trefor in Wales.

The first curling club was started at Loch Leven in 1668. The game was introduced in England in 1811 when some Scots gave a demonstration on the New River Canal in London. It caused a sensation and attracted so many onlookers it was feared the ice might break and the game had to be abandoned.

The Caledonian Club was formed in 1838 and established set weights and dimensions of the stones as well as the rules of play. They decreed the rink should be 46 yd. long. At one end is the dolly, set in a six ft. radius circle called the house. The Club was soon accorded the prestigious royal prefix. Queen Victoria, or more probably Prince Albert, was not, however prepared to grant the distinction on the nod. The Club officers were summoned to Scone Palace to give an account of themselves. There they were commanded to give a demonstration. The snag was, of course, there was no ice. However this apparently intractable problem was solved when it was realised the drawing room's highly polished floor would make an excellent substitute. By 1888 there were 480 affilated clubs with nearly 20,000 members.

One of the most significant developments in curling technique was the hack or single toehold cut in the ice. Previously players had to lay the stone while almost off balance. The hack, though, made it possible to slide the body forward virtually accompanying the stone over the first few feet. This considerably increases the impetus with which a stone can be made to cannon into any the opponent may have already set in the house. Stones started being made with hollow grinding in 1784. Having also acquired a handle, it was possible to give them a "curl" or swerve similar to putting a spin on a cricket ball. If the stone is going too fast it is allowed "to spoil". More often one of the team is called upon to "scoop! scoop!" which means industriously polishing the ice in its path. It can take the stone a further five yards. This requires a special broom set in a fabric case so that it does not shed inhibiting bristles on to the ice. It has a super dusting velvet edge.

Ordinary curling tended to centre on specialist Swiss hotels, the Bear at Grindelwald, the Palace at Villars and the Kulm at St.Moritz. They were the more luxurious hotels because they have summer tennis courts which provide the level base. Unlike the original Scottish frozen ponds and lakes, the ice has to be superlatively smooth with water sprayed not in droplets but as a fine mist producing a surface that almost springs underfoot. It also makes it surprisingly resistant to thaws.

In Austria, Kitzbühel for long had a local version known as ice shooting. Instead of stones, it was played with wooden cones with metal rings hung like bangles around the neck. These made up a prescribed weight, anything between 10 and 16 kg. No doubt much of its popularity lay in the modest area of ice required. As a result not just the hotels but every Kitzbühel pension had its "rink". When the Scots did arrive, they recognised its worth and rather than set up their national version preferred to join the locals.

The other ice rink game of any consequence at this time was bandy. It had much the same rules as hockey but used a ball rather than a puck and clubs rather than hockey sticks. It was also highly accommodating and teams could number seven or nine and could be made up with men only, ladies only, boys only, ladies and boys and even mixed ladies and men. It first materialized around 1880 among members of the Zurich Grasshopper Football club which was, in fact, managed by an Englishman. But it was another Englishman, Mr. Pennington Leigh, who introduced it into the Grisons. He could have hardly chosen a more opportune moment. Monotony had settled upon the visitors at St.Moritz and Davos and there was a strong demand for alternatives to skating and luging.

The St.Moritz Bandy Club was formed in 1894 at a meeting at the Kulm Hotel and General Sir Coleridge Grove was elected president. But really it owed its success to Badrutt.

He was far ahead of his time and, indeed, his ideas were more akin to the holiday camp. B & B was no longer sufficient. He realised there was a need for the all-in holiday with facilities for skating, luging and curling included. If bandy now promised to be popular among the guests, it was up to him to provide all the requisites.

So he made the Bandy Club a very handsome loan. In practice, though, it was no more a loan than the highly lucrative bet he had made that very first season. He made a special rink measuring 100 by 60 m. He incorporated a touch of affluence by equipping it with a 200 cu. m. overhead reservoir which could flood the ice in ten minutes. His efforts met with immediate success. Among the more auspicious pioneer bandy enthusiasts were Lord Helmsley, the Hon. F.N.Curzon and J.A.Bott. But no matter how distinguished they might be, a handful of players could not normally have justified such a large outlay. Badrutt additionally provided seating for 500 spectators. He knew he could rely on the patronage of the Arch Duke Ferdinand and his Consort who were inveterate supporters of virtually every winter sporting enterprise. No less he knew that in their wake would follow a large proportion of high society visitors.

The Davos bandy team was no less auspicious. They were led by E.G. Wynyard, a major figure in English cricket. Other distinguished players included A. Holland and E.L.Strutt. Yet, like the tobogganers, they seemed strangely reluctant to play away matches. In the end St.Moritz was driven to issuing ultimatums rather than invitations. But St.Moritz had become a formidable antagonist. By 1910 they had defeated Innsbruck, Munich, Leipzig and Berlin. As a team they were notable for their short, speedy passes. This was because they were used to the smaller indoor rinks in Britain. The Swiss, in particular, were more used to large outdoor rinks and so tended to make long passes right out on the wing.

Any and every sort of game was now becoming acceptable. There was even an attempt in 1896 at playing cricket on skates. St.Moritz, always seeking out rivals, challenged Davos. Ladies were included and the St.Moritz team starred Lottie Dod, a five times winner at Wimbledon. She more than proved her worth by taking five wickets for four runs.

A popular alternative to ice hockey; bandy is played with brooms and a soft ball

With all this diversity of sports, it is hardly surprising that comparatively few took up skiing. Indeed it could have only appealed to fanatics. There were no ski lifts and the trains only ascended above the resorts during the summer. Learning to ski therefore entailed painstakingly edging or herringboning up the slope. The run down would last a few seconds - if one was lucky. Much more likely a fall would be followed by a slide and wipe out all return on the effort.

No sort of style had yet emerged. This was hardly surprising because skis had to be ordered from Norway. Instructions did occasionally appear in some book or magazine. The degree of authority with which they were written is open to question. Most seemed to have been based on second hand experience and made even more obscure through indifferent translation. Indeed some seemed to border on mythology .

"On the descent, the ski runner leans back on his stick and shuts his eyes. Then he darts forward, straight as an arrow, and continues until he can no longer breathe. He then throws himself sideways on the snow and waits until he regains his breath, and then once again hurls himself downwards till once more he loses his breath and throws himself on the snow and so forth until he reaches the valley".

In practice a skier could really do little more than try and stand upright, keep the weight back, and run straight. Thus the most important attribute was to keep one's balance. If the slope proved too steep, the accepted practice was to slide across, do a kick turn and then slide back again. Sir Arthur Conan Doyle's description in "The Strand Magazine" in 1894 was remarkably comprehensive. He described ski-ing as "getting as near to flying as any earth bound man can". Other parts of his article were more prosaic: "In ascending you shuttle up by long zig--zags the only advantage of your footgear being that it is carrying you over the snow which would engulf

you without it. But coming back, you simply turn your long toes and let yourself go, gliding delightfully over the gentle slopes, flying down the steeper ones, taking an occasional cropper." At one point a ski came off and disappeared down the slope. He had to slide down on the other and was more than relieved when his companions found it.

Compared with today, the equipment was unbelievably clumsy. Each ski was a single plank of ash. Consequently the edges quickly rounded. This made it very difficult to hold a line across the slope and virtually impossible if the snow was hard. One manufacturer's solution was to protect the edges with celluloid envelopes. It was precious little good for they wore out, if anything, faster than the wood.

The soles of the skis were not much help either. Originally even skins were not available for skiers wishing to climb. To prevent backward sliding the skis had to be dipped in water to form a layer of ice on the bottoms. It was not very satisfactory. It was even less so on reaching the top. The skier had to do some hard chipping before making the descent.

Conventional sliding was assisted by ironing or using a cork to spread black wax on the soles. The cost of a pair of skis, with boots, was just £2.

The single lilienfeld pole was used for balance rather than for pushing. It was up to nine ft. long and was hopelessly unwieldy and more likely to hinder the skier.

The art of ski-ing was not made any easier through the tenuous link between foot and ski. The binding had one strap over the toe with a second behind the heel. Certainly they did prevent the foot from constantly falling out, but it hardly provided any lateral control.

Men wore ordinary shooting boots, large enough to wear three pairs of socks beneath and still not pinch at the toes. Also the soles had to be sufficiently strong not to buckle. They were soaked in oil and then given a final coating of grease which, supposedly, made them waterproof. In practice, however, they still absorbed sufficient moisture to turn into casings of ice around the feet. The necessarily tight toe strap further restricted circulation. So one had periodically to take off one's boots and try to massage some sense of feeling back into the feet. Arnold Lunn has described how the loss of a boot can be as disabling as the loss of a ski and his dismay when, during one massaging interval, his boot rolled off down the slope and the agonising moments he spent before his guide returned with it safely.

The Palace skating rink at St. Moritz

Outfitters treated winter sports the same as for shooting grouse on the moors. Men usually wore a Norfolk jacket and plus fours with stockings, sweaters, collar and tie and a peaked cap. Ladies wore tweed skirts with elastic around the bottom to stop any flapping. Lower still and Fox's puttees were wound around stockinged shins and ankles. They had an unfortunate tendency to work loose so that at any moment a a length of felt trailing might be trailing behind. Hoods were made in particular by Greensmith & Downes of Edinburgh.

The leading Parisian couturier, Paul Poiret, produced one of the earliest designer ski outfits for ladies. However the master evidently had little knowledge about the all-pervasiveness of snow. His design incorporated enormous open pockets dangling somewhere below the knees. It was never worn - not even at St.Moritz.

Inevitably there were the lady rebels who placed practical need and comfort above mere fashion. The daughter of the novelist Florence Barclay rode the Cresta wearing jodhpurs and was consequently deemed fast in a meaning beyond mere speed. Monica Rowley set tongues wagging in the skating world when it was evident she had left off her corsets.

The height of practical fashion at St. Morite in 1913

The impractical haute couture of Paul Poiret, 1913.

The considerable discomfort of ski clothes lay in the incompatibility of the two most suitable materials. Wool is warm but collects snow until it becomes a deadweight of ice. Waterproof meant the heavy, rubberised material as invented by Mr. Mackintosh. Unfortunately it excluded air as efficiently as it did water. Any exertion and the wearer was soon sweating and wet with condensation. As most ski slopes at this time had deep, untracked snow, even comparative experts found they spent most of the day wet through. So it was normal to take spare woollies, including a hat, gloves and even socks and a sweater. It was not for nothing that the Seehof at Arosa was advertising "a heating room is reserved for sweaters etc."

Even so such facilities had their disadvantages. While no one would have dreamt of stealing, there was still a tendency for such clothing to be borrowed. Not that anyone was particularly bothered because the borrower would be sure to return the garment in due course.

All in all, these pioneer skiers should be hailed as remarkable characters. They suffered prolonged discomfort combined with considerable physical effort and all for very brief moments of exhilaration. They were showing the way and Society was about to follow.

CHAPTER II
SOCIETY DECORUM
1900 - 1914

In just one season, shortly before the First World War, the guest list at the St.Moritz Kulm Hotel included the Maharanee Holkar of Indore, the Grand Duke Andrew of Russia, Prince Adalbert of Prussia, Princess Stephanie of Belgium, whose voice had reminded Edward VII of a foghorn, Prince Maximilian of Furstenberg and the Princes Henry XVII and XLII of Reuss. They would none of them have dreamt of arriving before 18th December and none would have been seen there any time after 28th February. All of which proves that by the turn of the century, taking a winter holiday in Switzerland had indeed become the height of fashion.

The majority did not start patronising ski resorts until the construction of mountain railways allowed them to journey from the lowland terminus in reasonable comfort. The line linking Landquart with Davos opened in 1890. The one from Chur to St.Moritz opened in 1904. It was a spectacular feat of engineering with 42 tunnels and 156 bridges. In the Grisons, the Lauterbrunnen rack and cog system linking Mürren, Wengen and Grindelwald was completed in 1893. It did not actually open for the winter season until 1908. Even then it was under duress. Sir Henry Lunn had, in fact, first asked for the trains to run to Mürren the year before. However the authorities refused to believe anyone in their right mind would wish to stay in such an isolated village. Certainly Mürren looks quite lonely, perched on its winter-bleak shelf above an almost vertical drop to the Lauterbrunnen valley. In summer this is enchanting with scores of waterfalls. Alfred Lord Tennyson describes the sprays of water as looking like "dropping veils of thinnest lawn, pausing and falling and pausing again". In winter, though, they are held in white frozen suspension.

But the hesitancy over opening the Mürren line was nothing compared to the incredulity over the branch on the other side of the valley reaching up to Wengen. This section was kept closed in winter due to avalanches and rock falls. To run it in the face of such hazards would mean re-routing the line with a gradient never more than 18 per cent - as against the existing 25 per cent. This in turn, meant boring several tunnels. So Sir Henry Lunn had to guarantee the railway company against financial loss.

On arrival the visitor would find uniformed porters, with the name of their hotels embroidered on their caps, lined up along the platform. The new arrivals would walk down the row and, on finding the right one, point out their luggage. Then they would get into the hotel sleigh, drawn by one or two horses, their heads tossing plumes in the hotel colours.

Arriving and leaving according to a train timetable created quite a new etiquette. The Kronenhof at Pontresina had an electric bell system linked with the station. Once the guests had been identified off the train, the sleigh driver would signal one of the Gredig brothers. So on entering the hotel foyer the guests would be greeted personally. The ladies would be given a box of chocolates before being conducted to their rooms.

The long and tedious journey out meant guests normally stayed four or more weeks. As there were no party groups, guests developed strong friendships. So when a visitor left for home, it became quite a social event. Friends made during their stay would come down to the station armed with gifts of exotic sweets and alcohol to speed them on their way.

Johannes Badrutt died in 1899. He had developed the Kulm into deep luxury. The dining room was the first place in Switzerland to be lit by electricity. The same year telephones were installed, even though it meant laying a direct line all the way from Chur. This early introduction meant that, even 50 years later, St.Moritz still had the reputation of handling international calls more efficiently than either the Zurich or Geneva exchanges.

In the meantime, one of Badrutt's sons, Caspar, had bought a hotel called The Beau Rivage set further down by the lake. He acquired it by accident. When it had come up for sale, he had put in a bid on behalf of a friend who had then welshed on the deal. So he decided to run it himself.

Caspar had inherited not only his father's business acumen and considerable capital but had his own special flair as an hotelier. He was already aware of a wealthy foreign element among the Kulm guests who rather deplored the noisier, indeed sometimes rowdier, English sporting type. He also calculated St.Moritz now enjoyed sufficient patronage to support a hotel that was in the world first class category. With this in mind, he renamed The Beau Rivage as the Palace.

Badrutt had also inherited his father's love for the lavish. He briefed the architects to turn the hotel, in the words of Raymond Flower, into "a combination of mountain schloss and baroque chateau with gingerbread features such as turrets and arrow slits, all topped by a great tower".

He spent a further fortune on the furnishings. Indeed Flower declares that the duty paid on the furniture imported from Germany amounted on its own to more than he had paid for the original building. He imported carvers from Austria and himself scoured Italy for works of art. His greatest find was the Rafael Assumption of the Madonna, which hangs in the hall. He claimed it to be the original from the Sistine Chapel, though the opinions of art historians tend to differ. He had his new hotel opened in 1897 in great splendour by Queen Mary while she was still Princess Mary of Teck.

All these grand people would not have taken kindly to dining traditionally at a single long table. So the Palace dining room was furnished according to conventional restaurants with individual tables. However the hotel was attracting so many distinguished guests that Badrutt allocated the alcove on the right for his extra special clientele. Before long it had become known, and with good reason, as The Royal Corner. Those guests of sufficient calibre advisably booked their table in advance along with their suite. Even today claimants have to be royal in riches, if not by inheritance. Elsa Maxwell tried to claim a place and when she was refused, took umbrage and the next train home in a flood of tears. However, the tone was considerably lowered when Andre Citroen insisted on having his pet monkey eat alongside him.

Others of the Badrutt family also took over hotels in the village, notably the Waldhaus and the Privat. Several other managements were also coming onto the scene. In 1905 The Grand opened and at once attracted a strange mixture of Jews and jockeys. It never became really fashionable. When Lady Linlithgow was asked why she always chose to stay there she replied "I come out for a rest and the only people I know at the Grand are the concierge and head waiter."

1911 was a particularly flourishing year. Chantarella, the "cure establishment" set some 1,000 ft. higher up the mountain, was enlarged. Suvretta House was rather austere for a hotel and was built by Anton Bon. He had originally come out on behalf of the Ritz group to negotiate for the Kulm. Typically he chose a splendid, isolated sylvan setting. It immediately attracted the more aristocratic element among the British. It also appealed to the Germans, including the Crown Prince, or Little Willie as he was universally known. He arrived with his strange entourage of two rather outlandish Australian girls and a jockey.

By now St.Moritz had developed from a small village into the substantial resort it is today. Approached from the south, with the flat white area of the frozen Great Lake as foreground, the Edwardian architectural blocks are set dramatically on the rising slope. It exudes all the glamour, history and power which it truly holds. Free from smoke and dirt, the buildings are predominantly cream. In the centre is the substantial architecture of the Palace together with its eccentric tower. Also outstanding is the leaning tower of the old church. Close by are the distinctive three cubes which form the Kulm. Crowding in on one side of the rising backdrop is the Crystal Hotel, formerly the Carlton, while there is the darker sizeable block of Chantarella in the background.

Many of the hotels at this time made much play over the Englishness of their fittings. The Alexandra at Arosa advertised not only that they had "a spacious lounge with English fireplace" but even specified the name of the English manufacturer of their billiard table (Burroughs & Watts). But they could none the less be fairly primitive in their facilities. After a fire, The Palace at Mürren had been rebuilt with reputedly the finest ballroom in Switzerland. The bedrooms, though, were without running water.

The more humble hotels could only be described as quaint. The water in the bathrooms of the Soldenella at Wengen was heated by a strange boiler set on the wall and fuelled with logs. So the bather benefited additionally from the scalding overspill from the heater above. What is more, the bather was not allowed to lock the door. Periodically the maid came in with more wood to stoke the boiler "when she took noticeable, leisurely and open interest in the naked incumbent."

Also at the turn of the century, the Society for the Propagation of the Gospel took upon itself to supply deserving clergymen with a working holiday. Initially services were held in the hotels. Soon visitors at the larger resorts were financing small chapels such as still flourish at Zermatt, Wengen, Arosa and Mürren. As most visitors attended, the services also provided an effective way of giving out important notices, such as avalanche warnings and safety rules concerning ski-jorers.

At a time when visitors might well spend three or four weeks in one another's company, social niceties assumed considerable importance. Yet these were peculiar circumstances. Visitors would be constantly meeting out luging, skating or curling to a degree when it would seem standoffish not to acknowledge each other without formal introduction. One of those infuriating self appointed arbiters of etiquette in the smart magazines decreed that "once one has tobogganed together, you can change from addressing one another as Mr. Brown and Miss Smith to Mr. John and Miss Mary". In practice anyone implicitly following these instructions would have been considered rather curious and definitely a prude.

Skiers were developing their own special etiquette. After all, it is only rational to assume that a lady prepared to go ski-ing has sufficient stamina to carry her own skis. "Ladies put on their own ski and manage their own bindings and it is not good manners to offer to assist them" was the strictly realistic guidance offered by Crichton Somerville, writing in 1907 in his book "Ski Running". He also said: "You may not instantly rush to the assistance of a lady who may have fallen".

The true sporting spirit was also cherished. Mostly the arrangements for any events were, by general consent, left to the English "since they are universally acknowledged to be past masters in the art of organising outdoor sports". It was a tribute which the British were apt, in their supercilious fashion, to take for granted. Yet it was a view widely held. A leading Swiss skier wrote: "The conception of (British) sport was much more developed than our own, clarifed through an age-long tradition..... we learned the meaning of a good loser, of the man who loses with a smile. We learned the meaning of fair play - almost a novelty for us for which we have no synonym in our mother language".

Behind this lay all the nuances of good and bad form. Heaven forbid that anyone should give even the slightest hint of gloating in victory or suggest undue depression in defeat. Taking part was what counted. Winning for the sake of winning was utterly repugnant to the British and was practised only by cads and foreigners. Indeed pot hunting was so reprehensible it became the practice to leave one's cups with the hotel where the management displayed them communally in a specially purchased display case.

In 1909 a Norwegian called Jakobsenki appeared in Kitzbühel. He was an exponent of several revolutionary ideas. He skied with a wide track and, besides christianias, he practised step and jump turns. Within a year or two his style had become all the rage throughout the Salzburg area though it was never widely practised.

At about the same time the single, long and highly inconvenient lilienfeld pole was at last discarded in favour of the two even length sticks used by the Laps. Amongst other things it made stick riding much easier. Two poles dragged in the snow make a far more effective brake than one. Also short poles can be held between the legs which is less tiring than having to hold them to one side. Although stick riding was soon considered very bad form, it was used even as late as 1913 by E.M.Thomas while he was winning the British Ski Association Championships.

However, beyond those areas frequented by the few knowledgeable skiers, everyone else in the Alps usually had to learn from books. "Dame Katherine Furse began to ski many years ago (she had in fact made the tour over the Furka pass 30 years earlier) but never did a turn till this year. In the summer she bought a book on ski-ing".

In truth, even in those early days she had quite a number to choose from. Within a year there had appeared "The Ski Runner" by E.C.Richardson, "Ski-ing for Beginners and Mountaineers" by W.R. Rickmers, a pioneer in mountaineering on skis. Most important of all was "How To Ski" by Vivian Caulfeild, which appeared in 1910. He replaced Zardski's theories after making the first really scientific analysis of ski dynamics. He considered that Zardski's use of snow ploughs and stem turns was a way of avoiding difficulties rather than eradicating them. His book had a huge impact. It became quite common to see skiers on the slopes consulting their copy, cursing as the wind turned over pages before they had time to find out why, yet again, their turns were failing to materialise. Then in 1913 Arnold Lunn added two periphery titles: "Ski-ing" which concentrated on ski holidays more generally and "The Alpine Ski Guide to the Bernese Oberland".

The other way people learned to ski was through clubs. The Edwardians were mad about clubs and every major resort had one for every sort of enterprise. They had, though, been long preceded in California for clubs in Onion Calley and Laporte had been founded in the 1860's.

The first club specifically for skiers in Switzerland was at St.Moritz in 1902. But the initial enthusiasm soon waned. The next year it re-emerged as the Ski Club Alpina. However by the following year it too had gone into terminal decline. The Ski Club at Davos was started a year later and due to the missionary zeal of the Richardson brothers, it remained highly active. The same year saw the foundation of the Ski Club of Great Britain. Perhaps it was significant that the first president, Edgar Syers, was primarily a skater. The first championships were held at Kitzbühel. It was still a Nordic competition and was won by E.C. Richardson.

The Davos club employed guides to give free lessons for adults. In time reasonable progress led from derisory floundering on the village slopes to mountain excursions and tours were conducted once or twice a week. Standardising the clubs was particularly useful in defining tests. These ensured a member did not have to wait until actually up the mountain before discovering a companion had been over optimistic in describing his prowess. To pass the SCGB test, skiers had to make two runs, with or without sticks, one finishing with a christiania and the other with a telemark in the opposite direction. Both had to be completed without falling.

However members were subjected to considerable discipline. Attendance at Sunday morning practice on the Church Slopes behind the Fluela Hotel was compulsory. The Club also undertook teaching the local boys - and with some success. It was largely to its credit that young Attenhoffer won the Swiss championships in 1917.

Another avowed object of the Davos Ski Club was to urge the local shops to stock proper Norwegian ski equipment. The Swiss products were considered rubbish. But the shopkeepers were either patriotic or, more probably, convinced they would lose money in some way. The Club met with such resistance it had to make its own arrangements for importing the skis along with such proven accessories as the limb-confusing brand- name Torgersen Handy Bindings.

These tours in turn led to set routes. Messrs Steele and Dandy made a major, if unwitting, contribution in this direction. They decided to emulate Conan Doyle by ski-ing over to Arosa. Instead they almost immediately turned right when they should have gone straight on. They were so hopelessly lost they had to spend the night in a shepherd's hut. So it was not until the next morning that they ended up at Küblis, a small village a long way down the railway line. And thus was discovered one of the longest and most famous ski runs in the world, the seven mile Parsenn. It was particularly attractive since it lent itself to a highly civilized routine. The usual form was to make the run in the morning. You had lunch in the train back. This left just enough time to make a second run in the afternoon arriving at Küblis station for a gluhwein before catching the last train back.

The run became so popular that before long the Club erected their Parsenn Hut. The owner of the only piece of bare mountainside at all suitable demanded an exorbitant rental. Not that the setting proved ideal at any price. In 1906, with one member still inside, it was swept away by an avalanche. However it was soon rebuilt and within its hot and steamy walls the perennial argument raged over how long it took to make the run. The obvious solution was to have a race. Thus was born the Parsenn Derby.

One difficulty inherent in all this competitive enthusiasm was the matter of prizes. Members would be detailed to go round begging the local shopkeepers. Hardly surprisingly the shopkeepers soon became fed up with it all. When they ultimately refused they were pestered for anything damaged or out of date. "Thus the prizes had a high percentage of chipped plaques, half strength scents etc."

Downhill ski-ing at this time only appealed to fanatics. To acquire even a modicum of prowess meant spending nine- tenths of the time climbing. So popular interest tended to be directed more to elaborations. Jumping and ski-joring do not require such energy. Moreover they attract admiring spectators.

The modern era of jumping began in Norway in 1840. The key discovery was that much further distances could be reached if the landing was on a slope rather than on the flat. Thus half of the vertical impact on landing is diverted into the forward movement. From that day on jumps have been gauged by distance rather than height.

When jumping was introduced into the Alpine setting at St.Moritz, in 1906, the British were instant converts, indeed fanatics. Alex Keiller of marmalade fame, coached by the Norwegian champion Harald Smith, was soon jumping 65 ft. Smith himself was drawing crowds of 4,000 as he reached 100 ft. on the Julier Jump. In true British fashion, the British Ski Jumping Club was duly formed. The choice of club colours was both apt and sympathetic. They were white for the snow and black and blue to represent the presumed state of a members' posterior. There were even ladies who jumped regardless of the encumbrance of their ankle-length skirts. The Countess Paula Lamberg won championships at her home town of Kitzbühel. Another intrepid lady was at St. Moritz. Inevitably there came the day when she fell. Her skirt was whipped up revealing red flannel underwear. After that she was generally known as Mademoiselle Fuscia.

Another elaboration was ski-joring. Harald Smith helped popularise this too. When he was not jumping, he was to be seen gliding effortlessly along the St.Moritz streets towed by a horse.

Soon the Kuverein was organising races on the Le Mans principle and pedestrians casually walking along the streets now had to look sharp. The most popular run started outside the Post Hotel and led down to St.Moritz Bad before coming back to finish just outside Steffani's Hotel. Formation of the inevitable club took a little longer and it was not until 1909 that Viscount Bury was elected the first president. One of the Club's most successful exponents was Lady Harmsworth wife of the press baron.

Ski-jorers could ski in pairs. The winning team of the mixed race in 1910 proved of peculiar interest. It comprised Lady Evelyn Guinness in partnership with Miss Hutton and with W.Griggs, the famous jockey, riding the horse. Much of the ski-jorers skill rested in negotiating corners. As the horse slows down, the reins

Ski-joring pairs. The ablest practitioners guided the horse as well. Licences were required to drive through the streets.

must be kept taut. This is done by raising the hands above the head and at the same time performing a step christie. Real experts gained those few vital moments just before the finish by winding in their tow.

The ablest practitioners guided the horse as well.

Some practitioners became so adept they dispensed with the rider. They held on to the tow with one hand and controlled the reins with the other. Not quite so adroit were the family groups. Father would be in front, of course, holding the tow and reins. Wife and one or two children would be strung along behind.

So it was hardly surprising when the police started receiving complaints of riderless horses careering along the St.Moritz streets. The authorities had to institute road tests. Later activities were transferred to the area of the Great Lake. Once there, ski-joring soon became linked with trotting events and was, in due course, incorporated with full blooded horse racing. This was taken up with such enthusiasm that by 1910 some of the leading owners, such as Prince Lubomirsky and Count Tassilo Festetics, were

Several famous owners raced their horses on the Great Lake infront of St. Moritz. The world famous Palace Hotel is in the left foreground and the three blocks of the Kulm are close to the church.

bringing their best mounts up from their stables in Vienna and Berlin. The course was made complete with railings and a totalizator which proved so popular it did 26,000 francs worth of business over the first season. Before long a stand and enclosure were added. At first those of a more nervous disposition feared the ice might crack under the weight. So a professor was brought up from Zurich and he pronounced it could support half a million people.

Visitors at Crans Montana adopted the idea with enthusiasm. They made a course on Lake Gremon and were soon elaborating it into a "Skidrome". Kitzbühel was another winter station where horse racing on ice became the rage. This, however, was derived from tradition. The local skills in working wrought iron had led naturally to the creation of ski chariots. With the Austrian love of parties, the events soon developed into something between the chariot races of Ancient Rome and the trotting races of the American South.

The popularity of curling among the British ran virtually parallel with the construction of artificial ice rinks. In 1887 the first two curling rinks opened in Britain. To the humiliation of the Scots, both enterprises were south of the border, at Southport and Manchester. The situation was not rectified for a further 20 years when at last a rink was opened in Glasgow and, eventually in 1912, an enormous rink was opened in Edinburgh. No specialist rinks were opened in London. In due course, though, both Princes in Knightsbridge and subsequently Westminster skating rinks were persuaded to allocate one or two evenings a week to curling.

Such all year venues inevitably raised both the number of curlers and the standard of play, particularly in Scotland. This, in turn, bred numerous clubs in Switzerland.

Largely because it is one of the few team winter sports, curling lent itself naturally to inter hotel competitions. The trend grew swiftly and soon reached the level of inter resort events. There was the Hudson Cup, an annual competition between the ladies of St.Moritz and Davos. But the game only became truly cosmopolitan in 1895 with the Jackson Cup. This is played alternately in the Eastern and Western halves of Switzerland. However each resort can enter only one team. Rather extravagant exceptions are made for Davos, Grindelwald and St.Moritz. They can enter as many as they wish. The advantage was fully realised by St.Moritz which won 13 of the initial 14 matches. They occasioned considerable excitement each year. "As the train came in, the Kurverein band struck up. The team members were greeted and embraced and conducted to a laurel bedecked equipage which was then drawn at a dignified pace through the village to the accompaniment of more music and huzzas from the crowd".

The success of these matches encouraged the Scots to organise bonspiels. The one at Celerina, with the first stone ceremonially laid by no less a person than The Arch Duke Franz Ferdinand, became particularly famous for its vivacity. By 1905, however, curling was going into serious decline. This did not suit Henry Lunn who had developed several resorts especially for curling. He set about reversing the slide by offering a cup for an international championship. His astute business sense was again confirmed. Nearly a hundred Scots rallied to the challenge. They travelled to Kandersteg along with an estimated three tons of granite. Some were so concerned they even kept their stones with them in the sleeping cars.

Curling, perhaps more than luging, found immediate appeal among the Swiss. The village tradesmen formed enthusiastic teams of their own and were always happy to play alongside or challenge visitors. But in contrast it did not seem to appeal to those Swiss living in lowland cities. Not, that is, until 1959 when Air Canada donated the Silver Broom trophy. This brought the game to international fame.

Hardly had bandy reached Switzerland than it was being challenged by ice hockey - and it soon became a losing battle. By 1910, for instance, play at Morgins had been restricted to an hour after tea. For the rest of the day the skaters had first claim to the ice. The results were sometimes strangely distorted, such as when Winchester played the world - and Winchester won. After that, bandy became extinct except in Eastern Europe. There was, however a freak revival in 1948 when it was surprisingly chosen as a demonstration event in the Olympic Games. It became an official event in 2002.

Ice hockey was, in contrast, destined for phenomenal growth. Indeed, as far back as 1875 it had become the preferred game at Princes, when they challenged Montreux to play a match "in the Canadian style". The British drew up what they declared to be the official rules and consequently dominated the International Hockey League - the Association was formed later. Then, in true British style, they organised a world championship which they proceeded to win. But ice hockey only really caught the public's imagination when Edward VII, while still Prince of Wales, together with his son, the future George V, arranged a match on the lake at Buckingham Palace.

Another innovation was the ski bike. By pure chance it was being developed almost simultaneously in both Switzerland and Austria.

The Kitzbühel version appeared in 1910. It required human scooting power. It had a conventional cycle frame of iron but had wooden runners instead of wheels. The handlebars were long and curved like Ibex antlers. This provided an advantage not so much for steering as for romance. The cyclist used it as a perch for his girlfriend. Rather appropriately, it was called a ski wolf.

At almost the same time, Christian Buhlmann, the local carpenter and wheelwright at Grindelwald, was developing a similar machine. Because he was a carpenter he reversed the use of materials. The frame was made of wood and he used metal just on the runners and the front steering bar.

Both models, however suffered through lack of any braking system. This added considerably to the excitement during races, particularly when they were in competition with skiers.

Some 20 years later the English made their contribution when Humphrey Cobb designed a snow bike of his own. His touch of originality was to make it articulated. He also overcame the brake problem by using a small float ski attached to each foot. He invented his bike so that it should speed him on his way from the Grand Hotel at Morgins down to the skating rink. For the uphill return he simply paid a village lad to take it back for him.

In the mean time luging was developing apace. One day in 1889 Stephen Whitney from Philadelphia was out with some high spirited friends at Davos. Rather than interrupt their scintillating conversation they tied the luges together. They found this so congenial they made the arrangement permanent by using 12 ft planks to fasten their luges in pairs. Thus, in principle, was bobsleighing invented.

Considering Mr. Whitney's agglomeration was undoubtedly makeshift it may well be asked what constitutes a proper bobsleigh? The Museum of Antiquities in Zurich displays what is claimed to be the first bob though it was not, in fact, made until five years later in 1895.

Another strong claimant is to be found at Kitzbühel. The pioneer bobsleigh, like the snow bikes and trotting gigs, had a metal frame. It had canvas seats set on wooden slats woven like the bedsprings of a cheap bed. The front 24 in. of both runners were made as a separate steering unit. They could be moved in parallel by a large steering wheel. However it was the Swiss design with cable attachments that came to be universally adopted. Then the Kitzbühel steering wheel regained popularity. It was found to be easier on the arms. The man at the rear has always been the brakeman, pressing on two iron spikes. He is also responsible for the initial push and part of his skill lies in jumping aboard at the last possible moment. The one, two or even three persons between are there largely for the ride. At the start they must lean back together to form a "good even lie". At the corners they must lean sideways in unison for if they skid they can overturn and then they will all be scalped!

Bobbers have always been conscientious over sex equality. The original St.Moritz club rules stated that in a team of three at least one must be a woman and if there are four or more places, at least two must be for women. The custom was also observed at Kitzbühel - though the gallantry was rather more questionable. While the team of four men were seated, the lady was provided with a handhold and had to stand precariously on the back. The rules made it clear that under no circumstances was she allowed to steer.

Although bobs may seem cumbersome machines, Tony Nash proved at the 1964 Olympics that they can be manoeuvred with considerable precision. He realised he could only gain a vital twelve hundredths of a second on the Igls run if he turned his machine precisely under the second O of a Coca-Cola sign. He did it and he won.

Initially the bobbers, like the lugers, used the roads. However their machines soon became so heavy they were shredding the surface. They experimented with an unfortunate attempt to toughen and flatten the surface using rollers filled with hot water. This merely melted the surface which immediately froze again producing an excellent sheet of ice. While the results may have been fine for the bobbers, it made a formidable hazard for all other forms of transport. It all proved too much for the long suffering locals. They took to placing rocks in the road just around the blind corners. The bobbers acceded the point and at last made their own special runs. At St.Moritz they continued freezing the snow and introduced embankments. They certainly sped down their

The disastrous experiment with a hot water roller. It turned the roads into sheet ice.

narrow corridor of ice but it was a bit too fast and there were several "horrendous incidents". The moment of sanity came after a crew had been hurled 30 yd. through the air. "It was sufficient to cause them to ponder carefully the good luck that had up to then attended their escapades". The result of this pondering was that rocks around the corners seemed the more preferable hazard. They returned to the road down to Celerina. By 1903, however, even they realised they should have a proper run, and accepted it must be snow covered rather than iced.

But again the citizens of Kitzbühel had forestalled them. The village run had been constructed back in 1896. It was 1,100 m. long with five hairpin and several minor bends. The first championships were held in 1909.

As with ski-ing, there was always the dreary process of returning to the top. Bobsleighs had become so heavy the new runs were planned to end close to the road. The local lads dragged them the short distance to the horse sleigh. Fights would break out among them until it was agreed that the first to touch the wheel had the right and could claim the tip.

Bobbing became so popular several resorts had to build a second and more difficult run. Besides reducing the frustration of long waits these more ambitious runs relieved the experts from tolerating the ineptitude of beginners. A second run was badly needed at Arosa as both skating and bandy were considered altogether too tiring for the TB patients. Even those too ill to bob could still act as timekeepers and gatekeepers. The second and considerably longer run was built in 1910. It started at the Old Church in Inner Arosa, running past the Grand Hotel right down to the Unter See.

Mürren also had a second run. Instead of a road, the Allmendhubel railway was extended a further 1,000 ft. At Wengen the authorities opened the section of railway up to the Water Station, immediately above the village.

All this evolution was only economically viable because bobbing was also attracting a large number of spectators. It is not only fast but carries a high degree of risk. At St.Mortiz there were almost bound to be one or two celebrities flashing past. They might even include royals, such as His Highness the Crown Prince of Germany, who was honorary president. Despite the ridicule of the British coterie, he was an adroit driver. Prince Henry of Reuss won the Bobsleigh Derby in 1908 and in the same year achieved the triple triumph of the Reckitt Challenge Cup, the Auffm Ordt and the Fleetwood Wilson cups. Winner of the Fleetwood cup in another year was the Hon. F.N.Curzon, brother of the Viceroy of India. Then John Jacob Astor, the American real estate millionaire, presented a cup and for the first two years proceeded to win it himself.

At the same time, luging had developed another elaboration called tobogganing, not to be confused with bobsleighing. It all came about in 1886 when, instead of sitting on his luge, a certain Mr. Cornish startled everyone by lying down upon it. Then, of all things, he proceeded down the slope head first "His legs alternating between a flourish in mid-air and occasional contact with mother earth". It was evident this prone position provided much better control and soon became accepted form. However there remained a few ladies who felt it was indecorous. They remained firmly seated.

Then in 1890 Major W.H.Bulpett designed a skeleton along Canadian timber style which, perversely, was called An American. It was unusually long and had spring runners. Further versions were made longer and longer till, at 150 cm., they were almost as long as their riders were tall.

Then A.J.Bott, who had been a keen oarsman, had the local blacksmith build him a sliding seat. It greatly improved the balance, sliding backwards for the corners and forward along the straits. He also introduced his "snubnosed" skeleton. At one point it became the practice to pre-heat the runners as it increased the speed. However the authorities took a poor view of the practice and quickly declared it illegal. Another direct result of the prone position was to fix rakes on the toes.

When transition from the road could be delayed no longer, Caspar Badrutt called in a young geometrician from Celerina. Together with Major Bulpett they planned a really formidable run with iced embankments. Typically Badrutt took full responsibility for the construction work. Also, typically, he refused a request to be on the founding committee for he felt it should be composed entirely of visitors. So in appreciation of his enthusiasm, his Kulm guests presented him with a silver megaphone, chosen because they feared he might lose his voice through constantly urging the workmen on to greater effort.

Following the same slope as the road, the run snakes three quarters of a mile, picking up its name as it passes through the village of Cresta, and ending at Celerina. It has hardly been altered since. Indeed it is the corners, echoing the road, that have made the Cresta unique. "Every variety of turn, from the sharp rectangular corner to the most gentle curve, is to be found", according to an early description. "The slope of the ground changes every few yards. There are leaps followed by sudden depressions which cause the machine to leave the track and skim through the air before touching the ice again. The aim in building the Cresta is to make it difficult - in moderation - as well as fast. It helps the most skilful and resourceful rider win." Indeed the winner of the first Cresta Grand National was a boy of 16 who was so light he was airborne for 12 yd. at a time.

Even though there is an earth base the tricky points vary from year to year. For instance, 1910 was notable for riders seen with cut chins, all acquired through going over the top of Bulpett corner.

Shuttlecock, however, is unique. It remains a perennial hazard. Indeed a special viewing platform had to be built alongside and immediately became known as the Vulture Perch. Everyone flung off Shuttlecock automatically qualifies as a member of the Shuttlecock Club. Indeed membership can be so comprehensive it at one time included a horse that had been seen to stumble within the vicinity. A distinguished feature of the Club's deliberations is the annual dinner when members eat surrounded by bales of straw. It is a touch that must have been of more than passing interest to the horse when it was brought over to attend the dinner.

In 1903 Major Bulpett set the Cresta record at 59.6 seconds. It meant he was travelling at 150 km or nearly 100 mph with his face barely six inches from the ice. It is an achievement which compares commendably with, for instance, the 54.21 seconds record set 70 years later in 1971.

Paul Gallico has written a vivid description of how it feels to go down the Cresta and gives an insight into the hold it gains on so many riders:

"'Rake' they told me, 'Rake all the way down and hang on for all you are worth'. The all clear bell sounded, the wooden barrier was raised. Someone gave me a push and within a few yards the ice walls, one either side, began to flash past. I dug in my toes and raked hard. It didn't seem to make any difference. Ahead of me looked a high curling wall of ice. I slammed into the side of it with a sickening wrench only to dip into what seemed a bottomless crevasse of gleaming ice. At the sight of this fearful pit, I don't mind admitting that I was close to panic...Ahead a high bridge shot up. Just as it seemed that I must split my skull against the bridge support the curve shot me through the tunnel..... my world was a nightmare of glittering blue-white ice, tearing wind, pounding and battering steel. My strength was failing. At any moment I would lose my frenzied hold. Suddenly I felt a sharp blow on the right side of my ribs, followed by an almost intolerable pressure. Then I was rising heavenwards (this was Finishing Bank, an upwards curve designed to slow the skeleton to a halt)... and then I was lying immobile on the sledge in soft snow, numb fingers still convulsively clutching the steel bar". And what did Paul Gallico then do? He went straight back to the top to claim another ride and see if he could do it a bit faster.

Alex Coomber, three times world champion, has described it, perhaps a bit more succinctly as like "lying on a skateboard and being towed down a motorway at 80 mph."

In 1895 it was found the "flagwallers" were no longer adequate and an electronic chromograph timing device was installed. It was precise to within a tenth of a second.

While there had been several serious accidents over the first 25 years, none had proved fatal. Then there were two fatalities within the same season. First down on the fatal morning, Compte Jules de Bylandt was travelling at 50 mph when he saw ahead a plank which one of the maintenance men had forgotten to remove. In desperation he apparently tried to propel himself over it hoping he might miraculously land on the skeleton on the other side. It was a gallant but hopeless attempt. He was killed instantly. The workman and the foreman were sent to prison for criminal negligence. However strong representations by the Club officials proved that Swiss legislation is indeed adjustable and they were released.

The same year Captain H. Pennell, who held the Victoria Cross, came off at Shuttlecock and died that night from internal injuries. Four years later and another two people had been killed and questions started being asked. Major Bulpett put his finger on the crucial point: It was the recent restructuring. In the desire to make the run faster, the embankments had been rebuilt so that they were almost vertical. This, he explained, meant that when people failed to negotiate a corner properly the increased G force pressed them right down into the run. It would be better, he declared, for the embankments to be kept as before. Then when a rider got into difficulties he would be automatically spewed off the top into the comparative safety of the snow.

For some time the president of the Club was the Hon. Francis Curzon. His family was famous for its pedigree and distinction. However the family was notorious for being only too aware of their superiority. True to family form, Francis assumed his opinion was unquestionably right and brooked no argument. His behaviour was so high handed he quickly became extremely unpopular. Other, and fortunately less contentious, aristocratic riders of the Cresta included Lord Northesk, Lord Northland and Lord Bledisloe. Outstanding among the plebeians was J.A.Bott, who won the Grand National five years in succession andconducted a 10 year rivalry with Thoma Badrutt. Just before the outbreak of the First World War, a promising youngster John Moore Brabazon, distinguished himself by winning the Novices Cup with consummate ease. He had already distinguished himself as the first Briton to pilot an airoplane. Another famous aviator who was a Cresta runner was Graham White. However he soon abandoned the Cresta for the Great Lake where he gave visitors air flips in his monoplane.

The fatal Cresta accident of Captain Henry Pennel, VC

35

Nor were ladies any less determined in riding the Cresta. The champion was Mrs.McLaren and following hard on her heels was Ursula Wheble who won the Women's Cup seven times. She was one of the two women prepared to start right from the top. The other rode with such complete indifference to danger it was rumoured that she was suffering from advanced cancer. If truth be known, many of the ladies made times equal and indeed faster than the men. But they exercised discretion and remained highly reticent over their supremacy. Other famous, though perhaps less adroit, lady riders were Lady Ribblesdale, the former wife of J.J.Astor and the best selling novelist Florence Barclay.

Eventually one of the ladies flew off the run and was badly bruised. The accident was made an excuse for banning women altogether. The committee tactfully explained that it was "for medical reasons". But these Cresta ladies not only had courage and determination but resourcefulness as well. They were not to be so easily thwarted. Quite a number found ways of going down after the run had been officially closed. There was even rumour that some were deceiving the authorities by dressing as men. However they triumphed in the end. In 1948 the men's skeleton bobsleigh

A tailing party of lugers ready for the start. "Snaking" may cause some to end up in a snowbank.

was dropped from the Olympics as being too dangerous. But in 2002 the skeleton bobsleigh was reinstated - but exclusively for the ladies.

Despite the obvious similarities there was quite a marked difference in temperament between those who preferred the prone position on a skeleton to sitting three or even five to a bobsleigh. Indeed they worked to a different clock.

The Cresta riders were usually aged at least 30 . They were more dedicated, indeed motivated almost by compulsion. They would be up by seven for the first run at nine o'clock while the ice was still hard. They considered the rest of the day to be an anticlimax. They might spend the afternoon leisurely ski-ing before retiring early to bed.

In contrast the bob fraternity were usually in their 'twenties and approached their sport with nonchalance. They got up late and did not make their runs until the afternoon. The camaraderie usually extended into the evening and indeed the early hours of the morning.

The final split came in 1897. As a result, the original luge became virtually obsolete. Its only remaining adherents were mothers and children. However, it did still retain some of its universal appeal in the form of tailing parties after dark. Indeed, being strung out along a rope trailing behind a horse and sleigh in itself requires a degree of skill. When the horse trots round a corner the line of luges tends to snake. This calls for neat footwork if the rider is not to be overturned in the snow bank at the side of the road. Another major threat is the village dogs, indignant at what they consider an intrusion on their territory. They are prone to run out, barking and threatening to bite.

Ignoring such hazards, Robert Louis Stevenson gave a graphic if glamorous description of such a night ride. "Then you push off; the toboggan fetches way; she begins to feel the hill, to glide, to swim, to gallop. In a breath you are out from under the pine trees and a whole heavenful of stars reels and flashes overhead. Then comes a vicious effort for by this time your wooden steed is speeding like the wind and you are spinning round a corner and the whole glittering valley and all the lights in the great hotels lie for a moment at your feet; and the next you are racing once more in the shadow of the night, with close shut teeth and beating heart. Yet a little while and you will be landed on the high road by the door of your own hotel. This is an atmosphere tingling with forty degrees of frost, in a night made luminous with stars and snow, and girt with strange white mountains, teaches the pulse an unaccustomed tune and adds a new excitement to the life of man upon his planet".

Skating was also undergoing a revolution, precipitated by the construction of mountain railways linking such lowland stations as Chur and Lauterbrunnen to the various resorts. Easier access now brought out members of the British skating clubs and Princes in Kinghtsbridge in particular.

All these club members, however, practised the new vulgar Continental style with its emphasis on dancing.. Its history, however, goes back at least to when Pepys is supposed to have danced with Nell Gwyn on the Thames during the great frost of 1683. But it did not really come to flourish until an American ballet dancer, Jackson Haines defined skating steps to be performed specifically to music. He introduced his ideas in Vienna in 1868 and they became so popular that it seemed perfectly normal when the Hungarian star Lilly Krobberger arrived for the championships in Vienna complete with her own orchestra.

There was a place for Continental skating in England as well. Up till then skating was only practised on frozen lakes so that there was no shortage of space. While a figure of four in the English school required about 3,600 sq ft., a pair skating Continental style required a mere 400 sq ft. and artificial ice rinks were becoming established.

One of the very first artificial rinks rejoiced in the name of a "floating glacierum". It was in Chelsea and the surface measured a mere 24 ft. by 16 ft. The refrigeration technique had been developed by a Professor John Gamage during his research to find an effective way of freezing meat. His formula, comprised ether, protoxide of nitrogen and glycerine. It was an expensive mixture and had its limitations. However it was a considerable improvement over previous attempts at artificial ice. This had notably included a concoction of hogs lard and melted sulphur which not only smelt but proved utterly revolting for any skater who chanced to trip and fall. .

Skating was only enthusiastically taken up by society when, largely through the initiative of the "Flying" Duchess of Bedford, Princes ice rink opened in Knightsbridge. It closed on the outbreak of the First World War and was, in due course, succeeded by the Westminster Ice Club, founded by Stephen Courtauld. Here, although there was much more space, there was still insufficient room for the traditional English style skater. The only tolerated exception was "Old" Colonel Anstey who persisted with his long brackets and rockers. He was considered rather tiresome in the way he would suddenly loom up and pass close to the centre of a skater diligently practising figures. Indeed it was all anathema to the traditionalists with their stately, stylised movements.

Continental skating had other advantages as well. While the English style undoubtedly afforded great fun, it did not, unlike Continental skating, offer much scope for competition. Similarly pair skating in the English style was limited to holding hands while the Continental offered all the flowing and rhythmic movements of ice dancing and the partners close to one another..

Exponents of the English style tended to be older and probably more crusty since they refused even to contemplate the Continental school. Rather they took refuge in ridicule. Henry Cobb wrote: "Combined figure skating appeals to me because it is English. The team spirit on ice. I like watching good Continental skating just as I like watching ballet dancing, but I pay other people to do my ballet for me".

In the same way, Miss Bland Jamieson was to write: "These exuberant international skaters seemed to be showing off and performing circus stunts. We looked askance at their black tunics and tight fitting breeches trimmed with Astrakhan fur". This was why they were contemptuously dubbed Lion Tamers. These diehards even claimed the Continental style damaged one's skating technique.

Outstanding exponents of the Continental skaters at St.Moritz were J. Keiller Greig, J.H.Johnson and the masseuse Grenandier. Very good looking, Grenandier would simply idle around the rink. Suddenly, apparently just as the mood took him, he would break into a dazzling display of world competition standard, for he had been world champion in 1898 and had given the first exhibition of the Continental style in London. After attracting quite a crowd, he would just as suddenly break off and start skating ordinarily as though he was quite another person. His wife owned the famous dress shop Lucille. So she was not given to wearing black tights but a multitude of different coloured petticoats which frothed as she whirled round the rink.

The Continental skaters did not allow the English school to go unchallenged. A moment of crisis occurred on the rink of the Bear Hotel. The Continentals had the audacity to ask Mr. Bosch to provide a band so that they could dance. Such an outrageous suggestion was instantly put down by the numerically superior exponents of the English style. However the Continentals rallied for a showdown. They simply hired their own band. The English school were forced to admit defeat.

Even the skiers were not above harassing them. When K.R. Swan, later president of the Ski Club of Great Britain, first put on skis, his friends mischievously took him to the top of the notorious Church run. Having successfully launched him, they watched with delight as he shot, completely out of control, down a bank and onto the rink scattering all the indignant skaters skimming around their tangerines.

The National Skating Association experienced its moment of truth in St. Moritz. They had spent years dithering over admitting the Continentals as a special section of the Club. But they had a traitor among them: In 1907 Edgar Syers stole a despicable march by announcing from London that he had formed a British club for the Continental stylists. The English school were furious. Not only had they been outmanoeuvred but Syers was not even a good skater. It was widely recognised that it was his wife, Madge, who carried him through all the pair championships they had won. With Princes as his base, the uppity Edgar Syers had acquired an almost unassailable position for his new fangled association. He had successfully inveigled the prestigious sporting Earl of Lytton into accepting the presidency. To add insult to injury, Syers had pre-empted the National Association and had already lodged an application for international status.

Within two years the National Skating Association had planned a terrible revenge. After protracted negotiations, Edgar Syers was coerced into agreeing to an amalgamation. A meeting to forge the link was held at the Kulm Hotel. There the English school made sure of their triumph. While passing a motion congratulating the secretary E.E. Mavrogordato for "the care and trouble he had taken," no mention was made of Edgar Syers. As a final indignity, he was not even voted onto the committee.

Usually about once a week the serious work on the village rinks would be given over to a gymkhana or fete.

The fetes tended to be the more serious affairs. They were held during the day time. There was usually a fine log fire burning at one side and nearby baskets of cakes provided light refreshment. The programme mainly comprised exhibition skating given by champions. There were also figure competitions for the more proficient visitors. The afternoons usually ended on a lighter note. The local skating professional would appear in pantomime kit pretending to be a beginner or drunk, barely staying upright. Then in the closing sequence, and perhaps mindful of their professional image, they would break into a dazzling display of twists and jumps.

Gymkhanas were altogether more frivolous with everyone encouraged to join in. They were usually organised by one or two of the local sporting clubs who used the entrance fee as a way of raising funds. One of the hotel bands would be hired for the occasion, Chinese lanterns were hung down the centre and on reaching the bottom, would split on either side. On reaching the top again, each would be joined by another skater so that the next time there would be four. They would keep doubling up until there was a massive column filling the entire rink.

Ice gymkhanas inveigled visitors into some remarkable high-jinks.

At Arosa, however, visitors were so besotted with tobogganing they even transferred their gymkhanas on to sledges in preference to skates. They devised numerous special skills. Armed with a walking stick, they would slide past a series of pea sticks set on the bank seeing how many they could knock down.

After a day of so many and diverse exertions, everyone would foregather for tea or, more probably, hot chocolate. In those hotels created for mountaineers there was little ceremony. A resident at The Bear in Grindelwald tells how "tea was served out of two urns with two large baskets, chained to the table legs to prevent theft, and filled with cakes. One just helped oneself to tea and as many cakes as one wanted and sat down wherever there was room. One old lady, who's husband was the uncrowned king of the British skating, was allowed a tablecloth and a teapot". If more refinement was preferred, there was always the Walter Restaurant. Since there was no traffic in those days, the tables were set in the main street with an uninterrupted view of those skaters still on the rink opposite. At Wengen the teatime rendez vous was the Schonegg, at Gstaad the Cafe Pernet and at St.Moritz there was initially the Scotch Tea House for muffins and scones with black cherry jam. But later and most favoured by fashion was the cafe of the rotund but twinkling Herr. Hanselmann. His great speciality was his Cresta Bun. Such patisseries normally offered a full range of appetising cream cakes. They were made from traditional national recipes, such as marzipan "potatoes" or there were cubes of meringue layered with chocolate cream and topped with chocolate crumb.

At this time, "apres ski" - and even the American cocktail - were still unknown. Guests had to find their own amusement during the dull dusk interval between tea and dinner. The serious skaters at The Bear would congregate in the entrance hall, passing round a dirty and increasingly damp towel for cleaning the blades prior to leaving their boots overnight on one of the big heaters. Most hotels had a billiard room where the men would repair. The ladies would knit or read in the lounge while the band played selections from the light classics.

Visitors usually arranged their after dinner amusements through a committee and all guests were expected to make a modest donation to an entertainments fund. Most of this was spent on prizes and other small items deemed essential for mounting pillowcase dances and confetti fights. Another passtime was preparing and presenting amateur dramatics. There was even a "spoof" amateur production engineered at St.Moritz by Hector Munro, the real name of Saki the novelist. Invitations were widely distributed for a performance to be given at a hotel noted for its stuffy and niggardly clientel. The chosen play was notoriously risqué and so was bound to attract a vociferous element. On the prescribed night the staid guests were completely ignorant and considerably embarrassed by the invasion of a noisy and salaciously expectant hoard of outsiders.

For many years Grindelwald had just the one band which would visit a different hotel each evening. The same arrangement, but qualified to suit the needs of the patients, applied to Arosa. It was financed by the village out of a kur tax of 20 centimes a day per person augmented by a franc table charge by the hotel. On such evenings the place was open to everyone. Because most visitors at Arosa were patients out for the whole season, everyone knew everyone else and most of them also knew one another's engagements. Hence messages would be flashed among the guests and parties would be got together with remarkable speed. However late nights were discouraged as being dangerously exhausting so that the band would normally play only between eight and ten thirty. But if enough couples were present, they could usually persuade the band to play on for another hour.

The resident bands in the big hotels were of a high standard and versatile. They were expected to play light music and particularly Strauss and Waldteufel beside the skating rink in the morning. Light classics were required at teatime and popular dance tunes after dinner. In those days a popular song lasted for months rather than weeks. So at the start of the season, the band leader would write to Chapells of Bond Street for copies of the current hits. In lesser hotels the quality could be varied. For long the Regina at Wengen was cursed by a band comprising a father and his five sons and all they seemed capable of playing was "Standchen". The penny pinching management of a Lenzerheide hotel assumed that guests could dance to a pianola. Chapells, however, made a mistake. As a result, if the guests wanted to dance, that season it had to be to the symphonies of Bach and Beethoven.

At St.Moritz the undoubted evening highlight of the season was the Race Week Ball. The race in question was the horse race on the Great Lake and the hotel was always Suvretta House. Typical of the light hearted mood that prevailed was the time when Lord Ossulston appeared dressed as a lady "so convincingly", according to contemporary reports, "that even his partners were not convinced as to his true identity".

Other evenings might be enlivened with tableaux vivants or such diversions as "A Spring Night's Dream" dance at The Palace accompanied by a ballet in which aristocratic and wealthy young ladies and gentlemen gambolled about dressed as nymphs and fawns.

But all too soon this pattern of wealth and frivolity was to be hideously eradicated.

CHAPTER III
THE BOISTEROUS YOUNG THINGS
1921 - 1939

In practice, the First World War completely bypassed neutral Switzerland. The only ski resort to be obviously affected was Mürren. The Swiss allocated it for accommodating English prisoners of war. Sir Henry Lunn's son, Arnold, was responsible for their welfare. He has described how on his return to the Palace, "I remember digging out my skis in 1916 from a sad row of depressed boards, all stacked and labelled and ready for the winter season which most skiers were to spend in the trenches. The first label that had caught my eye bore the name of a gallant young soldier who had fallen in the retreat from Mons."

Some of the most punishing fighting was along the old Austro-Hungarian border. The front ran from Trentino and Cortina south west right down to Montgenèvre, now largely covered by the Latte Via ski circuit. Probably more men there died through frost rather than by bullet. If a soldier was kept on guard longer than half an hour he was usually frozen to death. Even today the gun emplacements and shell holes can still be seen under the snow when going up the Lagazuoi cable car. The Rifugio Averau is on the actual site of the Italian Army general headquarters.

After the armistice, the social scene did not really pick up until the 1920-1921 season. Things were very diifferent. There was, for instance, Colonel Davis who, though not a good skier, had always been a centre of activity at Grindelwald. On the outbreak of war he had persuaded many of the younger element to join his Devonshire regiment. But like so many others, it had been decimated in Flanders. Now in the post-war years he returned to Grindelwald, but it was as a sadder, disillusioned figure.

The war had a devastating effect on European society. Gone were Little Willie, the princes and the serene highnesses of all the German states. At the same time, those Grand Dukes who had managed to escape the Bolshevik revolution were now utterly impoverished. Raymond Flower tells how one of the princes who had previously booked entire suites, called in at the St. Moritz Palace to sell his coin collection to an acquaintance. The impeccable intelligence network of a great hotel alerted Badrutt who came out to see him. Badrutt admonished him for not having given advance notice of his arrival. The Prince declared his poverty. But on returning to his humble pension he found his luggage had already been removed. He remonstrated with Badrutt: "But I can't even afford to stay here an hour" to which Badrutt replied: "The Palace will be honoured to have you as our guest for as long as you wish."

Not only were many Russian and German Princes cruelly eradicated from the guest lists but some of the outstanding names in sport were also missing. Among the Cresta riders, J.A. Bott, for instance, had been a casualty in Flanders. Certainly Mr. Moore Brabazon was back, though now he was being referred to as a veteran and had become a Member of Parliament. Fortunately neither Badrutt nor any of the other Swiss Hoteliers had subscribed to the overwhelming pessimism of the owner of the Gstaad Palace. He refused to believe that a generation which had suffered such carnage in the trenches would have the heart, let alone the wealth, to come out for winter sports any more. He was so convinced of the complete collapse of society and gracious living he could only envisage bankruptcy. He shot himself. Fortunately there was no loss of ton and the hotel retained its premier position under the capable management of the Scherz family.

Indeed even before the war there had been several signs auguring a prosperous future for those taking the long term view. Back in 1907 Karl Schuler, of the Post Hotel at St.Anton, was offering his guests the attraction of lessons in ski-ing. He hired the son of a local cheese maker as the hotel instructor. His name was Hannes Schneider. The venture was obviously a great success for at the end of the season Schneider was paid 100 kroner and booked for the coming year.

Another auspicious, if less obvious, event had occurred back in 1892 when an ardent Methodist organised an ecumenical meeting of churchmen at Grindelwald. But, as his son was to comment later, the result "was not - alas - the reunion of Christendom but the foundation of a travel agency later known as Sir Henry Lunn Ltd."

Before long Henry Lunn was sending 5,000 people each season to over a score of winter resorts.

He was quick to identify a small but influential sector of tourists - not that they would have admitted to such classification. The upper-middle and, indeed, the upper classes were ready to explore places abroad. At the same time they were not inclined to change their social environment. They had no wish to be associated with anything so vulgar as having a Lunn label on their luggage. Working on this premise, in 1902 Lunn initiated the Public Schools Alpine Sports Club. He ensured any associations were concealed by forming a subsidiary company which also did not include the Lunn name. He then persuaded a Harrow master to send a circular acquainting Old Harrovians and Etonians that the Grand Hotel at Adelboden had been reserved for their pleasure. The letter brought in 400 bookings made by, among others, the Bishops of Wakefield and Hereford. Pursuing snobbery still further, Lunn discreetly reduced charges significantly for members of the aristocracy. He calculated the prestige of their presence would far outweigh the cost.

Even before the First World War, the British were suffering under the most outrageous delusions of grandeur in relation to foreigners. After building an ice rink at Davos they haughtily refused membership to all foreigners and to Germans in particular who were forced to make a rink of their own. One of the early brochures epitomises how Sir Henry appealed to these sentiments: "Mürren has always been a favourite with the English visitor" adding, as though they might otherwise notice some unpleasant smell, "and has never been invaded by our Teutonic cousins in summer." It was only one of several examples of a chauvinist attitude. The owner of a Lenzerheide hotel had been so rash as to let rooms to a couple of Germans. Sir Henry's party staying there were so incensed they immediately dispatched a telegram in strong protest.

Other resorts adopted by Sir Henry included Montana, where he turned the sanatorium into the Palace Bellevue Hotel. It was under his guidance that Engelberg rapidly acquired a reputation for being almost as smart as St.Moritz.

In due course he quarrelled with the authorities at Grindelwald. So he made the simple hop over the mountain to Wengen and with a further hop across the valley to Mürren where he installed his son Arnold at the Palace. There, from the famous Room Four, with the centre of influence transferred at mealtimes to table number four immediately on the left, he rapidly built up the resort not only as a centre of holiday ski-ing but also for ski racing.

Sir Henry's dominance at Grindelwald was largely taken over by another pioneer of winter sports holidays. Quentin Hogg's ambition was to extend his Polytechnic educational experiments into foreign travel. So the clientele he introduced to the locals was a class of Englishman quite different from the Public Schools. To this end he took over the Hotel Bristol. At the same time the Bellevue was being patronised by a similar strata of society having been bought by Gordon Selfridge for his staff. Occasionally he even patronised it himself, not at that time being encumbered with his multiple girlfriends the Dolly Sisters. With such company nobody thought it particularly remarkable when a circus troupe arrived, celebrating a win on the sweepstakes. One memorable evening they took over the ballroom of the Regina Hotel and entertained fellow guests with all their tricks and contortions.

Not only were Sir Henry and Mr.Hogg popularising ski-ing but the sport itself was undergoing something of a change. There were two reasons: improved equipment and better climbing facilities.

There were all those railways, which had been constructed to provide the Victorian sightseers with a better view of the mountains, just waiting to be commandeered in winter. They had been constructed notably at Wengen, Mürren, Zermatt, Davos, St.Moritz and Villars. Doyen of them all extends the whole way up the 13,600 ft. granite tricorn to the peak of the Jungfrau.

Back in 1893 it had been a truly remarkable venture. Indeed the cog railway was only one of three competing schemes. One suggestion was to have the carriages set in a large pneumatic tube and shot up by compressed air like a grocery bill. The person who won the concession, Adolph Zeller , however, possessed the level head of an engineer. He also possessed the undoubted advantage of already being the director of a Swiss railway company. His solution came while at Mürren. He was watching a train on the opposite side of the valley creeping its way up to Scheidegg. Why not just extend the existing cog railway through two straight tunnels with a hairpin bend between? As each ramp would be seven and a half miles long they would have to encroach into the adjoining Eiger and Monch mountains. But that should present no greater problem.

His project created considerable controversy. "The Times" said it was a mercenary enterprise and took comfort in the belief that the "polar climate would render its execution impossible". With the name Jungfrau interpreted as virgin and with due artistic licence over the mountain's silhouette, the project offered a field day for the cartoonists. Some depicted the Eiger and Monch as two dirty old men leering at the young girl clutching at sheets of ice and snow in a desperate attempt to preserve her modesty.

Zeller estimated that to hew out each cu. yd. of rock would cost 40 francs. However, by completion the estimated total of 7.5 m. francs had more than doubled. It took 200 men working continually in three shifts, 18 years to complete. The workers' needs for a single winter alone made formidable reading and included four live pigs and 50,000 cigars. Wine was sold by the weight as chips off a red, frozen mass.

Today in the winter alone, 200,000 skiers give up a day to make the journey and see the incredible view. The Lake of Thun is so far below it seems possible to toss a snowball into it, though really it is 20 miles away. All around lies the snow. It is so white in the fierce dazzling sunlight and the sky such an uncompromising deep blue it all looks as flat as a crude stage set.

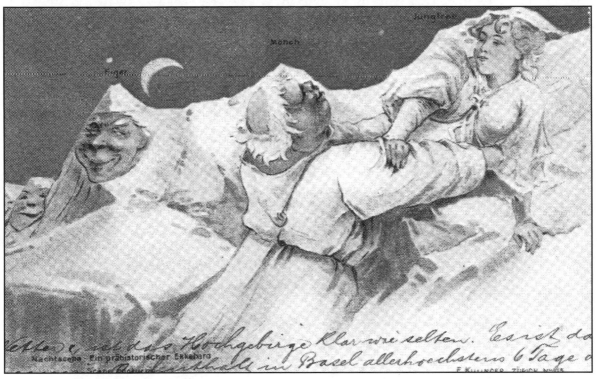

A cartoon suggests the Jungfrau is being ravished by the construction of the mountain railway.

With this engineering feat as inspiration, the more conventional mountain railways were opening the lower sections during the winter. Primarily it was to satisfy the large numbers of bobsleigh enthusiasts. But soon skiers were beginning to outnumber them, encouraging the railways to extend their winter services still higher. The "Bubble" section of Mürren's rack and pinion railway had an almost non stop service, the trains moving at a cracking 4 mph. The winter service at Wengen, which had previously extended as far as the Water Station, now reached as high as Wengernalp. It is a lone hotel memorable as the place where back in 1816 Byron penned part of "Manfried". The former director of the Channel Tunnel company, James Evans, is the life long honorary station master. A condition is that he visits it, in full Swiss Railway uniform, once a year. At this point, however, it acquired new significance as it registered the top of "the bumps". Another year or two and the service was being extended up to Scheidegg, perched on the shoulder between Wengen and Grindelwald. Used as a ski lift, the train allowed skiers to put in a good 5,000 ft. downhill within a day.

At St.Moritz the Chantarella funicular had originally been constructed purely to provide access to the hotel. However, as part of the 1928 Olympic development, a further section was built right up to Corviglia for the exclusive benefit of skiers.

The Gornergrat at Zermatt started a winter service in 1928. Initially it reached the 2,000 ft. up to the Riffelalp, just above the tree line. The following winter the service was extended to the Riffelboden. Then the year before the Second World War it was opened right up to the Observatory.

The principle was far too good to be confined to the Alps. Even while the Trans-Andean railway was being built the engineers were wearing skis in the course of their daily work. So it was hardly surprising that once the line was open, recreational skiers immediately patronised it as a lift.

All these developments inevitably led to the fine art of timetable ski-ing. This entailed a great deal more than merely timing the end of a run to coincide with the departure of the next train. Most of these high altitude railways had rolling stock of varying speed and comfort. It therefore became essential to recognise the faster and more comfortable models. Even boarding the trains required skill. It was necessary to stand exactly where the ski trucks would stop. By depositing your skis quickly you could be first in the carriage and claim a seat. However those who were highly accomplished in the art gauged the numbers waiting and stood aside. The intent was to let all the masses take the "hardarse" seats and still hold back until available standing room was crammed. The guard then usually opened the first class carriages so that the sophisticates reclined in luxury.

The work of a ticket collector was also fraught with hazards. In the early type of train he had to clamber his way along the outside swinging from carriage to carriage. The correctness of a ticket was paramount, no matter how well the individual might be known to the official. On one occasion it was not considered sufficient excuse when an unfortunate skier had his ticket held in a snagged zip pocket. He was taken off at Wengernalp. According to the lively imagination of Ken Foster, he was last seen by his jubilant companions, "pinned to the floor of the Wartsaal by the WAB who were taking him to pieces with tools borrowed from the engine driver".

The staff, however, were much more understanding once they were sure you had paid for your ticket. As there were no instant photo booths, it usually took two or three days for your photograph to be processed. So it became customary to flick through any available copy of "The Tatler" and cut out and paste in a reasonably suitable picture. Some of the inspectors would pretend not to notice. Others might proffer some cryptic remark such as "Yes, a very good likeness."

Rigid adherence to the timetable led to a less hilarious incident when the British ski team had only just made the connection at Lauterbrunnen. Regardless of the fact that half the team were on the train and half were not and that the same applied to their luggage, the guard signalled for the train to leave. Finding their appeals to his better nature of no avail, it occurred to some of the team they could delay departure by holding the guard hostage on the platform. A Swiss passenger interpreted this as an assault and weighed in with his fisticuffs. It unfortunately developed into quite a scandal.

The traditional funicular and, in due course, all types of ski lift, owed their existence to the development of cable spinning dating from 1825. Cable provides all the flexibility of the hessian rope but with a strength equal to its volume in metal. It was first used for mountain ascent with the Schatzalp funicular which opened at Davos in the summer of 1899.

It was a further 30 years before cable engineering was applied to aerial cars. First was the Hahnenkamm built specifically for Kitzbühel skiers in 1928. The prospect of spending six million schillings on the project divided the townsfolk. The Burgomaster responsible for town development was in favour but the Burgomaster responsible for the countryside was not. Eventually everyone agreed to the project on the understanding they could all use it in perpetuity at half price, It is a condition which rankles with the company to this day.

The cabin held 13 people and the door was on the front. The cable ran over a veritable forest of wooden pylons - 22 to be precise. Today there are just two, both made of steel. Unfortunately the cable kept jumping the pylon bogeys. Much time and money was spent developing an arm which would normally hold the cable in place but could be temporally switched to one side by the approaching cabin. Even so there were problems and on more than one occasion passengers had to clamber down a violently swinging 60 ft. rope ladder.

Sestriere had three cable cars radiating from the two futuristic- looking round tower hotels. But then the place was everything one might expect considering it was the brainchild of Giovanni Agnelli of Fiat fame. What is more, it had been enthusiastically endorsed by il Duce himself. Indeed Mussolini's two sons, one noticeably short and fat and the other remarkably tall and thin patronised the opening ceremony.

The first Hahnenkamm cable car held 13 skiers and was continually becoming stuck on its timber pylons

The Italians were already thoroughly unpopular through their invasion of Abyssinia. So the British contingent attending the celebrations made a point of writing letters of strong complaint to Mussolini personally.

So there was an understandable delay before the second Austrian cable car, the Galzigbahn, was opened at St. Anton in 1936. Unlike the Hahnenkamm, money for the St.Anton project came largely from just one local citizen, Itio Forarorri. He enjoyed the support of a minister in the Austrian Government; an arrangement that was to cause much woe. In the course of time the financial muscle passed to Viennese bankers. As they had no civic loyalties, they postponed all further development. The consequent overcrowding caused considerable damage to the reputation of the place.

At Zermatt, lift development was complicated due to the iron control the members of the bourgeoisie held over the village commune. They declared that their traditional rights to the grazing and timber naturally extend to include rights to erect ski lift pylons. Confident that the greatest advantage to any claim lies in staking it, they went ahead and erected their first cable car.

It was not long, however, before the true value of their holding became apparent and envy quickly brought them into dispute. So they produced supposedly 17th century deeds to three sides of the Matterhorn, each reaching to the top. Their argument was the more forceful since the bourgeoisie still held a majority vote in the Commune. In 1956 they re-financed the company to cover the whole of the Zermatt area. Thus they made sure of holding a clear majority of shares. It is also reasonable to presume that individually the bourgeois families availed themselves of a large proportion of the 20 per cent of shares made available to anonymous private investors. As a result the village commune and the rest of the villagers were left with a mere 28 per cent.

Skiers in the Austrian resorts wishing to go further afield than the lift system usually had to rely on the local buses for the way home. This in itself could be quite a hazardous affair as described by T.C. Bainter while ski-ing at Kirchberg:

"There were only a few seats so skiers would often trail behind it - an illegal but established practice. The bus leaving Kirchberg was an impressive sight. From within the passengers heard the assault of many skiers pulling against the back, the threshing of sticks and the despairing cries of those trampled underfoot. The pace at times was terrific and if you weakened and let go you not only lost your tow and your sticks but cannoned into the three or four people who had attached themselves behind. Whole parties would break away, stagger and flounder in the ditch".

Both funiculars and cable cars became the cause of a significant phenomena on the ski slopes. Passengers are all disgorged at one spot and consequently follow the same way down to the valley station. In some cases the way had already been trodden by generations of locals. It was usual to leave the hay in the mountain huts until the first snowfall. Then, part riding part sliding, it was comparatively easy to "toboggan" the load down to the village. The need to ski on hard beaten tracks became recognised by the Ski Club of Great Britain as far back as 1920. The second class tests at Mürren were amended to ensure the candidate was as proficient on hard snow as in soft. Of even greater significance, the piste crystallised the separation of Alpine downhill ski-ing from the Scandinavian cross country langlauf. It was a difference that soon became apparent in technique, in equipment and, indeed, in temperament.

Compared to the earlier social clubs formed around a particular winter sport, the clubs of the 'twenties and 'thirties came into being essentially through ski racing. Indeed early on these clubs were still about the only way a skier could acquire style. The situation was never more evident than at Mürren. Sir Henry Lunn had singled it out as a resort for the specialist skier and appointed his son Arnold as his permanent representative. Anyone arriving at Mürren under the auspices of the Lunn agency was automatically made a member of the Lone Tree Club named after a single, stunted shrub set prominently on the Hogg's Back rock. It acquired its fame through being frequently chosen as the starting point for races. Members were given elementary ski lessons free. Children had their own Beetle Club with its emphasis on training. The name was derived from the goggles with tinted celluloid lenses set in individual aluminium frames worn by the early motoring racers. Due to the associated glamour, the children eagerly adopted them instead of the usual eye shades.

But most influential among the Mürren clubs was the Kandahar, so named because Sir Henry happened to be acquainted with Field Marshal Lord Roberts of Kandahar. One of the founder members was A.C. Irvine of Irvine and Malory of fame. He distinguished himself by passing the second class test within a month of first putting on skis. Soon, however, the members had become so tight a clique that snobbery pervaded the whole resort. It was the only ski club where the application form required the candidate to state which school - public of course - they had been to. The Club did all it could to simulate the public school tradition. On club Nights each member wore a ribbon in the club colours in their lapel. Reminiscent of "The Eton Boating Song" and "Forty Years On", they sang such lyrical gems as: "Downhill, downhill, this is the racer's song" and "In powder or crust, run straight we must" so that one doubted whether the author's skill as a skier was any better than as a poet.

In The States the burgeoning Yale student club also had a songbook which profited by having a definite sense of humour:

"Here's to the skier who skis without a fall
We'd like to drink to him but there's no such guy at all."

The Kandahar sessions were extended once a year to London with a reunion dinner at the Cecil Hotel chaired by one, or better still jointly, by two peers of the realm.

Members were obsessed with rules, races, ties, badges and tests which everyone was for ever taking. They were of a high standard so that they became greatly coveted which further compounded the snobbery.

One woman member, returning after some seasons, purposely did not wear her gold K badge. If not actually rude, she found members would pay her scant courtesy. That was until the last day when she came into lunch wearing her gold K. badge. There was an immediate buzz of interest. When someone gushed "But why didn't you say you were one of us?" she replied: "Thank God I'm not" and stalked from the room. There was another occasion when the club was thrown into deep consternation. They were almost bound to elect a girl as she had won a major race. The dismay was due to her broad Huddersfield accent. One of the club's vainest moments came in 1929 when the King of the Belgians spent three weeks at Mürren and graciously accepted membership.

Elections to the Kandahar were held on Tuesdays. Candidates had first to submit to a visual inspection parading outside the staircase window of the Palace where they were scrutinised by members within. Presumably the King of the Belgians was not subjected to this ordeal. Ordinary members though were next taken out ski-ing under the surveillance of the entire committee. That evening there was a ballot with all the possible disgrace of being blackballed.

The basic characteristics guaranteed to gain membership were aptly defined by Edgie Boughton-Leigh: "The first essential is dash and therefore take everything straight and be the first to do it. To wait at the top of a slope preparing oneself for the plunge is fatal."

The great exponent of this cavalier approach was Chris Mackintosh. As a matter of principle, he took all the slopes straight and, as a result, he frequently fell. But he was so strong and skied so fast he would still make good time. He evolved his own peculiar style alternating telemarks and christianias in swinging curves. While not particularly graceful to watch he none the less created an impression of considerable power. This was indeed the case for he was an all round athlete with a double Oxford blue in athletics and rugby, in which he also played for Scotland. He was so strong a skier that in the Lauberhorn race he beat Zogg and Seelos, both future world champions. Arnold Lunn wrote of Mackintosh: "I never knew anybody who loved racing more or who cared less about victory."

His irrepressible exuberance was well illustrated when competitors and officials were wending their dispirited way up the Schilthorn in a raging blizzard. Having reached the end of their endurance, they decided that here was to be the start. Two porters in the entourage were sent down with instructions to stand ten yards apart at the bottom as winning posts. It was to be the usual geschmozzle or mass start. The official began explaining that he would count down: three, two... and before he could say "go", Chris Mackintosh shot off and was immediately swallowed up in the whiteness and without hope of recall. So all the other competitors started too, overtaking the two porters while they were only part of the way down. When Mackintosh reached the bottom he saw an old man walking along. He called out to him to stand still and thereby established him as the winning post.

Bill Bracken, another leading figure in the club, was a complete contrast. Although handicapped by a lighter physique, he was infinitely the better skier; always in control. He had learnt to ski in Kitzbühel where his father was among the first English residents. It was there that he learnt to ski christianias rather than the customary telemark. Even at 50 he was a formidable skier. When showing two young Austrian international skiers the way down, he left them clean behind purely through his superior skill in choice of line. He was eventually appointed head of the Mürren ski school. It was not only a unique but an apt distinction. He acquired a reputation for his consideration and patience with learners. He was a strange mixture of reticence and kindliness with fits of occasional, almost wilful, exhibitionism. A hint lay in his rather flashy clothes consisting of a very tight fitting red jacket and matching skull cap weighted down with ski badges.

If the men of Mürren were dashing, then the ladies were both elegant and courageous. One of the outstanding skiers was Doreen Elliott. She skied with considerable grace yet had such stamina she was one of the few women capable of rivalling the fastest men.

In his diary, Edgie Boughton-Leigh reported that three of the leading girls, Di Crewdson, Audrey Sale-Barker and Mavis Durrell were known as The Three Bears because they shared a small room. Despite this they managed to hold a virtual levee while they breakfasted in bed. Guests had to perch among a welter of last night's dresses and the coming day's ski clothes scattered all over the room.

But if the men could be snobs, the women could be bitchy. "Did you fall?" an innocent asked, after a competitor had completed a very icy course, to receive the no less icy reply: "Not since I first put on skis."

There were a few guests who had somehow found their way into the Palace Hotel although they were not club members. Doreen Elliott recalled the evenings when one man would solemnly dance holding a cushion as partner. Suddenly he would run up to a lady at one of the tables bordering the dance floor and blow cigarette smoke into her face. Another man came out each year with two pretty young "nieces". They were never the same but they were always accorded the same names "Day" and "Night".

The Kandahar and all the attendant enterprises was almost entirely the work of one man, Sir Henry's son Arnold. Throughout the 'twenties and 'thirties he encouraged a large number of young skiers into becoming regular visitors. They were the children of wealthy parents and consequently able to stay several weeks over the school holidays and vacations. They had the time to become top skiers.

Inevitably there was a lot of noise and constant ragging. Some wags, aware of Arnold Lunn's affection for the lone tree, doused it with petrol and set it alight. The next day a mock funeral procession was held of some of its parts. The "resident" comedian Alan d'Egville officiated, wearing a large nose, diminutive bowler hat and beating out a solemn rhythm on, of all tactless instruments, an empty oil drum.

At one of the fancy dress balls, Tony Viscount Kenilworth , in outsize baggy trousers, had found acclaim as a much ridiculed statue. Next day, he was persuaded to don them again and stand upon a plinth of snow outside the hotel entrance to be photographed. To his astonishment, he was unceremoniously "unveiled".

The funeral of Mürren's lone tree, conducted by Alan d'Egville - oil drum is in the foreground

Yet the high spirits and boisterous behaviour of these young people rarely got seriously out of hand. This was largely due to another astute move on the part of Sir Henry. In true Arnold of Rugby style he tamed the rowdy element by giving them responsibility. He arranged for the guests at each hotel to elect their own "working committee". They were held responsible for the good behaviour of members. Armed with the threat of "excommunication", they exerted a good deal more discipline than could the hotel management.

In this special atmosphere, the bright young things came to look upon the Palace staff more as family retainers. There was Schlumninger, the concierge, Fritz the barman, who was succeeded by another Fritz, together with Flora the barmaid and Peter who operated in the ski room. And above all there was Glanner, the head waiter.

The Palace is the dominant feature in a village which, from the opposite side of the valley, looks almost inaccessible on its mountain shelf. This was, no doubt, the reason why, in both the World Wars it was chosen as an internment camp for British forces. However that it is accessible is immediately apparent. The rack and pinion railway runs an eye catching straight vertical from the Lauterbrunnen Valley. Then it turns an abrupt right angle and continues absolutely level across to the village. Just as mathematically precise, the Allmendhubelbahn springs straight up from the village only conceding to the contours of the mountain towards the top. Over it all, on the skyline is the rock formation like a tilted mitre and called the Dying Pope.

In its prominent position, The Palace seems almost to overhang the precipitous drop to the Lauterbrunnen valley. This gives breathtaking views of the Jungfrau opposite. Then, besides the superb ballroom, there is the Inferno Bar in the basement. It has murals of skiers in outrageous but no less realistic poses drawn by Alan d'Egville.

But despite the fine public rooms and the fine life, the Palace remained an antiquated building. It was expensive too and in due course Chris Mackintosh persuaded many of the clientele to move over to the Hotel Alpina at 12 francs a day less. The much smaller Alpina was at that time highly distinctive through being painted a vivid blue. It was sited even closer and overhung even further the Lauters valley. According to James Riddell "One exercise of the young ski element was to throw plates diskus like out of the window to land, presumably, after considerable descent, into the Lauterbrunnen Valley".

James Riddell has described the behaviour at the Alpina, now free of the restraints of the Lunn management committee, as even more outrageous. The manager, Max Amstutz, an ardent skier and Anglophile, was incredibly long suffering. "The lounge was customarily used as ski repair and waxing rooms. Even timed descent of the stairs on ski was tolerated. Indeed the only time Max had been known to lose his temper was when guests tried to simulate an indoor snowstorm by tearing apart every cushion in the hotel." Then in the early hours of the morning, when they could not reasonably knock up the Palace, they would pursue their noisy way for bacon and egg parties at the Belmont.

Sir Henry Lunn also presided over Wengen set on the other side of the valley. In the very early days the younger element was not so gregarious. This was largely because Sir Henry only rented part of the Palace. So his Public School parties were spread over several hotels. Nor was he able to exercise any control over the bars. So on the whole the Wengen members were harder drinking and tended to ski only when the weather was good and they were not suffering too much from the night before.

Ruminating over these differences, S.B.Mais defined his preference for Wengen because "You can go into the bar and even if you haven't got your gold you can raise your voice and look your fellows in the face". However two factors were shortly to change all this dramatically. There was a growing element of officers from the newly formed R.A.F. The other factor was the foundation of the Downhill Only Club.

In those days of string and matchstick aircraft, flying meant a struggle against the elements under perilous circumstances. Ski-ing made much the same demands on a person. It was in this spirit that, for instance, Andrew Walser, later to become Air Marshal, held the theory that if you approached a fence fast enough it would give way. This no doubt largely explains his other boast: that his doctor's bill never came to less than 200 francs. One of the earliest British slalom champions at Wengen was known as "Stuffy", later to find world fame as Air Marshal Lord Dowding. Then there was "Mongoose" Seden who was in charge of R.A.F. parachuting. He too had a theory: There is no reason why skiers should not be pulled up the slope by parachute. To prove his point he lined up 14 or 15 guinea pig skiers along the Brooklands stretch. They hung on to the guide ropes, the parachute billowed and away they went. Unfortunately, though, they could not see beyond the canopy. So when it came to a barbed wire fence, while the parachute elegantly lifted itself over, the skiers were strung out in an ignominious line of doubled-up figures.

This mixture of companionship allied with the challenge for individual performance indeed encouraged comradely support. Once when Walser had broken yet another ski, his friends, according to a report by Kenneth Foster, "duly carried out their duty as they clearly saw it. They accompanied him to the start of the bob run down to Grindelwald. There they balanced him on his remaining ski and pushed him off down the icy chute of the run. Putting the broken ski in behind for good measure..... It is said that the outfit stationed at Grund to time out the bobs were startled when he clattered through their control."

All individual enterprise at Wengen was harnessed into a cohesive discipline in 1925. The Kandahar Club was looking for fresh fields to conquer. What better than the slope almost directly opposite?

And so they issued a challenge to the Wengenites. C.J.White, the unfortunate recipient of the message, was consequently forced the night before to raise a team by dredging the bars. And so it came about that assorted persons were forced out early the next morning to meet the visiting team. In the words of Kenneth Foster again, "The method of recruitment, being what it was, the Wengen team assembled on the platform displayed none of that brisk cheerfulness expected of healthy young athletes and they watched with increasing gloom as the Kandahar detrained covered with badges and supported by echelons carrying spare tips, extra bindings and rucksacks filled with exotic ski waxes".

After a terrible defeat, Kenneth Foster tried to revive morale during lunch. He pencilled badges which he initialled after the catchphrase of the moment "Downhill Only" though, in an unaccountable lapse, he initialled it as the D.H.O. These, he later reported, "were pinned to the hats and on the train up after lunch, the Kandahar team studied them politely but without comment".

Over dinner that night it was decided that the club should become a permanent institution. As clubs go, it proved remarkable in having eight officers who took charge of five ordinary members. But they took their duties seriously as was proven two years later when during a return challenge, Wengen beat Mürren.

The D.H.O. was fortunate in having Donald Dalrymple as its secretary. He was largely responsible for the way it flourished right up until his death in an avalanche in 1928. After a short decline, revival came with the election of another enthusiastic officer. Dick Waghorn was not only another airman but carried all the prestige as a winner of the Schneider Trophy.

For several years the locals had had their own Wengen Ski Club. It mainly comprised a clique of elderly guides. Under the excuse of prudence, they refrained from conducting their beginners and middle aged pupils above the tree line and looked upon the top of the bumps as a dangerous outpost. However the club was effectively stung into action when, in 1926, the D.H.O challenged it to a race. The W.S.C. won - but only just. Their performance was so poor the Swiss realised they must take themselves in hand.

The D.H.O and other visitors to Wengen were comparatively gregarious. This was partly because Sir Henry Lunn had wisely appointed Charles Dobbs as his local representative. He would spend hours discussing equipment and technique with the locals and his particular crony, the ski shop owner Oscar Gertsch. All four of the Gertsch children, who were no mean skiers, held the same values. This attitude was warmly reciprocated by such men as Tom Fox, L.F.W. Jackson,

Duncan Kessler and Charles Gardner. They skied with the locals as companions rather than as porters. Consequently they were pitting their prowess not only against the four Gertsch children but the other local lads including Karl Molitor, Heinz and Otto Von Allmen and Christian Rubi, all of whom were soon figuring prominently in the international field.

In contrast the Davos Ski Club was in a state of perpetual crisis. In 1927 it was rescued by Jock Marden and in 1929 by Arnold Lunn who renamed it after Marden and transferred its sphere of activities to nearby Klosters. At Andermatt there was The White Hare Club and at Villars the Visitors Club.

Club members were largely responsible for the rich local nomenclature of the main runs and landmarks. "Ma's Hell" at Villars, "Slip Cartilage Corner" and "Plum Pudding Hill" at Wengen.

Probably most famous of all was the slope alongside the railway up to the Jungfrau. It looks so steep from the top it almost invariably evinces the exclamation "Oh God". In due course it has become marked as such on the official Swiss maps. Mürren owed the basis of its prolific nomenclature to the British prisoners of war. It was they who first christened a long traverse as "The Hindenberg Line" and the place where two runs join as "The Menin Gate". There had been considerable ribbing between the regulars and Kitchener's Volunteers. Consequently one of the more gentle runs favoured by the older men was called " Regular's Ramble" while in retaliation the steeper route with its appeal to the younger and more impetuous was called "Kitchener's Crash".

The Kandahar Club, however, added considerably to this vocabulary. If it was a wood it might be " Olga's" (Olga Major, the first British Ladies' champion) or perhaps "Caulfeild's", another formidable section which the author was reputed to have taken straight. There was, of course, "Martha's Meadow", named after Martha Mainwaring, an unknown entrant for the Lady Denman Cup. She was supposed to have been coming from St.Moritz but as she had not appeared by the start it was assumed she had scratched. Betty Schuster, the favourite, was well down the course and in great form when, in the words of Arnold Lunn, "from just behind a rock a dreadful apparition appeared, a roughed and powdered female in wig, jumper and skirt.... and she set off in hot pursuit of Betty Schuster who was entirely put off by an unknown female skiing better than most men, and lost the race accordingly."

Martha Mainwaring turned out to be Anthony Knebworth up to another of his characteristic pranks.

Arnold Lunn has described how he persuaded the ladies to start their own club. When in their name he called a meeting none of them showed much interest. "I marshalled three or four rather bewildered women into room 4 and told them they were the founders of the Ladies Ski Club. The second meeting was held in my wife's bedroom. I read out the minutes of the previous meeting and put on record the resolutions for which I had moved and for which I had voted and the business which I had transacted while the founders of the L.S.C gossiped peacefully together."

Chris Mackintosh could also lay claim to part of the Mürren nomenclature. Officials, setting the course for a race, were debating whether pure sanity was not sufficient to preclude the need to place controls down a very steep slope. But they had not reckoned with Mackintosh who, coming upon them, said, according to Arnold Lunn:" 'What's wrong with taking it this way?' He dived down a slope, leaped 10 metres through the air where it steepened, rattled across the wood sleigh path at the bottom, held the abrupt outrun without a stagger, shot up the steep bank on the other side and finished with a cheerful christiania".

As from that day the spot has been known as Mac's Leap.

While the gilded youth played hard, they also took their ski-ing seriously. Most resorts, in deference to the few enthusiasts, would arrange perhaps two or three races throughout the season. At Mürren and Wengen, however, there could easily be 30 and all of them drawing enthusiastic supporters. The result was a chain of historical firsts. In 1921 the British held the first national Alpine ski championships in the world. The course was set on the Lauberhorn above Wengen and was won by Leonard Dobbs of Wengen. The first lady champion was Olga Major. Had it been today she would almost certainly have been disqualified. She was so nervous and hesitated so long over starting Arnold Lunn had to give her a push.

The next year Arnold Lunn organised the first slalom race according to his own fashion.

This time it was held at Mürren, though it was won by another Wengenite, J.A. Joannides.

The original slalom had been evolved by the Norwegians and assumed a rather drastic form. The racers had to go round such inhospitable objects as tree trunks and rocks. These were not padded so that the Scandinavian practice of marking for style might seem rather incidental. However the course was in cross country mode and comparatively slow.

So Arnold Lunn's slaloms, although essentially downhill, were not entirely original. Instead of obstacles placed haphazardly by nature, he placed poles in pairs or "gates". They were far more varied as they could be set "open", that is horizontally across the slope, or "closed" when they were vertical down the fall line. They could be formed in set sequences: Two open gates with a vertical between is a Seelos while five closed gates in succession is a flush. It at once became evident that because this new slalom was set on much steeper slopes it was no longer necessary to award points for style. Competitors who missed a gate were automatically penalised by the additional time taken to climb back on course.

Lunn's original rules stipulated that only one ski need pass through a gate. Chris Mackintosh showed up this deficiency with a characteristic prank. He went down the course bestriding one pole at each gate. As Arnold Lunn wryly commented some years later: "He escaped any penalty and the course setters spent much time setting right all the poles."

The Combined event was an almost inevitable evolution even though it was not in itself a race at all. Marks alone determine the overall winner of the meeting by incorporating results in the downhill, slalom and if relevant, the giant slalom. In 1924 the honour of staging the first of these triple convocations was divided between Scheidegg and Mürren.

Then Arnold Lunn carried out a stroke of sheer impertinence which he aptly compared to supposing the Dutch had persuaded the English to change the rules of cricket. For ten years he had been doggedly laying siege to the stubborn Scandinavian old guard then clogging up the supreme race committee, the Federation International de Ski. In 1928 they at last gave way and agreed to include Alpine races in the International calendar. But there was a proviso. It was not to be considered anything more than an experiment - and for two years only. Nordic langlauf and jumping still held pride of place. Of course, came the time for reassessment, and the Alpine races had already gained the overwhelming support they hold today.

The British have for long been in the habit of inventing a sport, drawing up an official set of rules and then organising international championships which initially they proceed to win. Quick off the mark, in both senses, Bill Bracken came second at Zakopane in Poland and again in the 1929 FIS Championships, forerunner of the World Championships.

The Poles had looked upon ski racing as an exclusively male event. They were completely confounded when they discovered the British team included ladies. Arnold Lunn had foreseen this and had previously inquired whether "the races were open to all?" Assuming the question referred to nationalities the Poles had without hesitation confirmed the fact.

The ladies proceeded to distinguish themselves under extremely difficult snow conditions. Their courage captured the admiration of the whole country. When later they entered a fashionable restaurant in Warsaw, all the diners stood up and applauded them. Audrey Sale-Barker went on that year to be first among the ladies in the Arlberg- Kandahar.

In 1930 Doreen Elliott won the first Swiss Ladies Open Championship and four other Mürren ladies were placed among the first twelve. It was the first year of the Lauberhorn race and Bill Bracken won the combined and was third in the downhill. 1931 proved the greatest year of all. Arnold Lunn organised the first World Championships for Alpine events. Esme Mackinnon won both the Ladies downhill and the slalom while other British ladies occupied places three to six in the slalom and second, fourth and fifth in the downhill. The Arlberg Kandahar proved just as great a British success with Audrey Sale-Barker winning the ladies cup. The men were not to be outdone and Bill Bracken won the slalom. 1933 and Esme Mackinnon again distinguished herself winning the Arlberg Kandahar while Arnold's son Peter came second in the Lauberhorn. In 1934 Jeannette Kessler won the AK. In 1936 there was another world triumph with Eve Pinching winning the combined. While not necessarily catching the headlines, the names of Mürren and Wengen visitors could usually be found liberally scattered among the leading places in most of the major races.

Another enduring race was evolved at this time and has remained exclusive to Mürren. It is the Inferno which covers a descent of almost 8,000 ft. from the summit of the Schilthorn to Lauterbrunnen station and incorporates three short climbs. To make it all the more unique as an Alpine race, there are no marker flags. Hardly surprisingly, such an unorthodox course calls for resource way beyond the normal ski champion. It needs astute judgement in choosing the best line and a mastery of a whole range of snow textures.

Indeed both physical fitness and stamina were essential for success in any of the early races. Thighs and knees of steel are all very well but today's racers would soon give up if they were expected to climb for an hour or two just to reach the start. Instead of immaculate pistes, carefully prepared days in advance, the normal course in the 'twenties would be tracked by just the two forerunners.

The Mürren races usually started by the Lone Tree - or what was left of it. The winning post was at the bottom of Martha's Meadow. Competitors were simply given a list of the nicknamed sections to be covered. Such directions were not made easier as several of these sections had "funk" alternatives for those who's courage failed. Indeed it was all so complicated, visitors were allocated a guide to ski alongside them. If they were lucky it would be Bill Bracken who made the whole procedure even more unorthodox by imparting nuggets of advice on how to take the slopes and where to turn.

This lack of convention extended across the valley. One day when the Mürren visitors were racing at Wengen, there was a white out. After the Mürren team had sportingly declined an offer to postpone the event, officials were posted down the course to shout and point the way. Despite these precautions one of the ladies became so hopelessly lost she did not turn up in the village until tea time.

Organisers were usually just as cavalier over safety. Particularly notorious were the 1936 World Championships at Innsbruck. The course ended with pure ice liberally punctuated with tree stumps. Peter Lunn has described: "When I reached the lower glades, I heard no cheering from the spectators, only shouts to be careful". The final toll was fearsome. Not only were 17 of the 54 competitors so badly injured they could not finish the course but three of the spectators ended up as stretcher cases.

In those early days it was held that if a competitor had not fallen more than twice before he was out of sight of the starter he had a good chance of winning. Indeed the shrewd competitor could use a fall to help get round the corner. The key was to keep the skis parallel while falling. Then, while remaining prone, it was quite simple to swing them round through the air into the new direction. After that it was merely a matter of springing up and continuing on ones way.

Racing for fun remained predominant at Mürren and Wengen even after such events had assumed true international status. For instance, in the Alpine Ski Challenge Cup in 1923, L.L.B. Angas was fancied as winner. Alas! three days before he "sat heavily while travelling at top speed, on a hard

lump of earth and was confined to his bed." But despite the recommendation of his doctor and the insistence of his friends, he was suddenly spotted ready at the top of the slalom course. The starter protested but was silenced by a long string of invectives. He started - and he won.

Chris Mackintosh's record for overcoming catastrophe is truly remarkable. In a race against the Swiss Universities he had hurt his ankle and had not been able to preview the course. "He consequently ran off the course at one or two critical points", yet still came in third. In an early slalom race, he fell heavily, lost a ski and again came third. But he really excelled himself when he collided with a tree, fell 20 ft into a river so that he was two minutes and ten seconds behind the winner - but was still in third place.

So it was hardly surprising when Mürren staged a crocks race. One entrant was without sticks because, in aspiring to take a second class test, he had sprained both his thumbs and had them in splints. Another had an arm in plaster and a third was heavily strapped up having only recently broken three ribs and was additionally suffering water on the knee.

In 1927 Arnold Lunn visited St.Anton. He thought to promote his slalom and set a course for the local boys. They were so enthusiastic Lunn suggested it could be made an annual adult event. When he returned a year or two later, he found his modest little cup had been set in a shop window and was surrounded by the Austrian flag. The village was en fete and the winner was to receive a year's free pass on the Austrian railways.

The Austrians had wanted to call the event after Arnold Lunn. He thought it unwise to "personalise" the cup and he recommended that the name should suggest the prestige of the two clubs Arlberg and Kandahar.

Three special commemorative badges were struck. One was for the co-founder Hannes Schneider, one for Arnold Lunn and one for Arnold Lunn after he had mislaid the first.

The Arlberg Kandahar was unusual in another way. It was a genuinely open race and competitors entered as individuals. Nationalism was played down to the extent that only the host country's flag was displayed. The spirit touched the spectators. They would often cheer competitors challenging their own countrymen. Chris Mackintosh acquired a reputation for enterprise even before the race began. One year he arrived in a private aeroplane, piloted by H.R.D. Waghorn. The next he came more conventionally by train. However he overslept and awoke at Landeck. Nothing daunted, he walked back along the line, astonishing the station staff as he emerged from the Arlberg tunnel with his suitcase, his skis and his face considerably blackened.

There was another race which came about almost incidentally yet solidified into a major event. It started in 1924 as an argument among Marden Club members, squashed into their steamy hut on the Parsenn. The matter in question was how long it should take to ski from the Furka to Küblis. There was only one way to settle the matter satisfactorily. It was to hold a race and Freddy Edlin agreed to present a cup. Everyone and anyone could enter and for that first race there were 53 competitors anxious to confirm their estimates. It was won by the local guide Peter Gruber. Indeed he, and occasionally one of his compatriots, won so consistently their victory almost became a foregone conclusion. Then a Belgian visitor considered it was not very sporting and hatched a plot. To make quite sure of success he quietly entered six top Austrian skiers. They broke the mould and after that the race became truly international. Over the years the numbers and nationalities have increased. Regardless of fame or ability, entrants are lined up in rows of ten for an old fashioned geschmozzle start. This means pandemonium until the best succeed in getting clear of those competitors tacking from side to side, interspersing their efforts with kick turns or snow ploughs. Yet during the first ten years there was only one serious accident.

A gschmozzle start. 1,200 skiers participate in the Vasa Lopp race in Sweden It covers the track taken by Gustav Vasa fleeing from the Danish occupation of Norway in 1521.

The timing of such long distance races depended on the stopwatch. It had been invented in the 1880's and was perfectly adequate for the mile and a half of the average downhill course. The slalom, however, is so short the finish is clearly visible from the start. Consequently the times separating first, second and third places are far closer. For instance in the 1936 Olympics, the time between the first three places in the downhill was two and three seconds; those in the slalom were 0.4 and 0.6 seconds. Fortunately the short distance allowed the time pieces to be linked by landline. This enabled the two watches to be synchronised. However, the finish still depended on the human element as the watch had to be stopped by hand. This was refined in 1948 when Longines introduced the electronic eye which recorded to within one hundredth of a second.

As equipment and training methods improved over the next 30 years, the margins between places in the slalom shrank by a tenth. The difference of 0.4 and 0.6 in 1936 had, by the Squaw Valley Olympics in 1960 shrunk to 0.05 and 0.06. Gina Hawthorn missed third place in the 1968 Olympics by a microscopic three hundredths of a second. The French girl, in a gracious gesture, handed her the pin off her bronze medal. So it was just as well that by this time Longines had developed the quartz clock. This remains accurate to one second within three hundred years.

Some of the international races were quite blatantly instituted to publicise the resort. The Hahnenkamm at Kitzbühel was inaugurated the year the cable car was opened. Zermatt inaugurated the Gornegrat Derby as a way of publicising that skiers could now ski down from the Riffelberg. In this case, however, its success engineered its own extinction. The course is so steep the winner would make the total drop of 4,800 ft in a breathtaking seven minutes plus a few seconds. It was later withdrawn from the calendar as it was considered too dangerous. Val d'Isére publicises the reliability of its early snow conditions by shoehorning the Premier Neige race into the pre-Christmas sector of the international racing calendar.

The rash of British racers that emerged during the 'thirties begat a new generation of authors. Alan d'Egville wrote "Modern Ski-ing" in 1927 and Bill Bracken's "Ski-ing Technique" appeared in 1936. There was " The Ski Runner" by Harold Mitchell and "High Speed Ski-ing" by Peter Lunn in 1935 while his father, Arnold, who had been first in the field with "The Complete Ski Runner" now followed with "Ski-ing for Beginners" and "Ski-ing in a Fortnight". The several other books Arnold wrote were concerned more with literary and historical aspects such as "A History of Ski-ing", and "The Story of Ski-ing", "Switzerland in English Prose and Poetry" and "The Englishman in the Alps".

Beyond instruction books and clubs, novices now had a third way of learning: the ski schools. They were a considerable improvement on the days when Sir. Henry had hired a guide for his first ski party at Chamonix. Arnold, then an impressionable ten year old, later wrote of the guide: "He regarded his ski with obvious distaste and terror. He slid down a gradual slope, leaning on his stick and breathing heavily while we gasped our admiration for his courage. Somebody asked him whether it was possible to turn. He replied in the negative, but added that a long gradual turn was just possible if one dragged oneself round the pole." Clearly he had not heard of Mathias Zdarski who, even then was giving lessons to classes with up to 100 pupils.

In 1906 a Viennese businessman, qualifications unknown, organised a ski class at Lech. Its only claim to fame lay in that one of the pupils was Hannes Schneider, in turn to become the Post Hotel instructor. Drafted into the Army during the First World War Schneider acquired further teaching experience under a Captain Bilgeri. The Captain was, at that time, doyen of the ski theorists Anagramatically his name was highly appropriate. Someone had pointed out that a military instruction book referred to "the skier's hind leg". This, it was held, suggested there was an officer in the Imperial Army who had four legs. Bilgeri was so incensed he challenged the perpetrator to a duel.

On returning to St.Anton, Schneider realised there was scope for something much larger than his original Post Hotel classes. His idea was a ski school in its own right and he opened it in 1919. His courses started with learning to walk and were designed so that by the end of the week the pupils could make a turn. When some of his pupils came back the following winter Schneider realised he must start advanced classes. This led naturally to promoting those skiers showing any real aptitude and the school was born.

Experience also caused him to improve the teaching technique. Originally pupils were taught a modified form of racing. It included, for instance, the "double ski turn" or snow plough. He soon abandoned it. He found that if he encouraged pupils to use stem turns right from the start they could bypass the snow plough stage altogether. He also set a basic curriculum. Each morning was spent in demonstration and practising technique. In the afternoons the class would go on a run. It has remained the universal arrangement among ski schools to this day. Schneider possessed awesome perseverance combined with an open mind and curiosity that meant he was not only constantly trying to improve his teaching methods but his method of ski-ing. He would spend many hours on his own, conducting painstaking trials and analysing his movements. For some time he had been completely confounded over ski-ing in breakable crust. He could have his skis pointing straight down, he could follow the full routine in making a stem turn - but he could not complete it. After persistent falling he suddenly succeeded. At first he could not understand why. But after persisting with experiments, he found the reason. He had, ever so slightly, lifted the inside ski.

Naturally he wanted to demonstrate his "lifted stem" turn and the best opportunity would have been the Swiss Open Championships. But it was too late to enter his name on the list. Nonetheless he went to Grindelwald and was heartened to see the competitors still using the telemark. Personally he was grossly prejudiced against the turn. In an over enthusiastic moment he had thrust his leg so far forward he had badly injured his foot .

Due to the fame now attending him, he was allowed to give an exhibition and went down the course last - and came first. He beat the official winner by several seconds. From then on his style became accepted throughout Europe.

On another occasion, having suffered an unusually heavy fall, he suddenly realised he was ski-ing faster and better than before. Again he painstakingly analysed his movements. This time he found that he was bending not only at the knees but at the ankles. Pondering the reason he realised this position lowered the centre of gravity and imparted far more stability. The stance soon became universally known as the Arlberg Crouch.

However, it was a position that easily lent itself to misinterpretation, even by his own instructors. As Jimmy Lindsey wrote in his memoirs: "One usually thought one was crouching when one was actually bending forward with the bottom well in the air". In practice, this misinterpretation actually blocked completing the turns, merely adding to a beginner's tribulations.

Schneider was a born leader but he easily lost patience and could make some very outspoken comments. But he was consistent. He was a strict disciplinarian with his pupils no less than with his instructors - and both appreciated it.

He made a point of treating everyone the same. When the King of the Belgians asked for private lessons, Schneider was short of instructors. He explained that it would mean taking an instructor away from an ordinary class, and made it abundantly clear that instead the King must join one too. Indeed he pursued this policy to a ridiculous degree. Later during the week one of the instructors complained there were four men persistently watching his class. "Don't worry. Don't pay any attention" Schneider told him. He did not explain they were bodyguards and that one of the ladies in the class was the Queen of the Belgians. Nor did he enlighten another of his instructors who had failed to recognise the Austrian Chancellor Schuschnigg among his pupils.

However Schneider did meet his match among the ladies. The German women took to making snide remarks about the French for wearing make-up while out ski-ing. When they started slapping one another Schneider capitulated and put all the Germans into a class on their own.

Despite all his careful organisation there were some strange situations. Once he was so short of instructors he had to inveigle the local butcher's boy into helping out. However, the boy knew his priorities and arrived to tell the class that he must first complete his rounds. Unfortunately none of his class understood German. So, not withstanding, they followed him round the back doors of all the hotels and restaurants. Far from being annoyed, the class declared their delight with the afternoon's lesson.

Early skiers using the lilenfeld pole

Ski schools were soon flourishing throughout the Alps so that by the early 'thirties there were 54 in Switzerland alone. After a while the head instructors realised they should get together and in 1933 they met at Engelberg to hammer out some sort of common style.

Skis, too, were undergoing major development. Herr. Lettner of Salzburg began experimenting with plastic edges but they proved too brittle. He met with more success when he used metal. He made them with a T cross section so that they could be actually embedded into the wood. However he found that when he ran this along the full length the ski lost much of its flexibility. So he made scores of interlocking sections each about an inch and a half long.

It was the metal edge that first made it possible to keep skis parallel throughout a turn. The next year, using Lettner's edges, Toni Seelos won the world championship. His margin of 10 seconds was the largest difference ever registered in international Alpine competition. It proved how much faster turns could be made in the slalom when the skis were kept together and parallel.

Hannes Schneider, with the Dutch princesses Beatrice and Irene, demonstrating the Arlberg crouch.

Not that everyone was immediately converted to metal edges. Many said they were highly dangerous. They warned of dire accidents such as lacerated faces and some even hinted at severed limbs. Even four years later Lillywhites were confusing the issue by advising customers that metal edges "spoil a new pair of skis and should only be put on during the second year".

The growing prevalence of hard beaten pistes marked the

demise of the telemark. One of the last strongholds was at Andermatt where the Franciscans from the local monastery continued to swoop down the slopes with their habits billowing behind making them look like a flock of brown birds.

The piste also facilitated the christie even though the heel was lifted clear of the ski. A partial solution came with the Amstutz spring. Kenneth Foster recorded how "it became fashionable to keep the spring on your boots and clank around the village like a knight wearing his spurs." This was followed by the Huitfeldt binding which had a cable around the heel so that it could barely be lifted off the ski at all. It was a quality perfected in the Kandahar binding.

All these developments encouraged a custom made ski boot. The heel had to be made with a deep groove to carry the tension cable. The sole had to be reinforced to ensure the tension did not cause it to buckle. At the same time, the leather in the entire boot was stiffened to give firmer support around the ankle. It became very tough on the feet. Anyone buying a new pair of boots spent the next two weeks hobbling in agony while "breaking them in."

Inevitably there were some bright ideas, even if they were not always successful. C.J.White had spikes hammered through the soles of his boots with corresponding holes bored in his skis. But when he tried to board the train at Wengen, the guard refused entry to the carriage. So he had to freeze in the open truck among the skis. He thereupon reversed his idea and had the holes made in his boot and the nails protruding from his skis. But when putting them on, prior to his first descent, one of the skis shot off down the slope. Appreciating the double hazard, he shouted a warning. However near the bottom and out of hearing was a young lady who considered herself adept at stopping such runaway skis. Her technique was to sit on them!

Professor Kreukenhauser leading an early ski school class.

The French and Emile Allais in particular found that a rigid boot clamped to the ski opened up a much improved technique. The weight could be put right forward and if this was combined with ruard, or flicking the heels clear of the snow, the entire turn could be made on the tips. So instead of the Arlberg crouch, Allais started his turns with the shoulders and allowed the movement to continue down through the hips, knees and finally the feet. Steep slopes imparted a completely new sense of elation since turns almost gave the feeling of diving down the mountain. Inevitably enthusiasts took the technique to extremes. They weighted their boots with lead and inserted wooden wedges under their heels. In this way their "vorlage" had them almost overhanging their ski tips.

Schneider's flair for turning what many assumed to be a romp into a chic pursuit revived the fortunes of an impoverished St. Anton. For centuries the village had been nothing more than a convenient stop for travellers crossing the formidable Arlberg Pass. One of the earliest persons recorded was Pope Leo. He found the journey far from congenial for he was overturned - or maybe tipped - out of his "snow carriage" into a snow bank. However, by the start of the eighteenth century travellers had better fortune with a daily coach service. At one time The Post Hotel had stabling for a hundred horses. Today much of the 16th century building still remains in the renamed Alt Post. While the stables have been demolished, the timbers are incorporated in the dining room and bar. Ralph Benatsky, lyrist of the musical "White Horse Inn", was later to mention the Alt Post in a song "Hearts in the Snow". The manager, however, upbraided him. No one with any self respect would drink cider. Benatsky agreed but pointed out that if he had to substitute the more acceptable red wine and still retain the rhyme, he would have to find an alternative to the Post Hotel.

In 1883 the liveliness of the village was boosted by 4,000 navvies working on a railway tunnel under the pass. Out of concern for the daughters of the village, they were housed in a camp some distance away. Completion was celebrated with a banquet held where the two ends had happily met. Inevitably for that period, it was christened the Franz-Joseph Tunnel and to this day there is an elaborate plaque to this effect set in the tunnel mouth.

The original farmers had included the Tschols, the Stroltz, the Grubers and the Murrs. The latter family for long held the village monopoly as butcher and also as doctor. They were now joined by the Italian émigrés from out of the ranks of the navvies, the Delasevers, Defsots and Scaralets.

In due course, the high standard of Schneider's ski school spread the fame of St.

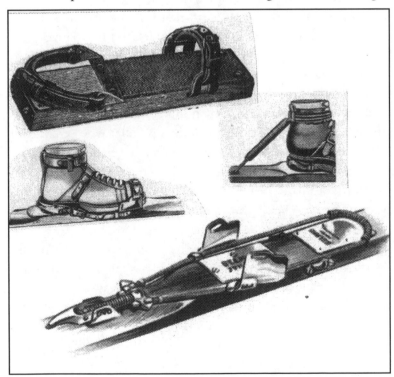

Ski binding progress: 1912 the Fleming Williams. 1935 the Amstutz spring and the 1952 Belmag binding, as illustrated in Harrods catalogues.

Anton far and wide. Most of this early publicity came through the budding film industry. It happened Schneider had gone ski-ing with the Swiss champion. They were amusing themselves chasing one another among the trees when they were spotted by a German film producer, Dr. Arnold Fanck. He immediately asked Schneider to feature in one of his films. It was still the height of the ski season and Schneider was extremely busy. So he consulted his long time mentor Karl Schuler, manager of the Post, who immediately recognised the potential publicity. Fanck's filming technique was highly unconventional. He would start with an idea but no script - and no money. But he chose superb settings and nearly always photographed skiers in deep snow. He gave it still greater impact through brilliant cutting.

To save hotel bills, Dr.Fanck had to shoot the film in a single day. He could not afford a guide, he could not even afford a porter. Schneider found he was having to perform all these duties.

Eventually Fanck had the film ready but he had no idea how it would be received. So it was sneaked into a matinee performance in a small cinema in Freiburg. The place was barely half full and the advertised programme seemed to have lulled the audience into a stupor. But Fanck's snow shots and Schneider's grace ravished them. At the end they stood up and cheered. However at that time film distribution in Austria was in the hands of a monopoly and Fanck considered their offer far too low. So the film was shown almost exclusively to universities and clubs.

Despite this curtailment, Karl Schuler was proved right. The next year Schneider asked his pupils how they had come to hear of him. Over half had seen the film.

A whole series of films, with such sugar sweet titles as "The White Dream of Arlberg", followed each other in quick succession. They were now having world wide exhibition and drawing more people to St.Anton. Perhaps the most famous was "Fox Chase" released in 1922. It was a return to the old theme but now with a pack of 18 skiers. At least, that was the intention but it was found the pack could not keep up with Schneider. So it additionally fell to him to give them lessons to improve their ski-ing. Even then their numbers on screen had to be reduced to 15 so that at any one moment three could be taking a rest.

At Zermatt, the peasant farmers remained doggedly indifferent to the potential of ski-ing. It might be booming elsewhere but it was no concern of theirs. The number of summer visitors was plummeting; it wasn't their fault - the mountains had not changed. It was Seiler who once again took the initiative. In the winter of 1927 he invited some influential guests to see for themselves. His welcome was on a much grander scale than Badrutt's party had been 90 years before. He needed 50 sleighs to bring them all from Visp, the nearest railway station open in winter. As though this cavalcade was not sufficiently impressive, he hired the village band to greet them as they drew into the village square.

It was sufficient to stir the bourgeoisie into reluctant action. That year they opened up ski runs on the lower slopes by cutting swathes through the trees. They also kept the Gornergrat railway open throughout the next winter. Even so, it did not grind its laborious way even as far up as the Riffelalp. It meant Sailer still could not open his hotel to skiers. The bourgeoisie were not worried; they were still smarting from the success of Sailer's initiative. But they also had sound reasons. Any ski run would have had to cross the avalanche-prone slopes of the Riffelboard. To make it safe would mean constructing nearly half a mile of galleries, not to mention a tunnel through the rock. However by 1934 even the village elders began to see that ski-ing might warrant such major financial investment. So they invited over some of the leading Mürren skiers to give their opinion. The verdict was a unanimous "yes". Not for the last time, the bourgeoisie lost their anticipated profit through their procrastinations. The work was finished only just before the outbreak of war so that the returns on their capital were postponed a further five years.

In complete contrast, Kitzbühel's local gentry had been enthusiastically participating in winter sports since the turn of the century. It is one of the charms of Kitzbühel that the inhabitants take their history for granted, incorporating the past into their everyday life. It is a walled town and everywhere visitors may go, they bump, sometimes literally, into history. The ski school office looks no more than a room bare except for a counter and a few chairs.

"The Fox Chase" with Schneider heading for the camera.

But it is in the tower of the main gateway. From there, at the time William the Conqueror was invading England, the wild Marguard of Chibuhel and his thugs were galloping forth and terrorising the surrounding neighbourhood.

The town happened upon prosperity because it lay on the main trading route to Venice. It was also blessed during the middle ages through the development of silver and copper mines. And now it thrives on its third blessing: snow.

Instead of individual steep roofed chalets, the tall thin houses are crammed together medieval style so that the outer sides form the actual city wall. The ways out are through tunnels between the houses and low enough for unwary novices to bang their skis tips against the ceiling. Stepping down into one of the shops in the Hinterstadt, there in the wall can still be seen the outline of a look out post. And sometimes it was used for a great deal more than looking out. After dark those young bloods seeking more excitement than could be found within the gates would use this way to clamber down and visit the stewhells in the mining camps.

Not that the older townspeople were all that innocent. The small building, now an insurance office at the end of the passageway close to Praxmair's Café, used to be a brothel. But because it projects beyond the main wall, the citizens excused themselves by considering it technically outside their jurisdiction.

In due course the mines were worked out. Then the populace was decimated by a terrible visitation of the plague. The Plague Chapel, standing today on the outskirts, was built in thanksgiving for eventual deliverance. It is one of a congregation of chapels constructed at various times to form a holy ring. The community hoped, with more fervour than realism, that it would protect them from avalanches. It was a precaution taken in several other ski resorts including Val d'Isére.

Kitzbühel's prosperity had, however, been irrevocably damaged. It fell on hard times. One visitor described how the pension landladies found tea so expensive they used the leaves over and over again until "the pots produced barely coloured water."

Indeed things had reached such a low ebb that the planners of the Zurich to Vienna railway completely overlooked the town so that the line was to pass some 30 kilometres away. A delegation was immediately dispatched to Vienna and successfully had the plan altered. But no matter how impoverished the City Fathers may have been, they were determined their town should remain unblemished. Rather than pierce their walls, they insisted the line must form a circumventing semi circle.

The Lambergs were among the first to become winter sports enthusiasts. They had for generations been a family of high distinction in the Austro-Hungarian Empire. When the mine owners sold up, they became lords of the manor. The Schloss Kaps remains their family seat though most of the building is now a conference centre. Interspersed on the walls are ferocious medieval battle weapons. Yet, true to tradition, it remains a family home. Delegates find themselves surrounded by portraits of ancestors; and very formidable they are too. Nearly all of them were leading politicians, generals or bishops of the Austro-Hungarian Empire and they were all holders of that most Noble Order of the Golden Fleece, the equivalent to the Garter. Then one of the dukes married his housemaid and the family were demoted to become mere counts.

Records show Count Hugo to have been a sleigh racing enthusiast. In 1881 he helped Count Anton Wolkenstein Trotsburg found the North Tyrolean Trotting Club. By the start of the twentieth century, the Countess Paula Lamberg had taken up ski jumping with such enthusiasm that she won the 1908 Ladies' championship . She reached 24 m. and this was at a time when the skier remained bolt upright in the air to land on the flat with a considerable thump.

Other local ski enthusiasts were Baron Bees and Burgomaster Harald who, if not titled, was at least a member of the landed gentry. Soon they were joined by another Burgomaster Franz Reisch. With a strong sense of the spectacular, Reisch caused a sensation through being the first to climb the Kitzbühelerhorn on skis.

And so the citizens had every encouragement to take winter sports seriously. A few years later and the Burgomaster was promoting the town as a winter resort. His ambition was to provide a major development every year. One year it was the construction of the Grand Hotel; another the Hahnenkamm cable car. It was even planned to build a funicular up the Kitzbühelerhorn. However, this had to be abandoned on the outbreak of the First World War.

Although Countess Lamberg died in 1928, the Kitzbühel gentry and Baron Carl Menshenger in particular, continued to set the pace in winter sports. Curiously it was the local expertise in metal working, a by-product of the mines, that was largely responsible. Early examples of this ornate craftsmanship can be seen in the gates of the church and the intricacy of the inn sign outside the Golden Greif. Came the winter sports era and the gentry of Kitzbühel had their skilled blacksmiths make them iron framed bobsleighs, horse sleighs and primitive snow bikes. Examples of them all can be seen in the local museum.

The races thrived and, true to the Austrian temperament, by 1934 they had become an elaborate social event. There were stands and a tea tent - something of a misnomer since it served exclusively grog and punch. In the evening there was a splendid race ball.

Kitzbühel promoted an even more daring variation of ski-joring. Instead of a horse the skier was towed by a light aeroplane and was kept in the air by kite. However the practice stopped when the Swiss champion slalomer Roger Staub was killed in a mid-air collision.

But it was in February 1933 that Kitzbühel was well and truly placed upon the map as an international resort. The world's golden boy, the Prince of Wales, later Edward VIII, arrived to learn ski-ing under the tuition of Count Hugo. He stayed however at the Grand Hotel, where he was constantly surrounded by photographers. There was one evening of consternation when it was suddenly realised he was missing. Distraught courtiers combed the town. They eventually found him, free at last from all the formality he so disliked, sitting in the Eggevert Cafe sipping beer and sampling Tiroler knoedles. With him was the, at that time still unknown, Mrs. Wallis Simpson.

On another occasion he had lunch at the exclusive Tennerhof Hotel. Much in the style of his mother, he assumed that the honour of his presence was sufficient to excuse him the bill. Not so the manager and, realising the situation, he jumped into his car in pursuit. He presented the bill just as H.R.H. was getting into the cable car.

Another place the Prince favoured was Praxmair's, a cafe which gave authentic demonstrations of Tyrolean dancing. Spectators might well recognise among the dancers their ski instructor or, perhaps, one of the shop assistants and even the man who kept the telescope atop the Hahnenkamm. They wore traditional lederhosen and broad belts with messages such as "Na bu" or "Sister Beware" woven in straw and which may have been in their family for a hundred years or more.

Après ski at Praxmairs. Kitzbhuel lads gave exhibitions of the
traditional ear boxing (watschentaz) dance

Dances include the Knappentanz which is derived from the mining days. The dancers carry primitive mining lamps and part of the routine is to hit their stemmeisen mining tool, a six inch strip of iron, so that it rings like an xylophone. The stelzentanz dates from the days before drainage. When the snows melted the only way to get about was on stilts. A girl wearing the mask of winter flits among the grotesque figures. Then as they gather round her, drubbing their stilts on the floor, she drops the mask and emerges as the spirit of spring.

Another favourite place for dancing in the 'thirties was the Reich. It was more conventional: "where the band played many Viennese arias, quiet sentimental valses and ballads from 'The Street Singer' and 'Die Fledermaus'". T.C.Bainter has also recorded that "on gala nights an enormous lampshade was let down suddenly from the ceiling so that it enveloped a dancing couple. How many men took advantage of the cover to kiss the girl was hard to guess, but it must have demanded speed and dexterity for the shade rose as abruptly as it fell."

Sir Henry Lunn had firm strictures on ballroom behaviour. Never exactly liberal, he had an unmitigated abhorrence of the modern dances. A member of one of his parties reported "The burning question of the acceptability of the Chamois-Shuffle and the Winkle Waddle never became really acute as the very few would-be exponents of the banned Bunny Hug consented to modify their transports as soon as they realised that their corybantic antics were not generally appreciated."

Later less outrageous "novelty" dances would become the seasonal rage. There was The Lambeth Walk and the Palais Glide danced to "Poor Little Angeline" or "The Isle of Capri". The steps were usually devised and promoted in the British Locharno dance hall chains. They were then made more widely known through verbal instructions from such top bandleaders as Victor Silvester and Henry Hall broadcasting from leading London hotels.

The one essential dance, however, was the Paul Jones. It had a unique social advantage. It provided an invaluable way for introducing new arrivals without any formalities. Holding hands, the men formed an outer ring revolving clockwise and the ladies moved in the contrary direction. When the music stopped, the pairs facing each other were partners for the next dance. Its success depended essentially on the men honourably accepting the girl opposite, no matter how plain she might be. Regrettably this was not always the case at Mürren. The shortage of girls was such that ensuring a partner might mean reserving a dance sometime during the day. So the moment the music stopped there could well follow a deplorable jostle.

The bar was another sphere in which Sir Henry enforced his Methodist principles. At the Mürren Palace it closed promptly at 11 o'clock. Furthermore the barman was forbidden to serve ladies at any time. They had to stand about outside and depend on boy friends for their supplies. At those hotels where Sir Henry had absolute jurisdiction there was no bar at all.

The cocktail, which had been invented during the American prohibition to mask illicit hooch of dubious quality, was becoming fashionable. Whether it was shaken or stirred was of small consequence. More important was the ice. At this time ice was still made using salt and a careless barman could easily let it spill over and ruin a screwdriver, a Manhattan or just a plain gin and tonic. A proportion of the Grindelwald visitors were retired Indian military. Experience in the Himalayan hillstations had taught them to appreciate glacier ice. With the close proximity of the glacier they always checked with the bell boy that the ice in their drink was not artificial. Indeed the best barmen had huge chunks hewn out of the glacier which they would store in the cellar.

However, patrons at the St.Moritz Palace liked something more expensive. It was not unusual, according to Raymond Flower, for 200 bottles of champagne to be disposed of within an evening. Gustave the head barman and his assistants made a point of not wearing watches. In contrast to Henry Lunn, their time was determined by their customers alone. Until the last one had left - and it might well be around breakfast time - the bar remained open.

The Palace bar had its fair quota of incidents too, as when one of Barbara Hutton's boy friends was rash enough to hit Georges Charpentier below the belt. Enraged, the champion boxer knocked him out. Unfortunately he was so incensed he did not let the matter rest there. He went on to knock out the staff who tried to restrain him and, for good measure, some of the guests as well. Next day Badrutt asked him - very politely - to leave.

In the really smart hotels, the time spent at the bar before dinner became a discreet indication of social status. At the St.Moritz Kulm and also at Suvretta House, most people dined at eight. At the Palace, however, the guests would not have even gone up to have their bath. By the time everyone had got dressed, dinner did not really get under way till ten or even half past.

Wengen evenings might include a moonlight ski party. A special train would be ordered after dinner. On reaching Scheidegg, everyone spent a convivial hour or so at the station bar waiting for the moon to rise or maybe acquiring suffcient courage to make the run back to the village.

An affectation prevalent among the bright young things at the Mürren Palace was to hold "supper parties". Dinner was part of the all in terms but it was thought very sophisticated to sit with your guests at a separate table for little more than the cost of such extras as champagne and caviar.

Things could become extremely boisterous there too. On club nights, Arnold Lunn could be relied upon to make an amusing speech. It was always supplemented by a highly amusing performance from "d'Eeggers". Alan d'Egville had made his name as a cartoonist in "The Sketch" and " The Bystander". He also had the gift of carrying his humour into real life. He would work up a funny situation into buffoonery and, encouraged by the guffaws of all the diners, would deftly develop it into sheer Marx Brother's anarchy. On one occasion the diners suddenly realised he had joined the army of waiters emerging from the kitchen, his napkin over his arm and carrying a gigantic covered dish. This he whipped off to reveal a large fish which he proceeded to drape over the head of a not very popular guest. He finished this particular interlude by trying to go out through the incoming swing doors, fighting against a stream of heavily laden genuine waiters. In contrast he could be quite sentimental yodelling while accompanying himself as adeptly as a professional Swiss accordianist.

Practical Gabardine Ski-ing Suits

Are Proof against Snow Damp

(Left):—
Men's Tunic Suits in Union Gabardine, proofed against snow and wind. It is tailored on loose easy-fitting lines, with 'two-way' collar, wind front and cuffs. May be worn with or without a belt. Navy or Fawn, lined with Natural Wool. In all fittings.

5½ Gns

Same style in All Wool Gabardine. Black, Navy or Fawn
7 Gns

(Centre):—
'Davos' A proofed Gabardine Suit with the verve of youth in every line. The jacket has a storm front and adaptable collar and the trousers cut on plus four lines are reinforced at the seat and knees. In Black and Navy only. S.S.W., S.W. and O.S. fittings.

5 Gns

Proofed Cap to match with patent leather peak .. 12/6

(Right):—
Men's Blouse Model made of Wool Gabardine in Navy or Fawn tones. This style allows ample freedom of movement and is very smart. The trousers are cut fairly full and fasten close around the ankle. Lined Natural Wool.

7 Gns

Ski-ing Breeches in Bedford Cord.
In Derby Tweed   2½ Gns

2 Gns

Warm Woolly Cap that can be pulled down to protect the ears. Various colourings.
From **4/6**

Gabardine Caps, in Navy or Fawn.
12/6

Wind Jackets, made from Brown Gabardine.
30/-

HARRODS WONDERFUL
SKI-ING BOOT

Specially designed with waterproof leather soles, which, being rigid in the waist and flexible in the forepart, give utmost support and ease of movement. Uppers of Tan or Black Chrome Calf. Light yet serviceable. All sizes 6 to 12 **45/-**

Gaberdene brings fashion to skiwear. Harrods catalogue, 1926

completeWinter Sports outfit
—many specially designed and exclusive to Harrods

MT. 20

RM. 2.

RM. 5

BLUE GREY SKI SUIT

in Barathea. Single or double-breasted style with zipp fronts and pockets.

(RM.2)

£6 6 0

WINDJAMMER OF DOUBLE POPLIN

One of the newest and best of pullover style ski jackets. Well-cut and made with knitted collar, cuffs and waistband in shades to contrast with the navy or white of the jacket itself. *(MT.20).* **30/-**

THE NEW 'VORLAGE' TROUSERS

This season's newest development in ski clothes. Tailored to give no pull on the knee when ski-running, and with the cut of Norwegian ski-jumpers' trousers—yet the freedom of ordinary trousers. Good fine quality Whipcord in shades of navy blue, fawn or French grey. *(RM. 5).* **45/-**

Figure above shows panel back jacket available in single or double breasted styles

HARRODS LTD

The Man's Shop—Ground Floor
Page 3

LONDON SW1

Men'swear influenced by the Mariners of England. Harrods catalogue 1936

Indeed d'Eggers' contribution to the festivities was such that regular visitors checked that he would be there before making their own bookings. Yet like many who are the life and soul of the party, he suffered the black dog of depression. His limited income made it necessary to rely on Lunns providing cheap rates in return for his remarkable gift for fun. While not often a winner he was also an outstanding skier.

In contrasting decorum, St.Moritz society was enlivened after dinner by Lady Diana Duff-Cooper's evenings at the Carlton. She arranged exquisite cabarets of near professional standards.

Universally one was expected to dress for dinner - black ties, not white. If someone's luggage had become lost en route, the head waiter would seat them in a corner even, perhaps, behind a screen. Towards the end of the 'thirties, it became the habit to invite one's ski teachers to supper. This practice became even more distressing when the ski teachers started appearing in dinner jackets. The natural reaction was to wear lounge suits.

All formality was waived, however, on the night of a fancy dress ball. As the making of costumes was a further way of passing the dull hours between dusk and supper time, they were frequently highly ingenious. Soon families or parties were wearing "team" costumes. This was especially the case at resorts like Morgins where the same proponents of English skating would meet year after year. The costumes made by the Jordan family won quite widespread renown. One year they were pieces in a chess set and in another they were different musical instruments making up a band. Then there was a Barnum and Bailey circus group. It included a horse with the rear end filled by a famous international rugger player. His prowess in the scrum was put to good use as he had a charming equestrienne pirouetting on his back.

Pyjama dances provided an economic alternative with ample potential for indiscretions. A captain in one of the Regiment of Guards appeared at the Kitzbühel Tennerhof in a frilly nightdress and convulsed all present with his posturing. But at breakfast next morning he learnt to his utter consternation that the village photographer had been present. Fearful that the pictures might be displayed on the board outside the shop or, even worse, be sent to his colonel, he at once set out and bought up all the prints and negatives.

It was not until after the First World War that fashion designers appreciated that skiers required clothes specifically designed for snow conditions. In place of heavy mackintosh there was an ideal material invented by Mr. Burberry of Basingstoke. He realised that cotton, when wet, swells and consequently becomes shower proof. Together with a professor in Edinburgh, he evolved a coating for the fibre which swells in unison and helps close gaps in the crossweave. He even insisted that the thread used in the garment should also be treated so that the holes made by the needle were moisture proof.

Being of a Shakespearean turn of mind, Mr. Burberry called his material gaberdine after Shylock. Its great asset is that it hangs well. Also it can be had in a multiplicity of colours. As a result ladies could wear stylish clothes which were still practical. Even so dark shades remained prevalent since they provided contrast rather than trying to vie with the snow. Men replaced their jodhpurs with shower proof trouser. Skiers, sufficiently good to be concerned more with wind than wet, wore leather jackets. For the rest Lillywhites started urging that "The Norwegian anorak deserves to become better known".

The first record of ladies wearing trousers was at Wengen in 1924. They were promoted by four sisters who, for some unrecorded reason, were known as One, Two, Three and Go. As the material was non-stretch and easily became baggy it was customary to sit with the legs straight out in front. Also the trousers tended to become worn at the bottom through being rubbed by the top of the boot. So if only for economic reasons, socks were usually worn outside and turned down over the top of the boots. This was incorporated into the 1925 fashions when ladies with any pretence at sartorial elegance were dressed all in black except for their socks which had to be in brilliant contrast.

It was also that year that Doreen Elliott had the first "Mariner of England" ensemble expressly tailored to her directions. It was a dark blue gaberdine suit. The bottom of the trousers flopped over the top of the boots, almost touching the skis, successfully covering the turned down socks. It was such an instant success that by the start of the following season it was incorporated in the Harrods catalogue.

Doreen Elliott herself emphasised the style by additionally wearing collar, tie and waistcoat so that along with her shingled hair, she looked fashionably masculine.

At St.Anton Lady Diana Kingsmill maintained much the same elegance. She sported a monocle which she kept firmly screwed in her eye not only when ski-ing but even when racing.

Several one season fashions came and went, such as a knitted hat to match the sweater. Then in the spring of 1938 skirts made a sudden comeback. Obviously it was less a fashion than a statement of the wearer's accomplishment.

The French women went their own way and took to wearing well tailored suits made in corduroy.

Fashions were also changing among skaters. When Sonja Henie became World Champion, she was still of school girl age. So she could without undue impropriety shorten her dresses to gymslip length. Once the trend had started, skating skirts continued becoming shorter rather than longer. In her early days Henie had her circular skirts lined in beige which co-ordinated with her tights and were duly finished off with beige boots. When other skaters started copying her she switched to an all white ensemble.

The first Olympic skating events formed part of the summer games and so had to be held on artificial ice rinks. In 1924 the inclusion of additional snow sports, such as bobsleigh and Nordic ski races, required separate Winter games. The French wanted to broaden the scope still further and, as hosts at Chamonix, chose curling as the "demonstration" event. It was won by Britain. Not surprising really. The team comprised a high proportion of Scots and there were only two other countries entered, Switzerland having scratched at the last moment.

In 1928 the games were held at St.Moritz and the authorities prepared for it with zest. They extended the Chantarella funicular up to Corviglia. Whereas previously it had required a three hour climb, the competing skiers were able to reach the top within minutes. A further 10,000 francs were spent on constructing the Julier ski jump. The cost proved justified when Jakob Tams beat the world record with a jump of 73 m. He would have jumped further had he not in mid air started leaning alarmingly to the right and landed with a spectacular but harmless fall.

His was by no means the only misfortune. There was a devastating thaw. The ice rink "blistered" so that contestants had to skate between the danger spots marked by red flags borrowed from the golf course. The suddenness of the thaw also upset predictions for the Cresta and the favourite, Lord Northesk was beaten for the gold by an American. Even the opening ceremony had a curious moment when a man appeared wearing not only skis but a grass skirt. It was feared he would try and interrupt the proceedings but, strangely, he made no demonstration and simply wandered off .

The cost for staging the games was so prohibitive there was serious discussion as to whether the entire concept of winter Olympics might not be abandoned.

However the 1932 games duly took place.in the United States at Lake Placid. An American, Eddie Eagan had already won a gold for boxing so that winning the bobsleigh made him the first person to win golds in both summer and winter meetings. The Germans were excluded because of their Nazi regime. However, Hitler won a prestigious victory when Garmisch was voted as venue for 1936, but only after he had "promised" not to promote anti-Semitism in any form. The arrangements were impressive and in every way impeccable. Yet the obvious intent to use the occasion for party propaganda successfully soured the atmosphere. A portent of things to come was when one of the leading Austrian skiers defected and raced for Germany. The Americans seriously considered a complete boycott while two outstandingly honourable Canadian skiers stood by their principles and refused to participate.

Fearing the worst, Baron Pierre de Coubertin, founder of the modern Olympics, excused himself from the opening ceremony. Tension mounted as Hitler opened the games in pouring rain. The British showed their contempt even as they entered the stadium. They used the outstretched arm of a Nazi at the salute as a rack upon which to hang their umbrellas. Everyone was keenly aware of the similarity with the Olympic salute when the arm is raised to one side. The Swiss contingent refused to salute Hitler at all. The Germans blatantly heiled, raising their arms to the front. Despite the excited declaration by the German broadcaster, the British made their salute very decisively to the side, so decisively that one lady skater hit her neighbour on the nose.

Later in the proceedings, the British skater Freddie Tomlins caused consternation among the security officials by breaking through the SS guards surrounding Hitler and asking him for his autograph. Hitler obliged.

It was the first time Alpine ski races were included. They were nearly spoilt when the Olympic Committee tried to override the Ski Federation on the definition of amateur. They declared ski instructors could not be included. This would have severely handicapped the Swiss team. Britain backed the Swiss, upholding ethics even though it considerably increased the odds against them.

For once Britain, with Evie Pinching, stood a really good chance of winning a gold medal. However nerves took their toll and she only came in seventh. Yet in the same season she showed her true worth by winning both the downhill and combined in the World Championships.

Olympic skating events throughout this decade were dominated by one person Sonja Henie. Mrs.T.D.Richardson has described how she made her appearance at Chamonix when the arrangements were so bad the skaters had no option but to practise on a curling rink. "Into this hurley burley there suddenly bounced a small, round, pink faced child - who promptly proceeded to do a spiral, a back scratch, free leg high in the air, followed by a sitzspin, to the horror and astonishment of all the purists present. One of them turned to my husband saying 'What is this, a puppet show - a circus?' to which he replied: 'No, that is the future of skating'".

How right he was. However on this occasion, Sonja Henie was judged last - though one perceptive judge gave her top marks. In the following years, starting at the tender age of l5, she was to become 10 times world champion and three times Olympic gold medallist. She completely revolutionized skating. Her programme would contain a breath taking sequence of skims, jumps and spins making maximum use of the tips of her skates till she seemed to be flirting with the ice. She also used her arm, indeed, she took ballet lessons from a member of Pavlova's company and this gave her a beautiful fluid movement like no other skater. She would end her display with a backward glide, almost on the toe of one skate and raising the other leg clear above the horizontal.

Just before the opening of the Chamonix Olympics, Sonja's father, a wealthy Norwegian bicycle manufacturer, asked "Tyke" Richardson for his opinion . He replied that, for a start, she could not skate brackets. Henie immediately asked him to train her but Richardson pointed out he was to be one of the judges. Even then her father failed to appreciate the nicety but assumed he wanted a reward - even maybe a bribe. He began by suggesting a case of champagne and followed it with a series of increasingly expensive offers ending up with a motor boat.

Once his daughter had achieved the ultimate success as an amateur, Mr.Henie went to Hollywood determined to batter the way through to making her a film star. He prepared a spectacular ice show, in which his daughter was to star, and invited the top people. His main quarry was Darryl F. Zanuck, head of Twentieth Century Fox. He refused the invitation. In the end Henie had him virtually kidnapped. Hardly conducive to winning a contract, it might be thought, though Zanuck did compromise by offering her a brief appearance. It was an appearance, however, that proved sufficient for Zanuck to revise his opinion. He ended by starring her in a dozen films. Her coquettish style was backed by gorgeous snow scenes and near fantasy such as a black and white chequered ice rink. One of her most successful films was "Sun Valley Serenade". It included the song " Chatanooga Choo Choo" with its railway rhythm ingeniously adaptable to skating tempo.

And so it was that, entranced by her free flowing grace, millions of filmgoers themselves caught the skating fever. It even gripped the Royal Family and that year the Royal Box at the British championships was positively crowded with George V and Queen Mary, the Dukes of York and Gloucester and the Princess Royal together with their entourage.

The international style had been flourishing abroad many years before it had become acceptable to the British. It was particularly strong in those Swiss resorts fortunate enough to have distinguished resident coaches. Even before the First World War there had been two such coaches at St. Moritz. At the Palace there was Bernard Adams. For the rest of the year he was the pro at Princes. The other was a Swede, Bror Meyer, who also officiated at the Manchester Ice Rink. After the war there were the brothers Gerschwiler, Arnold at the Kulm and Jacques at Suvretta House. However, after a row with the Kurverein, Arnold moved to Davos and much of the skating culture went with him.

Jacques retired but by then his star pupil, the British skater Cecilia Colledge was reaching the heights. At the Lake Placid Olympics, in 1932, Cecilia had been, at just 11, the youngest entrant ever in the Winter Olympics. At 14 she won the British title and under the most curious circumstances. English law forbade children to skate before a paying audience. There seemed to be only one solution. It was after midnight and before banks of empty seats that the judges watched her give her winning performance. By this time she had reached a pitch whereby she was closely shadowing Sonja Henie. It was simply bad luck that at the Garmisch Olympics she drew first place. Only a few spectators had arrived so that, once again, she was skating in a gloomy, echoingly empty auditorium. In contrast, when it came to Henie's turn, the place had filled, Hitler was present and her past success ensured high anticipation. It was late in the day, the lights were switched on and they included a spotlight which gave her performance a magic and sparkle that ensured her third Olympic gold. Cecilia won the silver.

Ice dancing, however, was suffering a dull patch. This was in part due to the ruling that one skate must always be on the ice. So besides the inevitable waltz, the only alternative was the ten

1900 Countess Lamberg landing on the flat

step. Then in the 'thirties there appeared the unlikely character of a British bank manager who, together with his wife, had won the ice dancing championships in 1937. While Reginald Wilkie may have been adept at both skating and adding up figures in columns, his most memorable metier was to choreograph figures on ice. In rapid succession he produced the quick step, the Argentine tango and the Paso Doble.

All this time the English style had been losing ground yet the diehards refused to change their minds. They still believed their most serious rival was ski-ing. "Only when experts in the English Style of skating begin to desert the rink for ski-ing will be the time to criticise English skating for its lack of variety".

The English School staggered on right up until the outbreak of the Second World War. At Villars it was for long nurtured by the author E.F. Benson. But eventually it could only be found at Morgins, where there was no mountain railway to lure skiers with the promise of easy climbing.

1921 Landing on a slope

Curling also was in the doldrums. It was only actively encouraged in a few resorts: Grindelwald, Wengen and Pontresina; all villages largely lying in the shadow of the mountains so that the sun did not spoil the ice. It received staunch support from such famous devotees as A.A.Milne, Sir Arthur Conan Doyle and Sir Henry Wickham, who had made a fabulous fortune after smuggling rubber seeds out of Brazil and establishing the plantations in Malaya. Curling was included as an Olympic event in 1932 and Britain won the gold medal.

Ski Flying 1950

Sex discrimination was rampant among curlers. Admittedly it had a logical basis. Initially women used lighter stones which lacked sufficient force to oust the men's heavier stones from the "house" of rings carved in the ice around the wooden dolly. Indeed the rules only recognised a ladies team if skippered by a man. Moreover they were only allowed to play their matches in the morning. When it came to competitions, they had their own Gossage Mirror. However by 1930, many ladies were using heavier stones and were forming a significant sector within the clubs.

While bandy was essentially for amateurs, ice hockey has always been predominantly for professionals. Skill and fitness are essentials not widely found among holiday sportsmen. For long the British had little scope. Throughout the 'twenties the only rink in Britain dedicated to ice hockey was in Manchester. But then ice rinks as a whole were at a premium.

The change came in the 'thirties spurred by the popularity of Sonja Henie's films. Within 10 years, 26 new rinks were opened. But ice hockey, like English style skating, requires a considerable area of ice. So if it is to pay its way it must attract a considerable number of spectators. This did not happen - at least not until the opening of Wembley Stadium in 1934 which did have sufficient spectator seating. Capacity attendance was further insured through the glamour of the Wembley Lions. They formed the backbone of the British team who won the gold medal in the 1936 Olympics.

Ski jumping was another event that had been included in the early Winter Olympics. Indeed it was in 1924 that Tullin Thams introduced his winning style. Instead of remaining bolt upright in the air, he leant forward from the hips. This not only makes the jumper more streamlined but traps a cushion of air under the body and increases the buoyancy. Two years later Dr.Reinhard Straumann published the first serious study on the aerodynamics of ski jumping.

In due course this led to the construction of a gigantic jump, 500ft high, which opened in 1934 at Planica in Yugoslavia. The distances shot up to around 280 ft. The whole concept seemed to be carrying the sport beyond dynamics and almost into ballistics.

The Ski Federation felt it had all gone too far. They tried to hobble further development by refusing to recognise competitions held on jumps designed for a distance over 90 m. But the highly spectacular form of jumping seized the public imagination and claimed recognition by defining the new classification of ski flying.

The first 100 m. or 330 ft. jump was made by Josef Bradl in 1936. The distance seemed so incredible the press invented an explanation - that the Yugoslav metre was shorter than the normal European measurement.

Such distances also had an effect on the ski flyers. Competitors now had sufficient time to lean forward from the ankles to the extent the body becomes parallel with the skis. Indeed, just to prove the point, the Yugoslav Marja Pecarn, while still in mid-air, scratched his forehead with his ski tip. Whereas parallel skis merely duplicated the aerodynamics of the body, it was then found that when the skis are angled in flight as a V extending outside the body area, they contribute to the lift similar to an aircraft wing.

Over the two years between the Anschluss and the outbreak of the second world war, most of Europe demurred from ski-ing in Austria. Kitzbühel, for instance, had become a hotbed of Nazi sympathisers. Notable was Count Schlick, then owner of the Schloss Lebenberg. He had married three times, and one of his wives had met a highly suspicious death falling from a racing car at Monte Carlo. His third wife was a very large and formidable lady with a penchant for hunting and smoking cigars. She became a close friend of Goering. Indeed Goering had been staying with them just before his arrest.

At St.Anton, however, the situation was quite different. The general attitude was set by Hannes Schneider. By now he had become very influential; deputy mayor and honorary head of the fire service as well as, of course, controlling the village main source of income, the ski school. So the Nazis had made a point of inviting him to become a party member. When he refused they felt snubbed. So they decided to hold a procession with all their "specially selected" members. Schneider's chalet was on the main street and so he sat on the balcony to watch. When he saw that the "selected" comprised all the lay-abouts, bully boys and half wits in the village, he collapsed laughing. All the other villagers followed suit. By the end the event had become such a fiasco the party's local branch had to be disbanded.

Soon after two small but by no means insignificant incidents came back to confront him. He had made one of his films with Hitler's favourite star Leni Riefenstahl. She had made a pass at him which he had ignored and she had taken umbrage. He further enraged the Nazis after they had engineered the removal of Gomperz as president of the Central European Ski Federation because he was a Jew. Defying Nazi threats of retaliation, he gave Gomperz a job with the ski school.

The threat continued to grow and Schneider was denounced in the local Nazi free paper. It suggested his films had made him filthy rich at the village's expense. The instructors in the school rallied round and signed a statement declaring the claim to be lies. It was noticed, however, that one instructor, Moser, slipped out without signing. He was already highly unpopular and when the instructors voted him out, Schneider acquired another black mark through failing to intervene. Moser became even more bitter when he tried to start a rival school and failed.

During the uneasy days of 1938 leading up to the Anschluss and the German occupation of Austria, Schneider noticed that most of his acquaintances were becoming too frightened to talk to him in public. In the street, young Nazi thugs would stand in the way and force his wife to walk in the gutter. It was only with difficulty that he was restrained from knocking them out of the way.

On March, 13th, the Germans invaded and Moser revealed his true self when he took over as mayor. That same night he ordered that Schneider be got out of bed and taken into "protective" custody. Fearful that there might be public outcry, the authorities took him to the little police station at Landeck further down the railway line.

It was the eve of the Arlberg Kandahar race and Arnold Lunn hurried out to see what influence he could bring to bear.

"The climate of fear is unmistakable. I snuffed it as I came out of the train at St.Anton. Near the Post I saw two Arlberg boys sheepishly murmuring 'Heil Hitler!' and giving each other the Nazi salute". Prompted by Arnold Lunn, the Ski Club of Great Britain, as race organisers, wrote to the Arlberg Club: "Unless Herr. Hannes Schneider, our Honorary Member, returns to St.Anton as head of the Arlberg School, which he founded, and as President of the Arlberg Ski Club, the race will not be held".

In the end, the Germans had to make do with the first Arlberg race bereft of its Kandahar suffix. There were no entries from Britain and several other countries followed suit. With the inevitable injection of Fascist militarism, the race proved a poor substitute. The next year the AK proper was run at Mürren, the start of a regular rotation among nations which still prevails.

As it happened one of Schneider's pupils had been Dr.Rosen, the solicitor who had defended Hitler after the first Munich putsch. He had enormous influence among the Nazi hierarchy and arranged for Schneider to be removed from the Landeck gaol to a more congenial life on parole in Garmisch. But it was another of Schneider's admirers, the American Harvey Gibson, who had the real clout. He was President of the Manufacturers' Trust which had made the previous German government a massive loan. It was a debt still unredeemed by the Nazis. It was made clear that pressure for repayment would become extreme unless Schneider was allowed to emigrate to the United States.

Until those first few weeks, the top Nazis had never heard of Schneider. Suddenly they found themselves confronted by the influence of all his friends. They capitulated and Schneider was allowed to sail for the States where Gibson arranged for him to work on the slopes at Cranmore in New Hampshire. There he found his Arlberg technique was already firmly established due to the number of Austrian instructors who had taken refuge from Nazism. Indeed one instructor had difficulty finding employment because, when speaking English, his accent was not considered sufficiently pronounced.

The Nazis substantiated their regime by cultivating fear. One way was to have unsuspected agents, like Moser, emerging from among ordinary villagers and suddenly wielding unbridled power. A number of Jews fleeing from Vienna took refuge in the only hotel of the then still obscure village of Alpbach. Then suddenly the head waiter, who had always seemed such a genial and amusing man, emerged as the Nazi agent. He applied a demonic ruthless efficiency to round them up for transport to the concentration camps.

CHAPTER IV
HAPPY DAYS AGAIN
1947 - 1965

The outbreak of the Second World War found Arnold Lunn, Sir Arnold as he was soon to become, again acting as steward for prisoners of war held at Mürren. During the first winter he was writing: "There are about three tracks at Half Way House, in soft powder snow. About an eighth of the rink is open. The small hotels are open but the big ones are shut." Indeed throughout Switzerland most of the hotels put up the shutters. Those that were uneconomic were pulled down. The rest received a Government grant so that they could be kept in good repair.

What Lunn did not record was that among the internees was a young skier who, on the outbreak of war, had walked across the Italian border. His name was Zeno Collo who emerged after the war as a highly popular world champion.

Billy Fiske, who had acquired a reputation on the Cresta for never coming to grief was, ironically, the first American to be killed in action. An irrepressible extrovert and widely popular, it was typical that on the outbreak of war he volunteered for the R.A.F. It was as a Spitfire pilot that he was killed during the Battle of Britain. He had started on the bob and had won gold medals in both the 1928 and 1932 Olympics. He had then transferred his allegiance to the Cresta and won practically every race in the calendar.

For the Army, ski warfare had begun during the Russo-Finnish war. Churchill, as First Sea Lord, decided that the formation of a ski troop would help bolster the Finns. Not many British could ski and those who could were almost entirely upper class. So it seemed logical to recruit from a highly fashionable regiment, the 5th Battalion the Scots Guards. The choice was canny for there were 700 volunteers, almost all of them officers. Even when told that only 20 would be acting commissioned, the numbers held at 200. The winter hardened Finnish troops were completely outwitting and outmanoeuvring the novice Russian skiers. So it was a shock to the British expeditionary force, who were actually loading at the port at Glasgow, when news came that the Finns had signed an armistice.

The unit was reformed on the outbreak of war. Having finished their training at Chamonix, they learnt from Lord Haw Haw that they were now to help the Norwegians. Narvik was the only winter port from where Swedish iron ore could be exported. It was believed the German invasion could be repulsed south of Lake Mjosa near Lillehammer. But hopes were dashed when the Germans succeeded in crossing the ice.

Eighteen Norwegians, who had been working with the British forces, foresaw a future need for military cross country training. So they escaped to Reykjavik and established a ski school. By the end of the war they had trained 10,000 British and US troops.

The training was highly specialised. For instance ski tracks can be seen ten miles away but they can be made to look confusing by walking in circles. Navigation procedure in the mountains must take into account the deception of heights. Uniforms have to be off white because pure white is highly reflective when seen against snow.

It was only occasionally that Switzerland was brushed by hostilities. There was the occasion when a British plane, obviously in difficulties, flew low over St.Moritz and from it blossomed several parachutes. The locals set out to rescue the crew from the snow and rocks. When one of them was reached he asked where he was. When told, he gave a gasp of surprise: "I used to work in a travel agent's office and the one place I always wanted to visit was St.Moritz."

Skiers completing the run at the Prariond refuge beside the upper reaches of the Isere, can see a memorial tablet set in a rock. It records the cruel fate of British soldiers, escaping from an Italian prisoner of war camp in 1944. Helped by two Italian partisans, they had successfully crossed the Glacier de Pisaillas when they were overtaken by a storm. It was unusually fierce for early November and they were only wearing suits. By chance a local almost stumbled over one of them covered in snow and but still alive. He was rushed to hospital. Then during the spring thaw the body of a man dressed in a lounge suit was found caught up in the Fornet Bridge. Returning to the valley, they found the bodies of a further 17 soldiers together with their two guides. They were only 50 m. from the refuge.

At St.Anton the final months of the war found the Alt Post in a rather curious situation. For some time the local resistance group had made the basement their headquarters. Then several top Nazi generals chose St.Anton as the place from where they would make a final dramatic stand. They installed themselves at the top of the hotel. The floors between in this remarkable sandwich were accommodating the local girls school.

The resistance group became quite high powered and members included Baron Heimele, later ambassador to Moscow, and the car racer Hans von Stuck. They decided to harass the Nazis fleeing Vienna. They successfully blew up the railway line in the tunnel where it would be difficult to repair.

A passenger on the first train to be held up was a sinister man in a long dark coat and dramatically broad brimmed hat. He did not so much introduce himself as materialise before the manager of the Alt Post. Would he help ensure the safety of the Hungarian Crown jewels? Closer scrutiny revealed the jewels formed only part of the treasure. They were in a gruesome mix with a large quantity of teeth with gold fillings. Altogether they filled three of the Alt Post's luxurious baths. The manager, mindful of the strange tenants already in his hotel, tactfully declined. So the sinister man split the jewels among several local householders. His scheme however came to grief. A local Nazi official noticed a woman whom he knew to be a poor widow, wound about with a mass of obviously genuine jewels. It set him on a trail that entailed digging up several back gardens. However five villagers managed to thwart him and in due course there were built five new hotels. In the mean time, the mystery man had disappeared and a French official, "call me Marcel", arrived on the scene. He took official charge of all the jewels he could trace - then he, too, disappeared.

The ski school at St.Anton had continued throughout the war even though it had little more than a quarter the normal number of pupils. They included a notably high proportion of beautiful women from Slovakia which the Nazis considered, like Austria, to be inland territory.

Came the end of the war and Dr.Salcher, the Nazi sponsored successor to Schneider, decamped in haste to Bad Gastein. There he reverted to his previous occupation as medical practitioner.

It is reputed that when the allied commanders were mapping out the various zones of responsibility they entirely failed to notice that their pencil line ran though the middle of a tiny mountain village. When this was eventually discovered, St.Anton was arbitrarily allocated to the French.

Enemy countries had been banned from participating in the first post war winter Olympics at St.Moritz. So the appearance of German and Italian contingents did not occur until the 1952 Olympics in Oslo. The Olympic flame was lit in the fireplace of Sondre Nordheim. Everyone was bemused when two ice hockey teams arrived from the United States, both declaring that they were the official representatives. The crucial moment came during the opening ceremony. As the German team entered the arena, the continuous applause died away. For a few seconds there was profound silence as the Norwegian people struggled with memories of the savage occupation they had suffered only a few years before. Then a small spattering of clapping could be heard. Then, ever so gradually it grew until eventually the Norwegians were giving full applause to their erstwhile occupiers.

Those particular games experienced another poignant moment. The death of George VI was announced while the games were still in progress. The Olympic movement uniquely saluted the sovereign head of a nation which during those vital months had alone held firm the destiny of Europe. The Olympic flag was lowered and the teams from nations throughout the world stood with heads bowed for a minute's silence.

There was another unusual ceremony when reparation was made to Anders Haugen. At the Chamonix Olympics he had been placed fourth in the jumping event. Subsequent calculations showed that the judges had been prejudiced the marks had been fudged and he should have received the bronze. So he now became undoubtedly the eldest person to receive an Olympic medal. He was 86.

The hopes of the Norwegian hosts were all pinned to their outstandingly brilliant skier Stein Eriksen. He was leading in the giant slalom when he slipped and even at that moment he was aware of a gasp of horror from the royal box. But he could perform the almost acrobatic feat of jumping from one edge of his skis to the other. With one hand actually touching the ground, it saved him to win the gold.

Also Bandy made its comeback as a demonstration event.

Another occasion that involved royalty at about this time was a slalom race held at St.Moritz to celebrate the birthday of Prince Michael of Bourbon Parma. Quite incidentally, it also heralded one of the most profound changes in winter sports holidays to follow the war. Competitors included the Shah of Iran and the Empress, Farah Dibhah, King Constantine of Greece and Queen Annemarie, King Michael of Rumania, King Simeon and the Queen of Bulgaria, Princess Mari Pia of Savoy, the Aga Khan and the Begun, Princess Sharem and Prince and Princess Victor Emmanuell. Among the men, Gunter Sachs came first and first among the royals was the King of Greece, taking fifth place. He was followed closely by Prince Victor Emmanuell. First among the ladies was the Empress of Iran.

It is much the same sort of list the Palace Hotel could have boasted any time over the previous 60 years. But in these first years of peace, its significance was not immediately apparent.

The first point was that high society was no longer content to potter about in the snow. It had taken up ski-ing seriously and had reached a very high standard.

Another major development is revealed by those who did not take part. It was an omission which confirmed that since the Second World War, the good and great were no longer patronising St.Moritz exclusively. Photographs in the glossy magazines showed that royal favour was now spread over several major resorts.

Prince Charles and Prince Edward stayed at St.Anton on school parties and would compete in the children's races. When Prince Andrew came back some years later he would become annoyed at the way the constant presence of his body guard cramped his style with the pretty girls. So he devised a cunning scheme. He would take the cable car up the Valluga and then hurtle down outski-ing his guards so that they lost him among the crowd. Then he would break off at the Ulmer Hutt and watch the bodyguard ski frantically past leaving him free to keep his rendezvous unencumbered.

The Duchess of Kent also skied at St.Anton and had a strange encounter on the slopes. An intrepid skier approached her and asked "Are you who I think you are?" To which she made the equally enigmatic reply "Yes, I'm afraid I am".

Queen Juliana, together with Prince Bernhard were wont to stay at the Alt Post at St. Anton. They also kept the royal train in a siding by the station. Much to the annoyance of the management, they preferred to invite friends back there for a quiet cup of tea away from the public gaze. Prince Bernhard was a constant cause for concern. While he would never overrule the advice of his guide, he loved to take risks and constantly had to be restrained.

Prince Charles later transferred his patronage to Klosters. Together with Princess Diana and the Duke and Duchess of York, he would be the guest of Peter Greenall of the brewing family. The locals treated them just like anyone else and remained utterly impervious to all the blandishments of the press. Prince Charles soon became firm friends with many of the locals and indeed invited several to his wedding: the doctor, the policeman who acted as his body guard, the Harmans who ran the ski shop and of course his ski instructor Bruno. Also there was Ruth Guler, proprietress of the epicurean restaurant. She is of such ample proportions it is said that just by standing in the doorway, she could effectively screen him from any photographers. Her father, Hans, was a ski teacher before he took over the 30 room Chesa Grischuna hotel. The bar has been particularly favoured by the famous leaving their chalets for an evening out - Audrey Hepburn, Mel Ferrer, Gene Kelly and Irwin Shaw among them.

They were by no means the only ones among the Royals to appreciate the privacy. King Gustav also went to Klosters where he found that he could walk the village street even more democratically than in Stockholm. Greta Garbo actually discovered she could go out on cloudy days without wearing her dark glasses.

King Juan Carlos preferred Courchevel and periodically threw the Byblos Hotel into disarray through his habit of booking at the last moment. Sometimes he arrived with his Queen and family. Sometimes he would come alone and meet up with his brother-in-law King Constantine who stayed at Des Neiges. Because his guards had to be good skiers they were mostly selected from among the stocky Spanish mountain peasants. Due to generations born in a hard climate, they are noticeably short. The King of Spain is not particularly tall but among them he provided such an outstanding target their presence seemed almost ridiculous.

King Baudouin of the Belgians stayed at Kitzbühel. During his engagement, his fiancé Queen Paula had, as was only proper, been allocated the Tennerhof's best suite. This, however, irked her mother-in-law-to-be who, up till then, had always had it for herself. The Queen Mother got her own back on New Year's eve. First Princess Paula came down in a superb red gown designed by Dior, set off with a simple solid gold chain necklace. Half an hour later her mother-in-law appeared. She was wearing an ensemble exactly the same even to the gold chain.

Field Marshal Montgomery was, in the eyes of the Swiss, the equal of royalty. By chance his skis and boots, labelled in his own hand, were found after their wartime sojourn in a hotel cellar. Photographs appeared in all the Swiss papers. He was the cousin of Lady Lunn, which naturally drew him to Mürren. He would make a right royal progress from the station to the Palace in his ankle length sheepskin coat and surrounded by dancing, flag waving children. But it soon became apparent that his personality was too dominant not to clash with Sir Arnold. Nevertheless he stayed on and in later years became a rather forlorn, isolated figure. He could often be seen walking with a youth he had virtually adopted as substitute for his estranged family. Sometimes he would step off the path into deep snow with a child like compulsion to check that the posts of a fence or a pile of firewood were properly aligned.

It was not just the nobility whose ski-ing habits underwent a post war change. There was tremendous broadening of the social classes.

It had been Sir Henry Lunn's strict Methodist principles, particularly over his hotel bars, that were widely considered to have been the cause of his company's collapse during the depression. He left, Sir Arnold later reported, barely enough to pay for his funeral expenses. So the late 'thirties had ushered in a new generation of travel agents. Erna Low and the Ingham Brothers, who specialised in Austria, made up quite small parties but offered a much wider choice of resorts. It meant they did not have to make any appreciable investment beyond the coming season. So on the outbreak of war they had simply put their business on hold until such time as peace should return.

The Swiss had a wartime joke with more than a grain of truth: "During the week we make arms for the Germans and on Sundays we make prayers for the British to win". Now, with the peace, the Swiss, wealthy through the proceeds of war, were greeting their loyal British visitors again. But the dollar debt to the Americans had made the British the paupers of Europe. A whole succession of chancellors imposed strict travel controls. Initially the foreign holiday allowance for the entire year, including the V form for the hotel, was £25. In the early days, the Swiss hoteliers were understanding. They charged modest rather than excessive profits. Particularly the long established family hoteliers, such as the Badrutts, the Seilers and the Gredigs of Pontresina, provided regular guests good suites at the cheapest prices.

The austerity educated British skating team was staying at the St.Moritz Palace prior to the Olympics. They failed to appreciate that the marvellous cream cakes were not part of the special all-in rate. So when the final staggering bill was presented, Badrutt had to be found and acquainted with the currency crisis. He listened politely. He thought for a moment and then said he would wave the charge on one condition - that he could have a signed photograph of the team.

But as the economic stringencies extended into a second decade, sympathy began to ebb. Nor were matters helped as the British became increasingly boring with apparently only two inexhaustible topics of conversation: one was the high prices, the other was the rate of exchange available at the various banks or, more particularly, the black market rates available through the various hotel concierges.

Before the war the Swiss hoteliers would compete among themselves to provide free accommodation to the representatives of the Ski Club of Great Britain. Now that there were more and wealthier visitors from other countries, there was a noticeable reluctance to continue the arrangement.

There was, in effect, a reincarnation of Sir Henry's Public School Club in the form of the Combined Services Ski Club. It was created essentially as an economy travel agency but instead of old boys from public schools it was for officers, gentlemen and their ladies. The Army took over first one, then two and eventually four hotels at St.Moritz. The Navy was strong in Austria, notably at St.Anton and Kitzbühel, while the R.A.F. was centred at Zermatt.

In so far as fashionable society was concerned, the British were largely spectators. While no one could afford to stay at the Palace, it was possible, just, to save sufficient to buy a drink at the bar. "Here", a cynic was heard to remark "beautiful people not staying at the Palace look at other beautiful people also not staying at the Palace".

It soon became clear that in their discreet way the British were spending more than ever. Extra currency was being smuggled out in quantity. Any pangs of conscience were dulled since the restrictions were imposed by "those wretched Socialists". So it seemed only sensible to spend the lot rather than risk being caught with the residue on the way home.

One currency dodger who became involved in a major scandal was the Socialist Lord Lever. The millionaire Mancunian mackintosh manufacturer would normally have had no trouble staying at the Gstaad Palace. But how did he manage it even though, by then, the allowance had been raised to £50? Added to this he was notorious as a ferocious gambler. There he was quite blatantly in the hotel lounge playing for astronomical stakes. He was spotted by a journalist and next day his exploits were splashed across the front pages. His reaction was to continue gambling - but in a private suite.

Indeed Gstaad society was flourishing to the degree the Earl of Warwick was able to found The Eagle Club in obvious rivalry to the St.Moritz Corviglia. The Eagle Club was set right at the top of the Wasserngrat, a situation that clearly implied that members of the Corviglia Club, set only half way up their mountain, still had some social climbing to do. But in practice The Eagle Club never achieved comparable status. Their oeuf la conte was never quite so delicious. No one at the Corviglia, whether Greek or not, would have thrown cream cakes at the Aga Khan. Altogether it seemed more a retreat for those who had been blackballed from the Corviglia, such as Gunter Sachs of the German steel family and Adnan Khashoggi, the unbelievably wealthy dealer in the shady world of international arms sales. At one point they even had an actor - Roger Moore - on the committee. The situation was made evidently clear when he arrived at the Corviglia Club, assuming an exchange membership. He was smartly shown the door.

Another facet essential for attracting society is a lively night life. At Gstaad, in fact, things started happening rather earlier - in the afternoon to be precise. Then Harold Lever's frenzied gambling parties might well be joined by Sir James Goldsmith and the murderer-to-be Lord Lucan. Such exhibitions of wealth were to become even more apparent in the 'eighties. Jocelyn Stevens threw a particularly sensational party at the Palace. He financed it from his hefty golden handshake on being sacked from Express Newspapers. After this Stevens, with his companion the former Vivien Clore, seems to have acquired the habit. His 1992 party had a circus theme and cost a reputed £250,000. But it ended in disaster. The millionaire advertising executive Frank

Lowe appeared as a lion but got his acrylic tail into the candle flame. Despite quick action by a waiter throwing him to the floor and smothering the flames with a tablecloth, he was taken to hospital with severe burns.

Another memorable party was held at Klosters by Virginia Hill, former girlfriend of Buggsy Siegel one of America's "Godfathers". Guests in fancy dress were asked to repair to the top of the Gotschnagrat. But the real novelty was that everyone was on skis. This

The peak of society. The Corvilia Club house, set halfway up to Piz Nair.

included the barman, his bar and the five piece orchestra. During the course of the night they made a gradual descent arriving level with the village shortly after breakfast time.

The parties held by Viscountess de Reeb at St.Anton were no less magnificent. On one occasion she decided that the caviar available in the village was not up to standard. She dispatched an obliging young and unknown Giscard d'Estain to fetch some of suitable quality from Innsbruck. But on the way back the train broke down. d'Estain showed the initiative that later made him Prime Minister of France: he hired a helicopter and thus delivered on time what must have been the most expensive caviar ever consumed.

Another promoter of high life was an Austrian playboy Hubert Praz. He had bought the Schloss Mittersill on the outskirts of Kitzbühel just before the Anschluss. So it seemed particularly providential that soon after it burnt to the ground. The insurance enabled Praz to emigrate and set himself up in some style in the United States. There he married Terry, heiress to the Avon cosmetics millions. After the war the couple returned to Mittersill which they refurbished as The White Rose Club. The declared intention was to bring over American ladies of the certain ages between 18 and 50 and who, above all, were rich. Under the guise of educational trips, they were introduced to impoverished Austrian noblemen in the hope some of them might marry. In fact the scheme met with a degree of success. Among the notable visitors to the castle, though not necessarily seeking suitors, were Henry Ford and Coco Chanel while Queen Juliana and Prince Bernhard spent their honeymoon there.

No less interest was being aroused at that time by the Marquess of Milford Haven. He was still in the public eye having been best man for the Duke of Edinburgh. He was staying at Kitzbühel's Grand Hotel, earning his divorce by blatantly cohabiting with a young beauty called Eva Bartock

There had also been a fundamental change among ski clubs.. Before the Second World War, the various clubs had been centred in specific resorts. In the post war years, these clubs went into decline. Only the Kandahar and the DHO continued to flourish. Instead the clubs became centred around some communal interest.

Among the first was the Anglo-Swiss Parliamentary Ski Meeting. It was started by Ernest Marples a junior minister in Harold Macmillan's Government. While he was in Davos his counterpart in the Swiss ministry of housing asked to see him. Marples made their meeting conditional on their ski-ing together and that any professional discussions must be confined strictly to lunch time. This proved such a success they decided to arrange annual meetings but with 10 MPs and that it should last a week with a race at the end. For the first two years it was the British who won. But ultimately the most dashing proved to be the wives. Audrey Sale-Barker, who had become the Countess of Selkirk, and Lady Ferranti, nee Hilary Laing, had both skied for Britain. One year, spectators were puzzled when Aubrey Jones refused to compete because of the bad weather; yet his number duly crossed the finishing line. Removing goggles the mystery skier proved to be his wife. In contrast there was John Cordle who could barely ski at all. But he was so determined to compete he went down the course upheld by an instructor on either side. Sir John Hunt was a guest one year but was not pleased when a newspaper declared that the conqueror of Everest was evidently faster going up hill than he was coming down.

When the French asked if they might join, the Swiss parliamentarians brusquely refused. So it was out of defiance that the European Parliamentary Ski Championship came into being. It included teams from Britain, Germany and Italy as well as France. The Swiss though abstained'.

The idea for the International Journalists Ski Club was born during a world conference at the Palais des Nations. After it was over, Gilles de La Rocque felt it a terrible pity that all the friendships forged by journalists during the interminable waits between interviews and press calls should just evaporate. Why not have journalists from all over the world meet for a week to exchange ideas and aspirations in the edifying atmosphere of the ski fields? So each year a meeting is held at a different ski resort. The club grew quickly even though at that time the cold war was at its coldest. After Yugoslavia had sent a team, Russia wished to be included too. With journalists from east and west sure they were conversing beyond the range of hidden microphones the Club assumed real significance. Occasionally a skier would wish to seek asylum and Gilles had to persuade them to abandon such dreams. One such defection and all eastern journalists would have been withdrawn and the whole concept would have collapsed. Within a few years members represented hundreds of leading newspapers television and radio stations from 36 different countries. Each meeting also included a round table conference discussing some major topic. Sometimes it was attended by the host country's prime minister. The first meeting to be held behind the iron curtain almost ended in disaster. The aircraft carrying the West's contingents had to circle Warsaw airport for three quarters of an hour before landing permission was granted to these unorthodox visitors. In reciprocity, the Russian team were the first Communist journalists allowed into post Civil War Spain.

Clubs for the disabled evolved in several countries independently. While there was no international meeting, they would sometimes pair up. Thus the British Ski Club for the Disabled was started when a solicitor, Hubert Sturges, happened to see a group of disabled skiers pass by his chalet window. He was so intrigued he ran out to make further inquiries and found they were Swiss. The French and Austrians also had clubs. The guide would ski behind maintaining continuous contact calling out "forward...forward... .." and giving intermittent instructions "turn left", "turn right" or "stop". Communication became much easier through using personal radios. Leg amputees have a "flyer" or mini ski on each stick enabling them to steer their "mono" ski with amazing adroitness. Other equipment has become increasingly sophisticated. Paraplegics have virtually caused the science of ski and bobsleigh manufacture to merge.

The International Police Federation have yearly ski meetings. The intimate knowledge of criminal techniques made itself manifest one year when a camera was believed stolen. Almost as quickly it was detected in the thieves' classic depository - a lavatory tank. On another occasion a trainer physically pulled a racer off the slalom course because he was impeding the Austrian about to overtake. No one put in an appeal.

Then there are not so much clubs as spontaneous "happenings." Once a year, 240 bankers, lawyers, fund managers, traders and insurance brokers descend on Courmayeur for the week-end. "Fuelled by Veuve Cliquot and bad jokes", it became a regular feature on the calendar. It seemed completely appropriate one year when a racer was accompanied all the way down by a windblown empty champagne case. Arriving just ahead, it obligingly cut the electronic beam providing the racer with a second's advantage. Almost as impressive, and perhaps even more competitive, are the après ski bar bills rung up at sundry Courmayeur hostelries. Winners have usually chalked up bills reaching well into thousands of pounds.

Another "happening" that just grew is the Whistler Gay Ski Week. It was started by Brent Benaschak to persuade patrons of his New York bed-and-breakfast to visit his other premises in Whistler. He meant it to be a discreet alternative to the raucous Aspen Gay Ski Week. However it quickly grew from having 200 participants to 3,000. The week traditionally ends with a bare chested "Mountain Top Tea Dance"

After the day's ski-ing, the ordinary visitor at St.Anton repaired to the Krazy Kangaroo, a barn of a chalet set half way up the nursery slopes. It was run by an Australian whose welcome among the locals was not ecstatic. His popularity was not helped by his habit of issuing late staying customers with sheets of cardboard on which they tobogganed back to the village. The ski instructors had to get up early each morning to collect the litter. Worse, the Krazy Kangaroo rapidly became the most popular night spot, drawing customers from the more conventional village bars.

Austrian commerce rarely welcomes foreign competition and all sorts of unaccountable things started happening. Various rumours circulated that the owner had made his money in London running houses of ill repute. Worse, the lights would suddenly go out; the water supply would dwindle to a trickle; deliveries of food and even drink would be unaccountably delayed. In the end, however, the objective was more effectively achieved through the proprietor's affinity with alcohol.

Throughout the 'fifties and 'sixties most skiers spent the evenings dancing to hotel or restaurant bands. They would happily jog to the hit tunes from the latest Broadway or West End musicals and other popular melodies. Regularly each year a seasonal dance would also emerge. But unlike the pre-war Lambeth Walk and the Palais Glide, they were of continental origin usually from the "Walk in the Black Forest" Horstmann band. As compositions, they were ingeniously tailored for the international holiday market. They had simple, catchy tunes, virtually meaningless words such as "Push a pineapple, Shake a tree" easy to mouth and furnished with jigging rather than dancing steps. Prompted by the band, visitors throughout the Alps easily picked up words and movements during their one week stay.

Under these circumstances, the choice of band was vital for the management. Those groups with a good track record were booked up months ahead and generously paid. Even so a band might prove inappropriate for the setting or their style might have fallen out of fashion. Thus a bar that had been popular one season might be virtually deserted the next.

So managements welcomed the arrival of the disco. It called for major expenditure to be made on electronic sound and lighting equipment which would be good for years. The only running cost was the wages for a reasonably competent disc jockey. The actual music was determined mechanically by "the top ten". It removed all the risk factor that had surrounded the live bands.

Not that discos were necessarily devoid of all excitement. At the St.Nicholas Bar at Courchevel the good looking barman caught the eye of Brigitte Bardot. All the clientele were aware of the drama. First she asked him to dance but he said he was not allowed to consort with the customers. Brigitte appealed to the management who pointed out that while they valued her custom, none the less there were all the other customers to be served. She did not consider this sufficient reason. She virtually kidnapped the barman and danced with him for the rest of the evening - indeed for the rest of the season. In so far as the management were concerned, that evening was the last they saw of him.

During another evening guests in one of the Courchevel hotels were leaning over their balconies under the impression they were watching a filming sequence being shot. Eddie Constantine was prowling around the floodlit walls grasping a knife and calling out "I'll kill him. I'll kill him". All very enthralling. But the guests would have found it infinitely more exciting had they realised that far from acting, it was for real. After a highly convivial evening in the hotel disco, Eddie had learnt that one of the waiters was attracting the attention of his daughter.

Even during the impoverished post war days, the British were unostentatiously reviving several of the traditional winter sports. Field Marshal Montgomery saved the Mürren Inferno race by decreeing that NATO forces should compete. The unique challenge of this cross country downhill race has proved so enduring that for the 60th anniversary race the number of entrants reached 70. Among them was Walter Amstutz who, at 84, had been an early participant. He completed the course in its entirety and then apologised for having taken so long.

Similarly the revival of the Cresta was in large part due to the persistence of the perennial John Moore Brabazon. A former Cabinet Minister and elevated now to the peerage, he successfully dragooned the three services into sponsoring teams. Before long the club had 900 members making a total of 8,000 runs each season. Lord Brabazon celebrated his eightieth birthday by making the run himself. His only comment on reaching the bottom was "Damn, I've bust my braces."

Among those who became Cresta fanatics were the cricketers Allan Lamb and David Gower, also Angus Ogilvy, Winston Churchill junior and General Sir John Hackett. Explaining that his performance was perhaps remarkable rather than distinguished, the General admitted "I once managed to come off Shuttlecock 11 times in 13 runs". The all time slowest run was made, much to his chagrin, by Errol Flynn.

But the aura of glamour and wealth that surrounds the Cresta is misleading. It is remarkably democratic. The most successful rider up to this time had been an Italian Nino Bibbia who achieved 229 firsts, 97 seconds and 84 third places. He is the local greengrocer. Another star rider was a cook working at the Palace.

Luge races were revived in the 1952 Olympics as an exhibition event and substitute since Oslo has no Cresta. In 1964 they were incorporated as an event in their own right.

The revival of the bobsleigh at St.Moritz was due almost entirely to the sponsorship of another Briton, the playboy Hubert Martineau. He was a millionaire who had become even wealthier after marrying the American Schwartz heiress. Because of a metal plate in his stomach, he was unable to participate in any sports but he was well known as a cricket enthusiast and had a private cricket ground on his estate He was also a qualified Skating Association judge. But at St.Moritz he is perhaps best remembered for his highly idiosyncratic Ice Martins Club. The constitution rules were strict and simple: No person shall seek membership; there is to be no subscription nor is any member to pay club bills or keep accounts. No correspondence will be answered.

Bobbing acquired true world fame through the newly developed Cinerama film process. Stomach churning shots were taken by the camera crew risking their lives standing precariously on the bob. The slipstream kept buckling the film so that it required repeated re-takes.

One of the most ardent bobbers was Prince Michael of Kent. His enthusiasm remained unimpaired even after the World Championships at Cervinia in 1971. He fell out and, with his legs trapped, was dragged along the ice at high speed. Even worse on that occasion, one of the Spanish riders was killed when flung against a tree. It must be just such danger that ensures old fashioned chivalry among bobbers lives on. When, during the 1964 Olympics at Igls, the British found their boblet axle had cracked, the reigning Italian champion Eugenio Monti loaned them his. As a result Tony Nash and Robin Dixon were able to relieve him of the gold medal.

The bobsleigh itself has developed until it weighs half a ton and looks more like the fuselage of a fighter aircraft. The run, too, has developed into a piece of high technology. It can cost £20m. pounds to construct - more if, as at Grenoble, it is inadvertently built to face south. It is a concrete structure set on pillars rather like a fly-over. It can embody as much as 50 miles of tubing and needs two days to get going at the start of each season. It must be brought below 20 deg F before the surface can be sprayed and then smoothed.

Luging also made its comeback, reaching undreamt speeds up to 70 mph. This is due to a highly idiosyncratic style lying down face up and feet first so that the ability to see where one is going is severely limited.

The war deprived the budding British skaters of the best of their years. Graham Sharp, world champion in 1939, joined the Army. Cecelia Colledge, world champion in 1937, became a driver in the Mechanised Transport Corps and Freddie Tomlins was killed on active service in the RAF. Of the trainers, Arnold Gerschweiler at the Richmond ice rink was now deprived of all his stars. Among the most conscientious of his many middle aged pupils was Air Marshal Dowding, seeking relaxation from all the stress of the Battle of Britain.

Due to labour and fuel shortages, most ice rinks in Britain were closed. This was not the case in the United States nor in Canada where fuel was of little concern. Consequently American and Canadian skaters were able to develop their technique apace. This burst upon the world at the 1948 Olympics at St.Moritz. Barbara Ann Scott and Dick Button astounded spectators with their theatrical athleticism. He had been trained by a former ski jumper whose insistence on always looking up gave him his distinctive style. The higher the jump the more time there is in which to perform elaborations. Button was performing triple loops and flying camels almost with abandon. Above all he did double axles which entailed one and half turns while airborne. It had, up till then, been considered a physical impossibility.

Indeed sheer strength became a major component in post war skating. Ronnie Robertson was a silver Olympic medallist in 1956 and famous for his spins. He was put into NASA's anti-gravity chamber and it was found impossible to make him dizzy.

In contrast, English style skating at St.Moritz was barely staggering into the post war period. Its survival was entirely due to Martineau's unstinting patronage. He was also financing what was, in effect, the first British ice show. He created it largely for his girlfriend and for her sake even supported it for a Continental tour.

Soon British skaters were again forging ahead. First there was Jeannette Altwegg who became World Champion in 1951 and Olympic champion the year after. A reticent Liverpool girl, she was perhaps the greatest exponent of compulsory figures. Her traces during the Olympics were declared to be geometrically perfect. But she went on to further win the hearts of all the world. She turned down highly remunerative offers to appear in ice shows and instead retired to help refugee children in the Swiss Pestalozzi village.

John Curry reached international standard while his performances were still sporadic. After a fall while making a triple jump he nearly gave up skating altogether. Then he received unexpected sponsorship from Ed Moser, the American safe manufacturer millionaire and regained his confidence when Carlo Fassi became his trainer. Thereafter he came third in the 1975 World Championships and first the year following. He completed his triumphant progress by winning the gold medal at the Innsbruck Olympics whereupon the press rewarded him by revealing he was homosexual. Whereas Sonja Henie had used classical ballet in her hand movements, Curry used it to harmonise the movements and carriage of his whole body with the music. It imparted a degree of effeminacy which hitherto the skating authorities had abhorred. But the effect is essentially visual and accordingly it was he who aroused the interest of the British TV public.

Stepping confidently into his boots came Robin Cousins. Much of his television appeal stemmed from his outstandingly strong jumps made all the more spectacular when seen through low camera angles. Tucks look particularly spectacular because the feet are drawn up into the body. However his potential, shown when he came tenth in the Innsbruck Olympics, was overshadowed by Curry's spectacular success. There was only one critic sufficiently perceptive to write: "He skated to 'Three Blind Mice' in front of nine blind judges." However in the World Championships of 1978 he came third and, despite operations for torn cartilages in both legs, he continued to work his way up; second in 1979 and second again in 1980. Expectations for that year's Olympics had now become so high that four and a half million TV viewers stayed up till four o'clock in the morning willing him to win at Lake Placid - and he did not disappoint them.

Television found an additional interest in ice dancing which had only become an offcial event in 1951. By this time the difference between dancing and pair skating had become little more than technical niceties, largely incomprehensible to the ordinary viewer. For instance, the man must not raise his hands above his head and spins must not be performed with the skating pair more than two arms length apart. Even the music was subject to pernickety segregation and for dancing it must have the emphasis on rhythm rather than melody.

During the 'fifties British skaters were as triumphant as the skiers had been in the 'thirties. Lawrence Demmy and Jean Westwood won the world championship over the five years from 1951 to 1955. In effect, they held it six times for they were also first in its antecedent, the ISU ice dancing competition held in Milan.

A further generatiion were brought on by Gladys Hogg, herself British pair and dance champion in 1947. First she trained Courtney Jones who, with June Markham and later Doreen Denny, won the World Championships from 1957 through to 1960.

In 1961 the programme was interrupted when the entire United States teams were killed in an air crash at Brussels airport. Even so the British skaters did not really come to the fore again until, with Gladys' still coaching, Bernard Ford and Diane Towler won the World Championships between 1966 and 1969 inclusive. They adopted the athletic approach with zest. Had one of them fallen during the climax to their routine to "Zorba the Greek", they would almost certainly have suffered serious injury.

As a culmination, in 1968 Britain took all three places at the World Championships in Geneva.

It happened that the next pair to catch the public eye, were each looking for new partners. A trial did not impress anyone except their trainer Betty Callaway. Then a grant from Nottingham Council cemented the partnership. By 1978 the former policeman Christopher Dean and insurance clerk Jayne Torvill were, due to the popularity of television, gaining a reputation far beyond immediate skating circles. They won the 1981 World Championships. In the European Championships, their dancing to the music of "Mack and Mabel" was so sensational the B.B.C. had to postpone the news for 40 minutes and viewers were able to applaud their record score of eleven sixes. But their finest hour came with the World Championships at Sarajevo. It was the first time competitors were permitted to lift their partners to the extent the man could raise his hands above the shoulder. Dean responded sensationally by throwing Torvill over his shoulder. At the end of the compulsory dance every judge awarded them the top 5.9 points. Finally for their free dance, they were awarded the maximum of a straight 5.9 for the first marking and a complete row of sixes for the second.

Sensation clothing, with a strict view to the interest of photographers and the television cameras, now became the key word. When in 1928, Sonja Henie had reached womanhood, she still had not lengthened her gym slip skirts. On the contrary, if anything she had shortened them. Other skaters followed suit. So the increasing inclusion of spins into the routines meant the colour of the ladies' panties became an integral part of their ensemble. As ladies skating became still more balletic, the Swiss Denise Biellmann took to spinning while lifting the other leg so high she could clutch the skate well above her head. She became almost as well known for her inch wide gussets as for being World Champion. With this latest licence to freedom, Rene Lakas astonished the world during the 1998 Olympics by holding Kati Winkler upside down. When she then proceeded to part her legs akimbo the International Ice Skating Association felt bound to declare that competitors would lose marks if they "tried to be more entertaining by producing moves that are gynaecological"

Style in ski-ing was undergoing no less a revolution. The combination of metal edges and the Kandahar binding enabled Emile Allais to perfect rotation. Starting at the shoulders the twisting movement progresses down the body. But even before the outbreak of war Allais was being challenged by the Swiss champion Rudolph Romand. He made more agile turns by starting the movement from the hips.

Soon after the war short skis were being promoted by the Kitzbühel ski school. They were intended primarily to help the beginner. Yet it was not long before they were finding equal support among good skiers. They proved particularly appropriate on hard beaten pistes where it was becoming necessary to make multiple short sharp turns. This in turn led to a new phenomenon: bumps. These mounds are created through numerous skiers turning in the same place. Their creation can easily grow out of control so that they are covering entire slopes and, indeed, complete runs. They called for a technique of their own. When bumps are slight it is easier to turn on the peak when a minimal area of ski sole is in contact with the snow. However bumps can grow so high they become humps and must be treated almost as though they are pillars. Then it becomes necessary to steer around the base.

The ski schools had to revise their programme to suit. Skiers with well developed thighs evolved "avalement" translating literally as bump gulper. It means running straight down the fall line hitting each bump full on and relying on the knees to absorb the shock. During the rebound the skis can be turned ready to pound the next bump.

Meanwhile the father of ski schools, Hannes Schneider, had permanently settled in the States and indeed until his death in 1954 he never spent more than a brief autumn hunting visit to St. Anton. Today his statue is in the main square outside the Post Office and his bust is at the foot of the stairs leading down to the bar in the Post Hotel. It is set on his table, purposely small so as to discourage more than one person at a time claiming his attention.

When the ski school was reopened after the war, it was run jointly and with considerable success by Rudi Matt and Sepp Farner. Rudi was the son of a local farmer. When, back in 1925, Schneider had suggested he should become a ski instructor, his father had replied "But what future is there in that?" Despite the fact that teaching left him little time in which to train, Rudi Matt became a distinguished skier in the international field. He won the Arlberg, Tyrol and then the Austrian, Swiss and German open championships and in 1936 the World Championships. As a ski instructor first and an international racer second, he had a far broader conception over running a ski school. He defined, set and pursued a highly successful policy.

Schneider had never looked upon instructors as more than local boys who could ski well. Rudi Matt however reasoned that if they were to teach eminent Vienna businessmen, not to mention politicians, they must have confidence. So all aspiring instructors first had to learn to teach in passable French and English. In due course, Emile Allais was to pursue the idea even further at Courchevel with several English only classes. Matt also insisted they should take a course in physical training and in first aid.

At the start of each season Matt would allocate several days for demonstrating the latest developments in technique. He would start with his ten top instructors. Each of these ten would then instruct up to ten more. By the third generation every instructor had been able to try out, test and question the latest theories. Each morning throughout the season, Matt would repair with field glasses to some promontory and methodically scan every slope to make sure each instructor was maintaining the standard.

Schneider heard of all this with a degree of scepticism. Rudi Matt however pointed out that whereas previously only 12 to 15 per cent of men taken on had eventually proved capable of teaching satisfactorily, now under his supervision, the percentage had risen to close on 90. Matt also eschewed the personality cult which had surrounded Schneider. Under Matt's regime few pupils would have been able to name the principal. Yet the school acquired increasing fame till it was widely acclaimed as the best in the world.

For several years the instructor to the racing class was Robert Falch. The majority of his pupils were Americans for only they could afford to remain out long enough to stay the pace. Just how fast became clear one season when two Czechs, one Canadian and a Swede, who were all Olympic runners, independently joined the top class to brush up on their technique.

Only two events marred the time Matt was a director of the St.Anton ski school. The first was in 1961 when a pupil badgered an instructor into taking the class down the Ulmer run although it was closed. An avalanche down the Schindlerkar engulfed them. The school was sued by, ironically, the relatives of the man who through his insistence had brought about the calamity. However, the instructor and the school were exonerated.

On the other occasion, the instructors demanded the school should be run as a co-operative. They went on strike and set up a rival concern at St.Christoph. Matt and Farner tried to break the strike by importing students from Innsbruck University. But neither venture met with success. While Matt received numerous complaints, the rogue instructors gathered no pupils. So a compromise was reached and the school was run as a modified co-operative.

The path of the Zermatt ski school was not proving particularly smooth either. The family Juliens decided that the Biners held too strong a control. So they set up a red anorak rival with classes meeting at the other end of the village. This split lasted several years, but, in true Zermatt tradition, the bad feeling continued much longer. Visitors to the office of the amalgamated ski school were confronted by a Juliens and a Biner sitting at adjacent desks. Neither would exchange a single word; neither would deign give the confused visitor any indication as to which of them should be addressed.

Matt always warned his instructors against becoming too familiar with their pupils. He had a set procedure. If he found an instructor ignoring his warning, he gave him two chances and on the third offence he dismissed him. Such high principles were by no means observed at all resorts. One Austrian village received in one season notice of 70 paternity cases against ski instructors. In another, an instructor was sacked after seducing a pupil in a hayloft. This had become known because they had fallen through a trap door and the girl had been taken to hospital. A plea was made to the head of the ski school that the instructor had been deliberately seduced by the girl. "I do not mind" the head replied, "my instructors taking their pupils to haylofts but I do expect them to know which haylofts are safe".

At Kitzbühel instructors were officially named "The Red Devils" as much, one suspects, for their après ski prowess as for the colour of their jackets. Occasionally, during the morning after, human frailty might be glimpsed and more than one instructor dozed and fell of the chair lift. Raymond Rhiner, the charming, popular and very extrovert instructor for the top class was wooed by and, in due course, married to the American Armour meat heiress. Transported to San Francisco, papa-in-law offered him a whole range of highly salaried but ineffectual positions within the company. Raymond refused them all preferring to return to Kitzbühel and continue as a ski and swimming instructor.

Pravda, one of the famous Kitzbühel ski team, also married an American heiress but, after the trauma of a serious car accident, took up permanent residence in the States.

The war years also saw considerable advances in the technology of ski manufacture. Primarily it entailed the bonding of wood and metal. Back in 1916, W.W.Moredy had experimented with metal skis but they had proved to be too heavy. The real development came during the Second World War when Gomme, famous for manufacturing G Plan furniture, was under contract to the DeHavilland Aircraft Co. They discovered how electrical resistance can fuse the molecular structure of wood and metal. This, in effect, makes the two materials an integral whole.

In 1947 Donald Gomme extended this technique to skis. He also extended the principles of aircraft design to the ground plan. The result were skis highly flexible longitudinally. This lends itself to schussing. At the same time it had torsional rigidity so that it did not easily twist. This made it manageable on icy piste. This went far to combining the properties of the ideal skis: satisfactory on the hard piste yet able to aquaplane gracefully in deep snow.

Unfortunately one season the Gomme venture became literally unstuck. The bonding was faulty and skis everywhere had tops flapping against the bottoms. Gomme lost heart and sold the patents to the Swiss manufacturer Attenhoffer. While actually on his way to sign the contract, the old man had a fatal heart attack and died at the airport. The Attenhoffer sons took over the patent. While they retained the bonding process they completely failed to appreciate the advantages of the ground plan. It was a formula that was not resurrected until manufacturers were able to take advantage of computer design. Gomme also developed a water-repellent and tough plastic sole which gave his skis additional speed.

Just when Gomme was patenting his idea, in America Howard Head, who had also worked in the aircraft industry, began thinking along similar lines. Instead of a metal wood sandwich, he merely enclosed the wood core in an aluminium casing. He had set out to make skis lighter. By the end he had failed and, in fact, his skis were slightly heavier. However, quite inadvertently, he had stumbled on the same major advantage, torsional rigidity. But he, too, failed to appreciate the importance of the ground plan of skis. He did, though, introduce a plastic sole that was not only tough but which largely eliminated the need for waxing.

He launched his skis in Europe at almost double the price of others on the market. He made them seem more exclusive by stamping a small manufacturer's number in white on the smart all black ski. He backed them with a major and very expensive public relations exercise. As a start, top instructors in every major ski school were given a sample pair. They were consequently hailed as the definitive ski. Buy a pair and they will last for life - or so it was claimed.

Technology was also a major factor in the development of skiwear fashions. A French manufacturer discovered how to combine wool with twisted nylon thread. The result was figure hugging stretch pants. By incorporating a strap under the instep they remained smartly taut without becoming baggy at the knees.

Ski racers underwrote the trend. With tenths, even hundredths, of a second separating the placings, wind resistance became a significant factor. Several teams appeared for the 1960 Olympics in skin tight uniforms. The significance was emphasised by the Canadians who, more traditionally turned-out, in panic tied bits of string around their arms and legs. Thereupon skin tight trousers became the vogue. The durability of nylon meant the sleek line could be further enhanced through wearing sock tops under the trouser leg.

Doyen among ski pant tailors was Ernst Webster working from a shop, little more than a hut, set back a bit off the main street of St.Anton. Each year he would visit Harrods where skiers would be measured to be sure their trousers were improperly tight. Splitting seams became inevitable and instructors took to carrying sheaves of safety pins along with their first aid kit.

Nylon can be quilted and was first used for anoraks for the allied forces in the sub zero climate of Korea. It was soon adopted by skiers as a great advance on doubled gaberdene. Finally nylon's easy cleaning properties makes it practical to wear lighter shades, even white, with impunity against the pure driven snow.

So great were all these potentials that by the 'fifties Dior was designing haute couturier ski suits - and these were actually bought and worn by skiers. However by far the most important development over the war years was the ski tow.

Historically the first ski lift must have been the Eurika mine in California. The ore bucket lift was fired up at week ends so that it could carry miners to the top of the mine head and the start of a formidable schuss. Back in the 'thirties an astute Wengen farmer had provided a horse and sleigh and took skiers up the woodpath to the top of the nursery slopes. As his custom increased so he expanded his business into providing a trailing rope and those not in time for a place on the sleigh could, at a reduced rate, hang on behind. Then Méribel introduced an obvious adaptation of the funicular consisting of a large sledge at the end of a cable. It was little more than a platform with a number of chairs screwed onto it.

The idea of a mechanical drag lift seems to have occurred to several people simultaneously during 1934. At Davos an engineer, Gerhard Mueller, harnessed parts of a motor bike to a cable loop spliced with tags to provide hand holds. In the United States, Pomagalski was experimenting with a tractor and rope. At about the same time George Morton, who later invented the ski mobile, was erecting his own tow, powered by a T Ford at Vermont. However all three prototypes had the ropes and tags dragging along the ground often making them frozen and too slippery to grasp properly. A partial solution was the "meathook". A wooden anchor was attached to an individual line that was spliced into the overhead cable. It supported rather than carried the skier.

Even so these early ski lifts, like the funicular sleighs, had to be comparatively short. The only flexibility lay in the pendulum movement of the individual drag. So should the ground undulate too severely, skiers either had to bend double as the cable dragged across a rise or reach up desperately as they descended into a dip.

Initially this was no serious disadvantage as the early lifts were erected on practice slopes. They were not intended to do more than cut out the tedium of side stepping and herringboning to the top. The ski lift revolution made its most immediate impact in Austria. The Government invested a large proportion of its share of Marshall Aid in ski lifts. Almost within the year, Austria had become a serious winter tourist rival to Switzerland.

Several of the Swiss traditional resorts were already facing a problem but of a different kind. It was the discovery of PAS, a simple and reliable cure to tuberculosis. It meant that Davos, Arosa and the other cure resorts found themselves lumbered with literally acres of empty beds. The only obvious solution was to promote ski-ing from being incidental into becoming a major attraction.

Even the dedicated existing ski resorts had to revise their priorities. It was to be seen most clearly in the skating rinks. Before the war every major hotel in a ski resort had its own ice rink. After the war, the only rink in the village was maintained by the Kurverein and it was usually deserted except for school children. Now that there was no need for tedious climbing even the skaters had gone ski-ing.

CHAPTER V
THE MIDAS TOUCH
1966 - 1987

Whenever a skier contemplated the metal box attached to the revolving overhead cable it should have been with something between wonder and incredulity. The lines on the early drag lifts were spliced into the revolving cable. They simply pulled people up the more even sections of nursery slopes. The lifts were never intended to do more than save beginners time and energy. But once the lift lines were linked by spring-loaded housing the whole face of ski-ing changed. That vital metal box provided just the right amount of line to support the skier no matter whether fat man or child. At the same time it let out just enough to allow descent into a dip and withdraw sufficient slack when breasting a crest. Once drag lifts could carry skiers over varied terrain, they could be extended to considerable lengths. They became useful for advanced skiers as well as beginners.

The next logical development was the chair lift. Averell Harriman had the idea it could be a luxury his patrons at Sun Valley might appreciate. So he set some of his engineers to make it all possible. They found the solution in the Honduras docks where there was a hoist specially designed so as not to bruise bananas. That skiers should be so lucky! ever since generations have had the back of their shins bruised by the chair's leading edge. But this blemish did not exist through want of testing. Harriman sent his assistant to check it was possible to get on and off while on the move. The hay, spread on a concrete test bed, did not prove a satisfactory substitute for snow and initially the assistant suffered numerous knocks and falls.

With a variety of lifts available to suit all situations, quite small resorts were brought almost into the same league as those with funiculars and cable cars. Everywhere village mayors were presented with a bewildering choice. Not only can the various types of lift cover various types of terrain, but at different speeds and capacities. A chairlift could carry 2,000 skiers an hour over tree tops and rivers and a gondelbahn around 3,000. A cable car carried an average of only 1,500 but it could cross deep valleys and extensive rocks falls at a much greater speed.

Additionally there was the problem of increasing passenger loads. The march of progress is marked by the Schatzalp section of the Parsennbahn funicular. It was built in 1899 and was designed to accommodate 60,000 summer visitors. Naturally Victorian ladies and their escorts expected to ascend in decent composure. Between the two wars, skiers steadily built up a winter traffic. Instead of the ladies with their easels and parasols, their place was taken by skiers with seven foot skis and sticks with baskets the size of pram wheels. Since ski-ing is a more energetic pastime, they were fortunately prepared to put up with considerably more hassle. By 1937 their number had, at 245,000, almost quadrupled. However transport capacity was enlarged without too much difficulty. A carriage was added to either end of the cable. Due to the quality of Victorian engineering, everything still worked safely. However the post war years saw the passenger load rise to 413,000. By this time 91 per cent of the passengers were using the funicular in winter. The only remedy, short of installing a completely new system, was to increase the speed by increasing the horsepower. This, together with porters prepared to push passenger posteriors until the doors could be closed, made it possible to carry a further 35 per cent.

It is a quirk common among skiers that, while prepared to bash slopes and bumps with enormous zest, there is strong and vociferous protest against any suggestion of walking. So once drag lifts had acquired sufficient length, they were aligned so as to eliminate walking.

Kitzbühel led the way by erecting "The Circus" atop the Hahnenkamm. It comprised three lifts arranged so that each started from the end of the previous run. In this way it was possible to move perpetually around a circuit of four and a half kilometres without taking off one's skis.

But it was the custom built ski resort which provided the ultimate opportunity for a walkless lift system. The concept was too large to be based on a circle. First a place was chosen where the ski slopes looked ideal in precipitousness, snow retention and protection from the wind. The runs were planned like the spokes of an upturned umbrella and were virtually sculpted from the mountain side. Only after all this had been settled was the location of the actual village decided.

When Courchevel was on the drawing board, several additional and specific stipulations were required. It was anticipated that many of the skiers would be beginners or have reached only medium skill. So it was decreed that no gradient must be steeper than six per cent. There must, of course, be some black runs, such as the Jean Blanc and the Jockey, which would qualify for international racing. But even these were made completely safe not only for racers but for over ambitious amateurs. The steepest sections are at no point less than 50 ft wide. Plans even included a number of superfluous pistes. They could be held in reserve for when the more popular runs needed repair or became snow bald.

Overall responsibility for ski-ing at Courchevel was given to Emile Allais. Beyond his renown as an international racer, he had administrative experience through having helped build resorts in the Andes and California. His guiding principle was simple. Skiers are on holiday and do not want to waste time. Consequently ski conditions must always be as near perfect as the weather will allow. He would have his men out preparing the piste by five o'clock in the morning. If it had been snowing, they had to be on the job by three. So when the first intrepid skier emerged, be it nine o'clock or even half past eight, all lifts would be working and all runs in immaculate condition.

Allais extended his concept to every aspect of ski-ing. Dashing champion though he may have been, he could still appreciate the feeling of blind panic that can grip the ordinary skier in a white out. There is that awful fear of losing sight of one marker pole before being able to see the next. So instead of sparse painted sticks he had the piste markers designed to stand out clearly in the mist. They pointed emphatically in the right direction. They even showed green to the skier on the piste but red for anyone who had strayed.

Packing the piste was another matter that claimed his attention. The most effective way was to have columns of men ranged in lines stamping the snow. But it was far too labour intensive. So

Piste roller, circ 1948

he set about designing his ideal roller. It had to be effective yet not so cumbersome that it could not be pulled up on a ski tow. Andree Payert, an engineer at St.Anton was also wresting with the problem. He was experimenting with a slatted roller weighted by two men sitting on it. But even that was considered too extravagant of manpower. Allais then had a moment of inspiration. The ends of the rollers should be able to open like a biscuit barrel and the weight could be made by filling it with snow. In practice, however, the time spent at the top loading the snow and at the bottom clearing it out took far too long. Also there is little to be gained by, in effect, using snow to flatten snow.

Payert, in the mean time, was successfully leading the way to mechanisation.

A rescue service is another obligation expected of every resort. In the very early days all skiers were expected to know the universal distress signal - waving a flag. If they had been so negligent as to be ski-ing without a flag they waved an item of clothing set on a ski stick. It had to be waved in an upward semi-circular movement six times a minute with intervals of one minute. It was also mooted that anyone seeing such a signal should respond with similar gestures, but only three times a minute. Then they must rush off to tell the chief of police. Rescue was one of his responsibilities together with the issue of weather warnings.

The Parsenn was one of the first areas to have a bloodwaggon. Back in 1927 it was nothing more than a jumbo luge not even long enough to carry the casualty lying full length. This, complete with the attendant rescue service, was instigated by Freddy Edlin. It can be fancied he still keeps vigil over casualties for his ashes are interred in a rock, marked by a plaque, at the top of the Furka lift. Roland Palmedo introduced the idea into the United States at Mount Mansfield, though that was not until 1938.

Allais' bloodwaggons were far more sophisticated. The actual stretcher was a separate unit set on the toboggan chassis so that it could turn within its own length. It was also easier on the casualty whenever it tilted or had to be lifted into the ambulance. Perhaps most reassuring of all, it was furnished with a dead man's handle to stay any untoward disaster should the patrolman fall.

Bloodwaggoners annually tested their prowess with an international race. It was reassuring to know that upsetting a sledge meant instant disqualification.

All this should have been of considerable interest to Eddie Constantine. He did not really like ski-ing but was loth to mar his macho image by admitting it. So he sought reassurance through drinking several whiskies at the top restaurant. But then his companions discovered an unattended bloodwaggon and offered to take him down on it. Unfortunately they too had

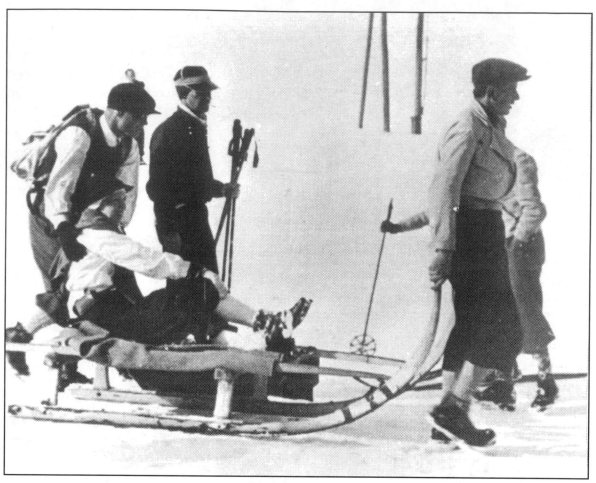

The St. Anton bloodwaggon circa 1935

been imbibing and were ignorant of the safety brake. So hardly had they started than they fell. Any fears Eddie may have previously held were as naught compared to finding himself strapped helpless as the sledge hurtled down out of all control. He was extremely lucky when he at last came to a stop without having overturned or hit a rock.

Allais also combined the first aid service with the ski patrol responsible for slope upkeep. He stationed pisteurs with bloodwaggons at two or three specific spots. They were always ready to respond to any telephone calls. But most of the 60 men were scattered over the slopes conducting minor repairs to the piste. So they often happened to be already close to a casualty and could administer first aid even before the official message had reached the nearest centre. In an average season the patrols were bringing down 300 stretcher cases while a further 300 were brought down by helicopter. .

The time skiers saved by taking ski lifts instead of climbing had some unsuspected effects on ski culture.

It even led to changes in the basic principles of ski school organisation. This was because pupils could spend more time physically imitating their instructor. Professor Krukenhauser, head of the State Training of ski teachers in Austria, estimated that pupils were learning four times faster.

Instructors had already become concerned at the way pupils became demoralised if they were sent down a class. This speedier learning pattern made it no longer necessary. Through remaining among faster skiers, dullards seemed to acquire the additional incentive.

Another consequence of the ski lift was the demise of the pack lunch. Ever since visitors had sat on their luges for a picnic, every hotel in every resort throughout Switzerland and Austria had, as if by some mysterious mutual consent, produced almost identical lunches. They included slices of ham, tongue and beef, separately wrapped in greaseproof paper and with accompanying rolls, one plain, the other buttered, a foil wrapped triangle of processed cheese, a hard boiled egg, a twist of salt in a bit of blue paper, a small bar of chocolate and an apple and an orange. All this was in a pristine white paper bag tied up with red and white twisted string. Basic etiquette insisted you bring any residue back to the hotel rather than bury it in the snow when spring would have revealed it in all its tawdriness.

But lifts now made the average skier so mobile it became easy to reach one of the mountain restaurants. Indeed those at cable car top stations often became so well patronised they changed over to fast food service.

All this custom made ski resorts expand their lift capacity in relation to the number of visitors' beds. From the start Sestriere had proved a model example. It had only 1,500 beds while the lifts could carry 6,000 skiers an hour. The French resorts also had a good record with, for instance, Tignes at 14,500 : 36,000.

A few of the most fashionable resorts felt they could happily disdain such figures. Their clientele considered it as important to be seen as to ski. At one point, 40 per cent of visitors at Flims never put on skis the whole time they were there. Gstaad has the contradictory combination of unreliable snow conditions, only to be expected when situated a mere 3,650 ft above sea level, yet is still one of the most fashionable resorts with a dozen four star hotels.

The clue to all this lies perhaps with the film director Alfred Hitchcock. He boasted that, during the 32 seasons he had stayed at St.Moritz, he had not once attempted any sort of winter sport.

But those resorts which had grown fat on a thriving summer trade remained unconcerned as their ski lift capacity became hopelessly inadequate. With the numbers of skiers increasing constantly throughout the 'fifties and 'sixties, these resorts treated their patrons almost with contempt. Davos, St.Anton, Kitzbühel and Zermatt were among the worst offenders. At one time, anyone wishing to reach the top of the Gornergrat before mid day had to join the queue before seven in the morning. At St.Anton, it became necessary either to ascend along with the milk and vegetables or join a lengthy queue which, at weekends, meant waiting five hours. With four different entrances to the Galzig cable car station, it became quite an art. The ski instructors had their own door. Second preference was given to their pupils who had a separate entrance. Then there was the way in for the ordinary skier. Finally there was a side door for those who paid a few schillings extra and the first 20 in that queue were given preference over the rest.

The banker owners were the problem at St. Anton. Sited in Vienna they were unconcerned over the resentment caused by their refusal to open up the Rendl ski fields on the mountain opposite.

In the same vein, they retained books of coupons long after all other resorts had changed to abonnements. It meant that within a week the skier paid between five and six times more than at other resorts.

The bankers' only competitor was Cornelius Starr, who had made his millions through his American International Underwriters insurance company. He incidentally also owned two Hong Kong newspapers and the United States ski resort of Stowe. So it must have been on a slight whim that he decided to finance a chairlift to run almost parallel with the Valluga cable car. The Kapal is comparatively short, for it ends 1,000 ft. lower on a neighbouring peak. But it opened up several excellent deep snow runs.

Starr also befriended one of the local ski champions, Toni (Rubber) Spiess, and underwrote much of his training costs. However he withdrew his support when he had reason to believe Spiess was making approaches to his pretty young wife. But Starr's acumen was proven in the World Championships when Speiss was a clear five seconds ahead - then his safety binding opened. He has never really overcome his feeling of bitterness over the unfairness of it all.

Starr was enraptured by ski-ing and would give fabulous parties. On these occasions the hotel would bring in extra staff to cope with the rows of instructors retching in the lavatories. When Starr was told of the Austrian custom of tipping the band by sticking 20 schilling notes into the instruments, he went about sticking notes not only in the instruments but the pockets of the waiters and they were not for twenty but a thousand schillings. When Cornelius Starr died the Credit Bank bought his Kapal interest and its monopoly became absolute.

Other tycoons were making similar investments at other resorts. At St.Moritz the Greek shipping billionaire Niarchos approached the Kurverein over building a cable car up to Piz Corvatsch. It was not a new idea. Schemes had been floated as far back as 1906, again in 1934 and as recently as 1948 but they had all failed through lack of capital. So Niarchos was offering a rare opportunity when he put £500.000, a sizeable amount at that time, down on the table. Rather than being grateful, the Kurverein drove a hard bargain. Niarchos could have the honour of owning 5l per cent of the shares, but the local Silvaplana community must retain absolute control.

Later Niarchos went into partnership with Loel Guinness for construction of the Piz Nair cable car. This led to another of his supposed ambitions: to a make a gift of a cablecar to each of his three children.

No less opportune financing occurred on the Courmayeur side of the Mont Blanc lift system. It is suitably recorded at the top station. There is a plaque set in the rock giving glory to God for the mountains. Beside it is another plaque commemorating Edouard Angelli for providing the capital for the enterprise.

Jet air travel, the fluctuations in currency exchanges and the rise in property prices encouraged the wealthy to buy their own chalets. Count Theo Rossi, Herbert Von Karajan, Prince Constantine of Lichtenstein, all became residents in St.Moritz. The Shah of Persia, in dubious taste, added a copper dome to his chalet. Another chalet of curious regional design belonged to King Farouk of Egypt. He was so bored in exile he spent most of his waking hours in a night club, throwing the shoes of the beauties in his party onto an overhead shelf.

Another resident who also had sad memories of St.Moritz was Aristotle Onassis. His daughter Christina refused fellow shipping billionaire Goulandris, the man he wanted her to marry. Instead she took up with Luis Basualdo, one in a celebrated line of comparatively impoverished Argentinean polo playing lady killers. However, no sooner had Basualdo become intimate friends with Christina than he was off to St.Anton to woo another heiress.

Brother in law and fierce business rival Stavros Niarchos not only owned a chalet at St. Moritz, he also had a major interest in both the Kulm and Chantarella Hotels. Not that there was much difference between them since his chalet had 30 rooms, its own cinema and swimming pool. He also had a daily private aeroplane service landing at nearby Samaden reputedly so that he could have the newspapers three hours ahead of normal delivery.

At Gstaad royal chalet owners have included King Baudouin of the Belgians, Prince Rainier and Princess Soraya. Among the world citizens were the Kennedys, Sir Yehudi Menhuin, Joan Collins, Elizabeth Taylor, David Niven and Julie Andrews who financed the main street Christmas lights each year. Aleco Govlandris had a chalet sufficiently magnificent for him to entertain two kings and the Prince of Wales all at the same time.

Queen Juliana wished to buy a chalet at Lech. Austria, however, has a law preventing foreigners from owning property. Hence the peculiar codicil whereby Dutch nationals have been made an exception.

Ski-ing was becoming so popular that all the traditional resorts would have soon become swamped. At the same time the Swiss franc became a symbol of stability while there was a prolonged crisis over the French franc. Consequently an estimated 300,000 French crossed the border surreptitiously carrying suitcases holding an average 40,000 francs necessary to buy a place. Their numbers were increasing at 20 per cent a year. Soon there was not a ski resort in Switzerland without its block of holiday apartments.

So it was not surprising when General de Gaulle decided to stop this foreign currency haemorrhage. His solution was simple. There are mountains in France so the French must build their own ski resorts. The result was that wherever an open snow field seemed likely to appeal to skiers it would be sized up for its potentials. Almost between seasons, there arose Avoriaz, Morzine, Les Arcs, Flaine, Val Thorens and a score more.

Historically the first custom built resort dates from the Great War and was also in France. Baron de Rothschild could not bring himself to be in close proximity to the Boches. Since that ruled out Austria and Switzerland, he hired a team of Norwegian ski champions to scour France for likely places. They recommended a spot which admittedly already had two small hotels and was called Megève. So the Baron, together with his friends, converted and developed the place It consequently became very grand. Not many bars can rival Les Enfants Terrible at the Hotel du Mont Blanc with murals decorated by Jean Cocteau. Colonel de Linde remarked it was the only resort where his ski instructor insisted on carrying his pack lunch for him.

Another wealthy skier seeking a resort was Giovanni Agnelli who accordingly dreamt up Sestriere. Early on it attracted several British notables, including Lord Farnham and the Duke of Grafton who soon became known as The Ducal Seat because of the position he so frequently assumed in the snow. The British ski team also arrived and disgraced itself. They ripped the coat of a cable car attendant while he was trying, astonishingly, to prevent them from overcrowding the cabin.

Meanwhile in New York, Averell Harriman was looking to buoy up the sagging number of winter passengers on his Union Pacific Railway. He set out his concept in an office memo. It was brief but its value must have been a million dollars a word: "It has occurred to me that some day there will be established a ski centre in the mountains here of the same character as in the Swiss and Austrian Alps". Just like Baron de Rothschild, Harriman sought an expert to conduct the search. Unfortunately there was a muddle and the invitation was addressed to Count Felix Schagotsch instead of his brother Frederich. Felix was elegant and charming but no more than a social skier. So a far from disinterested local farmer had little difficulty in convincing him that his land around Sawtooth Mountain would make ideal ski slopes. He obligingly furnished him with snowfall figures. Unfortunately Felix failed to ask whether they applied to the mountain peak or the valley. The venture was crowned by Steve Hannigan who had gained his reputation in public relations by "making a sun drenched paradise out of a Floroida sandspit called Miami". Without having been nearer to Sawtooth Mountain than New York, he called Harriman's new resort Sun Valley.

Harriman also sought publicity by personally inviting Darryl Zanuck to spend a few days ski-ing. If, he reasoned, Zanuck became a ski enthusiast then all Hollywood would follow in his wake. It turned out that Zanuck was not a natural skier. He was not even a natural sportsman. There followed several agonising days before he could be persuaded to declare that ski-ing was fun. After that the stars came duly trooping: Spencer Tracy, Katherine Hepburn, Garry Cooper, Claudette Colbert and many more.

Harriman's venture proved such a success he can claim credit for the week end ski break. This gave him special satisfaction for it meant his Union Pacific Railway was notching up highly profitable two-way journeys concentrated within the two lax days of the week. The numbers rose quickly. In 1935, 3,600 left New York for the snows. The next year the number was 11,900. He had the trains equipped with ski repair and ski wear shops and there was even a coach in which ski monitors gave instruction. Weekend destinations were not announced until three days before hand, the decision being made according to up to date snow reports. Indeed Sometimes they were almost literally up to the minute. One train destined for Bear Town instead carried on to Pittsfield since the snow conditions there were reported as being better.

Indeed the ski trains became so glamorous, whole areas of Grand Central Station had to be cordoned off to contain the crowds who turned up to watch the great and good carrying their strange equipment.

Also during the years immediately before the war, the Duke of Bedford took a fancy to a pretty village in the Savoie called Les Allues. By 1936 several of his friends had built chalets alongside him. In due course there appeared a four bedroom hotel and a primitive ski tow. After the war another British ski fanatic, the financier Peter Lindsay, also came to appreciate its potential. He spent many painstaking months buying up chicken runs, pigsties and other sections of village property until he owned sufficient to develop the area as Méribel. Fortunately he also appreciated the importance of keeping the atmosphere of the original village. It is an asset retained to this day.

Brand new resorts had, in fact, been emerging even during the turmoil of war. The German occupation of France had deprived Geneva ski enthusiasts of their neighbouring resorts in the Haute Savoie. So instead they repaired to the nearby hamlet of Verbier. Once the war was over, Tessier, a solicitor from nearby Martigny, joined with colleagues recently returned from the Belgian Congo to develop the place. The access road was opened in 1948 and they formed the Societe Telesege in 1951. Tessier had planned to keep the number of beds to 15,000. However the incentive of success soon had him increase it to 23,000.

Another development had been heralded even earlier. In the 'twenties Arnold Lunn had commented on some snow fields around and above St.Bon. "Despite different characteristics, they are admirably suited for the creation of large resorts. The slopes are magnificent, well exposed and the danger from avalanche is small". He showed considerable foresight for now the magnificent slopes are sprinkled with Courchevels. Each of the old villages within the Courchevel cluster is distinguished by its height above sea level.

Arnold Lunn's enthusiasm began to assume physical form when the French champion, Jean Blanc, annually organised a race from the top of La Loze down to St.Bon. Even so the local authorities were puzzled by his persistence in asking permission to put up a lift. They failed to see any attraction in these remote slopes marked by some cow houses which could only be reached along a mule path.

Indeed the entire area was in decline. Even at its most prosperous, the village of St.Bon had never boasted more than 650 inhabitants. By this time, they had dwindled to under 500. Nearby Moriond was indeed close to being moribund. It had never got further than 200 guest rooms and a feeble effort to start a ski school.

But after the Second World War the municipality was rejuvenated with young blood. Pierre de la Gontrie became President of the Savoie Department Council and Francis Mugnier became mayor of St.Bon. Together they took a fresh look at all the potential around them. They reached a startling conclusion: "Instead of seeking a village where we could develop the snowfields, we were seeking the ideal snowfields where we could develop a village." They accordingly looked around and decided that Jean Blanc's cow houses marked the spot. Today one of the houses is registered as a national monument and another has been incorporated into a very expensive restaurant.

The planning of the runs was considered so important that the Regional Surveyor was called in right at the start. Indeed it was before the start, for Albert Chules had to spend the first winter in a tiny hut with neither running water nor electricity and often with snow three feet deep between him and the iced-up well. Fortunately he had unbounded enthusiasm. One day he was doing his best to accommodate a VIP who had come to check progress. At lunch he remarked the water tasted peculiar. Albert made some technical excuse and forebode to explain the taste was bleach because the woman in the chalet on the slope above was having her washing day.

In the aftermath of war, there was very little private capital available. It would have been useless trying to finance the resort in the same way as had been found for Megève and Méribel. It was clear that initial backing must come from the local authorities.

Right from the first it was planned to link Courchevel with the two adjacent valleys; the intermediate Méribel and Les Menuires beyond. There was no doubt that the success of the entire enterprise depended on persuading the extremely conservative peasants to give up smallholdings that had been in their family for centuries. It was a formidable, many said hopeless, task. But nothing could daunt Francis Mugnier. Astutely he decided to start where he was best known and trusted, the area that was soon to be known as Courchevel 1850.

He was right. To begin with the locals were highly suspicious of the whole concept. It took all his power to persuade them to agree. Altogether he negotiated the transfer of 500 hectares of privately owned ground. This covered sites for hotels, shops and the lower ski slopes as well. But it did not properly extend to the upper areas, an omission that was subsequently to cause a number of problems.

Naturally several of the smart land owners wanted to keep their property, anticipating that the value would appreciate considerably. But having major tracts of land held in limbo would have retarded the entire development and put the programme beyond control.

So a by-law was passed: anyone purchasing or holding land must build according to planning permission within three years. This was considered so important that the penalty for failure was drastic in the extreme: confiscation without compensation. In practice this was exercised on 17 unfortunate would-be development moguls.

In contrast, anyone prepared to invest in the approved fashion received every encouragement. For instance, there was Arlette Casalta who arrived by jeep in 1947. She had been dispatched there to oversee the construction of the post office. Her initial accommodation consisted of two cellars with the lavatory situated across the road. She all but despaired. However she happened to go into the only hotel then open and there she saw the most wonderful cakes. If there is one thing Mme.Casalta cannot resist it is cream cakes.

And they were to prove her fortune.

The commune desperately needed funds to put up a new ski lift and the only easily disposable asset was the ground for an hotel. Bids for the property came in from all over France. Mme. Casalta realised it could be something good. So when the then manager unwittingly revealed that he had bid two million francs, she put in a bid of her own of two million plus 5,000 francs. She won. But, of course, she did not have the money. However the notaire in charge of the negotiations was evidently impressed by her abilities. "Come back in a couple of hours" he told her. She did and in the interim he had telephoned round persuading his friends that this was a good investment. The money was hers. Every year since she has enlarged the hotel. From being 15 rooms with a one star rating, Les Trois Valleés now has 55 rooms and four stars.

Another early success was Boix Vives. He was a local potato merchant who bought and ran two ski lifts and in time made a handsome profit. So handsome, in fact, that by 1956 he was able to outlay 250,000 francs buying control of a little known ski factory called Rossignol.

The haute couturier Jacques Fath also decided that Courchevel was a good investment and bought 15 chalets and for several years let them to his friends and acquaintances.

It was not long before the amount of capital put up by private enterprise, including the Rothschilds, was five times the department's original investment. But perhaps the growth is most impressively shown through the municipal cash flow. Before the construction of Courchevel the annual budget of St.Bon had been a million francs; after it had become fully developed it was 800 m.

The development rapidly spread to the outlying villages. Eventually it absorbed Moriond which consequently became Courchevel 1650. Then all further building was halted holding the area at 64 hotels and 30,000 beds.

Like most French ski resorts of "instant" construction, Courchevel was the responsibility of a single organisation with a single architect appointed to provide the whole with an all embracing style.

The architect of Courchevel was Laurent Chapis. He aspired to make the buildings harmonise with the mountains by having every roof sloping one side only. He later adjusted this in favour of the "butterfly" roof. But he had to give up this idea as well since the central gutters were prone to leak. Some declared that in his obsession for being in harmony with the mountains he was quite happily relegating the human occupants to secondary importance.

None the less Chapis was soon acclaimed a leading authority on mountain architecture and had a major influence on Val Thorens.

A more convincing success is to be found in the brick cube buildings at Les Arcs. They so hug the contours of the mountain they are barely visible from Bourg St.Maurice in the valley below. From above the snow is held on the flat roofs making them just as indistinguishable. The style has been integrated almost to the same degree as did Robert Adam. It extends even to the design of the boot scrapers outside the shops.

La Daille, on the outskirts of Val d'Isére, is another example of building in harmony with the surroundings. The slate coloured ragged silhouette is, at a distance, almost imperceptible set against a vast mass of grey rock, too steep to hold any snow. The colours also ingeniously reflect those in the Isere flowing close by. The style has been repeated further up the valley at Val Claret, but there the effect is lost. The background is snow or pasture which show up the ragged grey buildings to considerable disadvantage.

Flaine appears from a distance to be one long concrete coffer slung along the bare mountainside. So it is not surprising to learn that it was developed by a major cement company. Its weighty presence made itself felt early on. The local mayor did not wish to see his modest ski resort completely overwhelmed. So he refused access to the builders; until, that is, one morning when he was astonished to see none of the village ski lifts were working. Urgent enquiries revealed that the cement mogul had bought out the local ski lift company. It was made abundantly clear there was only one way the lifts could be set working again.

In the mean time all those resorts that had grown from original villages were undergoing a disastrous architectural lapse. It seemed that any contractor could acquire permission for any design so long as it conformed to the mayor's desire - a desire that assumed many forms. Every sensible villager knows better than to be in dispute with the Mayor. Consequently resorts such as Val d'Isére and Cervinia became a mishmash of over blown chalets and concrete apartment blocks with the occasional individual fantasy lodged between.

During the 'nineties an attempt was made to remedy the situation in Val d'Isére. The local architect "discovered" a neighbouring village where some of the houses had a pillar stuck onto one corner. He acclaimed it as the local style and had one slapped onto the facade of every new building. He considered it of no consequence that it sometimes obliterated the view from any corner window. Others were built so high they resembled stilts rather than pillars.

Another essential for the modern ski resort is easy access. All the traditional Swiss places can be reached by train. Some of the older villages, notably Zermatt, Mürren, Wengen and Saas Fee are positively inaccessible to cars in winter. It is a shortcoming which, in these environmental conscious times can be turned to good account. At Zermatt only the municipal dust cart, the doctor and the fire brigade are permitted an internal combustion engine. All other transport has to be by horse sleigh or by one of the electric cars which look like rolling telephone kiosks. While the harness jingles cheerfully, the almost silent electric cars creep up from behind the pedestrian and nudge their way past.

In 1974 the City Fathers decided to broaden the restriction and authorised a diesel bus service linking the bottom stations of the three lift axis. This was not favoured by Imboden who owned many of the electric cars and almost all the horse drawn sleighs. Initially his protests were ignored by the Burghers; his family had not been in the village for three 300 years. So he canvassed 3,000 regular visitors to write in protest. On the New Year's Eve, he led a torchlight procession with 5,000 demonstrators. The village fathers capitulated, the bus service was withdrawn and peace returned.

Although St.Moritz at one time had electric trams, it too drew a line against the use of cars in winter. It was a situation that particularly irked Andre Citroen since he had just produced a car he felt sure could cover the Julier Pass in deep snow. It had skis on the front and a caterpillar track at the back and was in fact a large precursor of the snow cat. His protest was joined by the hoteliers who calculated that the exclusion of cars was costing them two million francs a year. So the St. Moritz authorities also capitulated. But not the locals. They expressed their displeasure in their customary fashion - by throwing stones.

Situated along the main artery of Austria, St.Anton followed the opposite course. Monster articulated lorries had to inch round hairpin corners between the centuries old chalets. Progress tended to be further complicated by jay walking skiers. Then in 1972 the railway tunnel was augmented by a road tunnel. It ran not only under the Arlberg Pass but also the village itself to emerge clear on the far side. This made it possible to declare the village centre a car free zone.

During the three years the tunnel was under construction, the wheel turned full circle. The 1,100 navvies were again housed in a special camp outside the village. This time, however, it was not for the protection of the village maidens - or so it was claimed. It was to leave the accommodation free for skiers.

In complete contrast most of the custom built modern resorts can be reached by road only. This can also cause an acute problem. There have been peak weekends when traffic to Moutier has been in gridlock for 72 hours. So when the Olympics were allocated to the Savoie area, millions of francs were well spent improving the access roads. Just one road tunnel cost 170 m francs. Les Arcs supplemented its approach road by constructing a funicular.

At Verbier the planning authorities made the mistake of allowing every chalet to be built with a garage. The traffic has become such that those carrying skis in the street slip at their peril.

Initially aeroplane flights were just another tourist gimmick, but increasingly they have become a major means of access. The first essay in altitude flying came to St. Moritz in 1908. Baron Auffm 'Ordt persuaded Badrutt to underwrite accommodation at the Palace for himself and his mechanics. Eventually, after many weeks of tinkering and false starts, he managed to get the plane to take off - for three metres. Two years later Captain Engelhard arrived with two Wright aeroplanes. But the thin atmosphere at high altitude occasions considerable loss of engine power. Also low temperatures have an adverse effect on benzine. In the end the Captain considerably improved on the Baron's record with a flight lasting just over half an hour.

During the 'thirties, science advanced sufficiently for Graham White, having become disenchanted with the Cresta, to provide flights on a regular basis.

But it was not until 1961 that the pioneer Alpine aviator Michael Ziegler introduced a regular light aircraft service at Courchevel. In the first year, he transported 4,500 visitors to and from Orly or Le Bourget. In addition he took up 8,000 skiers to experience the superb off-piste runs among the 20 neighbouring peaks.

Courchevel's Altiport did not so much have a runway as a snow apron. It ends abruptly with an alarmingly precipitous drop like a ski jump. Contrary to all normal credence, this enables Pilatus and Piper Cub aircraft to glide-off rather than take-off - and all within a mere 30 yd. Such an extreme venture had its moments of drama. Once, after the aircraft had taken off, a patch of oil was found in the snow. The pilot was radioed and spent some minutes flying round and round while the ground crew scanned the underside through field glasses for any visible defect. All seemed in order and it was with trepidation that it was brought in to land. It was some time later that the pilot realised it had not been oil but it was the spot where she had spilt a thermos of black coffee on the snow.

Before long the altiport had three trained Alpine pilots working full time. One was the first woman to hold the special certificate. One passenger, having his first sight of the foreshortened runway, actually panicked when he found his pilot was wearing her favourite multi-flowered hat.

Enough to cause passenger panic: A Pilatus about to take-off from the "ski-jump" runway of Courchevel altiport.

Before long the terminal was made replete with bar, restaurant, control tower and custom office. Its pioneering approach was recognised when it was also made a training centre.

Such developments require massive capital investment and that in turn demands high powered marketing. In the 'twenties it took the form of a poster of the St.Moritz girl and created a sensation. Initially she was starkers except for a flimsy drape of sunbeams.

But after the Second World War it was no longer sufficient to rely on the traditional poster. Even the power of cinematography came into question. St.Anton had indeed benefited mightily from the Hannes Schneider ski chase films. Forty years on and Salzburg's tourist numbers doubled through the appeal of "The Sound of Music". But the cinema dismally failed to deliver when James Bond went to Mürren "on Her Majesty's Service". Perhaps skiers were no longer sufficiently engaged by spectacular ski heroics even when performed by George Lazenby in the company of Diana Rigg. The villains seized control of the cable car. One of Bond's skis had to be blown up by remote control when it was supposed to be shattered by bullets. Not, of course, that it was of the least concern to Bond. He continued just as effortlessly all on one ski.

Not so in real life. During one of the practice runs Bond missed a turn and ended ignominiously in the bob run.

There followed a desperate race with a distinctly audible thud as one of the villains failed to slalom a tree. Then there was a spectacular long distance shot when another of the villains failed to notice the 1,000 ft sheer drop to Lauterbrunnen. By pure chance, the weighting of the dummy caused the arms and legs to flail the air grotesquely.

The late 'thirties had shown what more conventional promotion could do. When Baron Mersheng was appointed director of publicity for Kitzbühel he doubled the number of visitors within the first two years.

109

The shocking posterposter after the sunbeam draped lady had been adequately censored.

Marketing became a more exact science when Courchevel set out to target a specific section among skiers. Rather than attract home market the policy was to seek a more cosmopolitan clientele. This meant soft pedalling publicity in France and concentrating on foreign countries. The project met with such success that whereas in 1960 only five per cent of visitors came from abroad, a mere four years later and the figures had risen to 15 per cent and eight years on it was 30 per cent, 8.5 per cent of them British.

The first resort that was not only launched but actually created with a precise type of patron in mind was La Plagne in 1965. The creator was Robert Legoux, a banker and therefore well placed to raise the necessary finance. His strategy was strangely casual. He relied heavily on a friend whose sole qualification was president of the Old Boys Association of the l'Ecole Polytechnique. Everyone attending this highly prestigious training college is almost certainly destined for a top job. They proved highly amenable for 60 of the first 100 apartments were sold to these high flyers. Brilliant though they may have been, it soon transpired they could be easily hoodwinked over matters rustic. Monsieur Legoux did not shrink from making prefabricated extensions to the original village and no one noticed. He even imported chickens to scratch in the street. The villagers were quick to enter the conspiracy. When the daily tankers arrived, they would discreetly siphon the milk into suitably antiquated churns. The mandarins apparently failed to notice the lack of cows in the immediate vicinity.

The launch of Avoriaz the same year was perhaps more logical for it was entrusted almost exclusively to an advertising agency. Here the intention was to concentrate on the up market left wing element of society. Symbolic to this end, Johnny Hallyday was enticed into buying an apartment at a ridiculously low price. The only drawback was that he almost immediately sold it again at a comfortable profit. Rustic life was pursued to even greater extremes. As cars were prohibited, reindeer were brought in to pull sleighs of all sorts. Unfortunately the reindeer did not co-operate any more than had Johnny Hallyday. They made a point of jumping out of their enclosures and taking to the mountains. They had to be replaced by horses.

There was one further and rather more serious drawback to the Avoriaz marketing plan. It soon became clear that people holding left wing views are not necessarily inclined to buy apartments at ski resorts. So the image had to be drastically altered to emphasise family comfort and "l'air sportif".

Le Corbier opened in 1986 to even more razzmatazz, not least because the figure behind the development was Christian Guerin, a former jazz drummer. He symbolised the immediate post war generation and the St.Germain des Pres club scene of the 'fifties. It was reasonably assumed that all those who had gone to such lengths to shock their parents would, after 25 years, have settled down with family responsibilities. Sufficient responsibilities indeed, to have saved enough to buy a ski apartment. Yet it was assumed they still retained some, even if small, hankering for their rip roaring past. Accordingly the inauguration was entrusted to a Paris impresario with an apparently limitless budget. He brought down a trainload of film stars or, more accurately, starlets. Together with the inevitable gaggle of journalists, they enjoyed a three day all free junket. Certainly the journalists kept their side of the bargain and produced an incredible 40,000 lines of newspaper copy - the equivalent of about five novels.

In complete contrast, Les Arcs, another concept of Robert Legoux, was created with the utmost discretion. Shares were offered on a personal basis among the 200 plus listed members of the establishment. Most negotiations were conducted in low murmurs in only the most elegant

Edi Reinalter demonstrates the French rotation technique

Paris salons. Marketing - what a vulgar word - was conducted by a princess widely known to enjoy a close relationship with a Government Minister. Only essential facts were released to the press.

Beyond France, Anzere, like Verbier, was developed largely with Belgian money. Unlike Verbier, however, the marketing policy proved wanting. Logically enough, it was aimed at the super rich. Unfortunately they proved to be so super they had no need to let out their apartments when not themselves in residence. So except at the New Year and Easter, the cable car and ski lifts revolved in exclusive emptiness. For several years takings proved hopelessly insufficient to finance the planned expansion.

One of the earliest forms of marketing had been to appoint a champion ski racer as head of the ski school. Rudolph Rominger had been made head of the St.Moritz ski school on the strength of winning the 1936 World Championship . So when, in 1948, Edi Reinalter, on his home ground, won the Olympic slalom gold, the St. Moritz ski school doubled its prestige by appointing him joint head. In the same way, David Zogg was appointed head of the ski school at Arosa. Not that the formula proved infallible. Karl Schranz projected his racing temperament into the business of running of the St.Anton ski school and soon had to retire. Kitzbühel came to be considered a major teaching centre through their "White Wonder " team. Between them, Hias Leitner, Ernst Hinterseer, Anderl Molterer, Christian Pravda, and Fritz Huber won five gold, four silver and four bronze Olympic medals and eleven gold, seven silver and five bronze medals in World Championships. Toni Sailer was a little younger and his achievement of all four downhill medals in the 1956

Olympics was in a class of its own. Toni Sailer is the son of Rudi, the local plumber who had himself been a prominent skier.

At Cortina Toni had already won the slalom by four seconds and the giant slalom by 6.2 seconds.

The downhill began while it was snowing and the competitors were ski-ing virtually blind. The finish was down a small glade with numerous little bumps. Here the crowd waited and no skier appeared. The first to be sighted was way down the starting list for all his predecessors had fallen. Then suddenly there appeared a figure obviously in full control. It was Toni Sailer. Almost at the finish he hit one of the bumps and his skis crossed. The crowd gave a mass groan. But with almost super human effort he jumped and uncrossed his skis and, through good fortune, did not land on another of the bumps. As he completed the course the crowd let out a great roar and but for the barriers would, in their enthusiasm, have crushed him. After an experimental period in advertising and singing in a Vienna nightclub, Sailer returned to Kitzbühel. His style inaugurated the inside shoulder technique. However business interests did not allow him time to accept appointment as head of the ski school. So his brother provided the Sailer name while Toni undertook the less demanding work of the children's classes. His team mate, Ernst Hinterseer, set up his own ski school a short distance further down the valley.

It was soon realised that the prestige of a ski champion not only promotes the ski school but the entire resort as well. After Toni Sailer won the Olympics, Kitzbühel found it necessary to provide 3,000 more beds and six more ski lifts. Similarly it is estimated that, entirely due to Guy Perillat's ski triumphs, French resorts were enlarged by a total of 100,000 beds.

Guy Perillat and the Austrian inside shoulder technique

So it seemed only natural when a grateful village commune granted Sailer a plot of land big enough to build a handsome hotel.

The only other skier to have won triple gold in the Olympic Alpine events was Jean Claude Killy from Val d'Isére. The fastest time had been made by his serious rival, the veteran Karl Schranz, winner of the AK eight times, the Lauberhorn four and the Hahnenkamm three times. He had missed participating in the the Squaw Valley Olympics after having been spotted the night before the race, living it up in a Reno night club and he had been sent home in disgrace. Once again he was the great hope of Austria. He was eliminated, having missed a gate. But he insisted there had been a "phantom" gatekeeper on the piste. He was accorded a second run. This time, though, he was slower.

Killy's triumph has been fully utilised in his home village. The entire area has been encompassed as l'Espace Killy. He, too, was prevented by business interests from being associated with the ski school. Nor did he inspire the French ski schools to initiate a "national" style. None the less, he has considerably influenced style through suggesting skis should be kept apart to ensure stability and that the weight should be more evenly distributed. As both precepts are in accord with natural inclination, they have found general acceptance but, some may say, at the expense of grace.

Even though lifts eliminated the tedium of climbing, the appeal of ski-ing could never have touched so many people had not the sliding down been made equally facile. The Scandinavians have for long considered ski wax to be a key component in cross country ski-ing. Indeed formulas are considered so personal it is an affront to question anyone too closely. They may incorporate six or even ten ingredients such as , Burgundy pitch, Canada pitch, balsam of fire, Venice turpentine, oil of cedar, glycerine, camphor and castor oil and spermaceti, the waxy part of the sperm whale making it amenable to acoustic signals . But for Alpine skiers the crucial factor proved to be

113

the Koflak sole. It made skis so manoeuvrable it changed ski-ing style on the piste and brought wedeln within everybody's aspirations.

Technically wedeln is starting one parallel turn but interrupting it with a turn in the opposite direction. As a substitute for complete turns, it provides controlled descent in a comparatively straight line. It was a movement that had, in fact, been demonstrated before the Second World War. However the waxed wooden soles made it so strenuous it was little more than a gimmick to be displayed by the super fit, notably Bill Bracken and Vivian Caulfeild's son Barry. So wedeln did not make itself generally manifest until Toni Sailer won the 1956 Olympics. It enabled the Austrians to elaborate it as the "inside shoulder" technique and make it their national response to the French rotation.

Racing technique was also subtly influenced by changes among course setters. When Sir Arnold had evolved the slalom, the course setters, burdened with their bundle of poles, started from the bottom of the slope. As they climbed their way up, they naturally moved quite widely from side to side. But then lifts made it easier to carry up the poles and start setting the course from the top. This meant they could slide straight down. As a result, the line of gates almost imperceptibly became more vertical. This encouraged competitors to go faster and take greater risks. Anderl Molterer was the first to realise that the straighter one can approach a gate the higher the acceleration and the less the friction. He proved the apparent contradiction that, in the giant slalom, it is faster to step actually up the slope before entering the next gate.

During the 'sixties the ski manufacturers toyed with fibreglass. While it was enthusiastically adopted by the racers, it proved too heavy for the holiday skier. Since then plastic, and more recently carbon fibre, have become the crucial ingredient.

One way of gauging how much ski equipment is worth is by the value put upon it by thieves. In the early days people left their skis outside a cafe. It was assumed that no thief would risk the time necessary to find a pair that fitted his boots. So it was their sticks that skiers would take with them inside. Today plastic skis, and no less the bindings, are so expensive it is economic to renovate and re-sell them. Consequently thieves started working on a commercial scale. Gangs from such nearby lowland towns as Milan or Lyons drove lorries to the very door of an hotel or apartment ski room. It is easy to prise open the lockers with crowbars, load the lorry and leave the resort within minutes.

Plastic has also brought about a revolution in ski boots. Initially it was too weak and wherever a crack appeared a hole had to be punched to dissipate further tension from making it worse. 1959 almost proved fatal for Lange. They used ABS Royalite and by the end of the season almost their entire year's production had been returned split. Once these initial troubles had been solved, plastic showed its true value. It can form an outer shell providing sufficient support for a padded boot inside. This banished for ever the two or three weeks agony of pinching and chafing unavoidable while the leather was being "broken in".

Clips had been tried on boots during the 'thirties but the leather had proved too insubstantial. Plastic proved sufficiently strong to accommodate them. They too brought relief to the wearer since it was no longer necessary to acquire calluses on the inside of the fingers through constantly pulling the laces ever tighter.

Safety bindings were another important development though they contributed less to style than to confidence. The early examples were simply a strap looped under the heel cable and screwed into the ski behind the boot. When the skier fell forward and levered the back of the boot upwards, the loop pulled the cable off the heel. Unfortunately this was not effective during a torsional fall. None the less they were better than nothing. They were strongly promoted by the Ski Club of Great Britain though most of the shops refused to put screws into their hire skis. Unfortunately the ski tiger viewed the total safety binding concept with utter contempt. This was despite an accident rate of one in ten. However attitudes noticeably changed after Herr. Marker persuaded the Austrian team to adopt his far more expensive metal contraption. The immediate result was the number of ski accidents was reduced by 65 per cent. or five per thousand visits to the slopes. As Dr. Michael Turner rather unscientifically expressed it: "driving to the supermarket is eight times more dangerous than ski-ing the steepest black run."

Now that the boot could be automatically ejected from the binding, the next problem became the loose ski. The obvious solution was the 15in. longthong. However it became stigmatised as being dangerous. This was just as misplaced as all the warnings had been over metal edges. Then in 1963 an American Mitch Cubberly invented a spring loaded spike which dug into the snow when released from the pressure of the boot. It was universally acclaimed as the Toad Stabber and was soon elaborated with an aesthetically more pleasing fellow prong.

High technology was also touching speed skating and curling, though not necessarily advantageously.

Salt Lake City spent $27 m on a rink for the speed skaters. The substructure was made with specially fine grained concrete. The refrigeration pipes were placed over it so that there would be no hot or cold spots. The actual ice was built up in 25 layers, each sprayed-on using hand held hoses. Even the atmosphere in the hall was strictly controlled so that there would be no condensation.

High tech, however, can become too tech. The competitors were evidently unaccustomed to such perfection. During the heats several stumbled and fell. Gradually a largely unknown Australian Steven Bradbury came to the fore qualifying for the quarter finals, then for the semi finals. And yet his times were very disappointing. The full truth only emerged during the finals. The Korean Kim Dong-Ung was in the lead when he tripped. Apolo Ohno, the American hope, was so close behind he could not avoid him and others in the field piled up too. So for the third time Bradbury came first through being last. The largely American crowd booed him and Ohno, who had been first to scramble to his feet, received his silver sitting in a wheelchair.

After the Second World War curling had largely slid into abeyance. It was kept alive mainly in Scotland. It was also strong in Canada, nurtured by the Air Canada Silver Broom trophy. It was made a full blown Olympic event at Nagano. Now it, too, was being brought into the world of technology. Scientific tests were made possible after a Canadian University produced a laying machine. It laid any number of stones with identical force. Then Edinburgh University's department of materials, science and engineering came up with an electronic broom. It was stuffed with an ergometer and a strain gauge load cell so that it registered horizontal and vertical forces. A wire running up the handle electronically downloaded the findings onto a computer.

The results of this research became clear during the 2002 Olympics.

The curlers themselves remained genuine amateurs. Rhona Martin, the British captain was a Dunlop housewife. The rink was the only place in the Olympic complex where there was a smoking room. But all seemed lost when the British team was beaten by the Germans. Then the Germans were beaten by the Swiss. This brought the British back onto the rink. Over three million British TV viewers tuned into the final. There was increasing tension as the two teams scored in parallel. Eventually everything depended on the final stone. Overcoming the tremendous tension, Rhona laid a perfect stone, knocking the Swiss out of the house and replacing it with her own. Typical of the amateur spirit, she dodged the outstretched arms of her team members to commiserate with her rival captain.

As sports equipment has become more sophisticated and expensive, so manufacturers have found that, like resorts, marketing becomes more effective when associated with a champion. Just as skiers believe their technique will improve more if the ski school is managed by a big personality, so they believe that, by using a sponsored brand, some of the champion's lustre will be shed upon them.

Before the war, the Olympic Committee tried to counter the threat of commercialism by insisting that competitors should have only one pair of skis for all the events. They were so insistent competitors had their skis marked. Certainly in the years immediately after the war the manufacturers were reticent. They provided skis free to the national team for "testing". If they over calculated the number required, no one objected if the surplus was sold. It was just chance, of course, that when photographed, they held their skis so that the manufacturer's name was clearly visible. Avery Bundage, the Olympic chairman and scourge of commercialism, was not so accommodating. He forbade the showing of the top side of the skis. The manufacturers countered by printing their names on the soles as well.

Soon manufacturers were subsidising training throughout the year.

It was in 1965 that the canker of commercialism attacked the very heart of the campaign against "shamateurism" being conducted by Arnold Lunn as well as Avery Bundage. It appeared right there, during his own Arlberg Kandahar race. In the past the AK prize givings and subsequent dinner had always been outstanding for good humour and friendliness. This had largely been generated through the personality of Schneider who, off duty, was the embodiment of all that is Austrian fun and charm. He would be the centre of hospitality, dispensing refreshments and bonhomie in equal proportions. He had even been known to hold his dancing partner by her arms and whirl her around in the centre of the floor as though they were a pair of skaters. The prize giving was made even more hilarious whenever Alan d'Egville was present.

Now winners were finding silver cups were no longer sufficient. They required such prizes as rolls of cloth which were easy to resell. When they came up to receive their award they would blatantly feel the texture to gauge which would realise the highest price.

The skaters were even worse. They discovered a successful ploy for inflating the value of their "expenses" when appearing in "amateur" exhibitions. Even before the war Sonja Henie had acquired a reputation threatening to cancel appearances due to "extreme fatigue". She made it blatantly clear the only way to overcome this malaise was the offer of a gift. As time went on these gifts became more and more extravagant if they were to be effective. It reached the pitch where the Norwegian American Society had to present her with a sports car.

Her successor, Barbara Ann Scott started experiencing similar fatigue. However when she too reached the sports car category, Avery Bundage threatened to withdraw her amateur status. She was forced to return it - but for no longer than it took her to win the Olympic gold. Then she announced her retirement and the car was re-proffered and re-accepted.

But relations between the French, Austrian and Swiss ski teams had also become tense. The prestige attendant on their respective ski "techniques" had progressed beyond pride and was assuming national values. The turning point came during practice for the AK . The French trainer had brought the ladies team down the men's course. He was stopped by a controller. It was against the rules but hardly a heinous offence. What caused such consternation among Sir Arnold and the authorities was the reaction of the trainer. He knew the controller was a volunteer, but none the less he roundly abused him. Other teams also began taking liberties.

The committee issued a warning and reluctantly felt they must take the unprecedented step of naming names.

Now manufacturers with little or no association with ski-ing, such as Marlbrough cigarettes, were entering the fray. They believed that ski-ing's strong association with sun, health, athleticism and glamour, would be ideal for promoting their products. Came the 1988 Winter Olympic events and IBM paid 200m francs for the privilege of being associated with the five ring emblem, Credit Lyonais 150m, and so on down to Renault at 50m.francs.

The FIS, having gamely withstood constant battery over a number of years, finally capitulated when the manufacturers were joined by the politicians.

Stalinists felt it necessary to prove that Communism was superior to Capitalism in every way. This applied to sport as much as to anything else. To uphold this precept, all the iron curtain nations blatantly flouted the amateur status. Even while the Russians were assuring the F.I.S. that their entrants were genuine amateurs, "Pravda" was publishing details of the cash prizes they were receiving.

This gross disregard for true sportsmanship became blatant during the Oslo games. The East German bobbers took the advantage of weight to such extremes that they ignored skill of any sort. The average weight of their crew was around 20 stone and one "competitor" was so enormous he could barely walk. It provoked the authorities to write weight restrictions into the rules.

The Russians were equally happy to go to the other extreme. For the 1978 international pair skating events they produced a partnership of one and a half. While the man was of true championship standard the half was a girl around the minimum age of 12. Her advantage did not lie so much in her technique as in her lightness. She was lifted and thrown in more and more daring moves. The validity of this technique was proved by Marina Tcherkasova and Sergi Shakhrai. Much of their victory in the 1978 World Championships was due to their quadruple twist lift. Those conventionally mature entrants from other countries who dared try emulate them were having to retire through injuries. When the couple tried to repeat the move after Marina had become fully grown, they found it physically impossible. .

Having blatantly cheated with their competitors, the Russians turned to influencing the judging. At Cortina the iron curtain countries awarded outrageously low marks to the American skater Carol Reiss. They could not possibly have done this by accident. Before displaying their marks, skating judges tell them to the referee who calculates the average. Thus, should they find their points out of line to an embarrassing degree, they have ample opportunity to revise them. This time they were so blatantly biased they were not only booed and jeered but came under a hail of garbage so that they had to take cover.

In the 1976 European Championships the Czech judge defied instructions and awarded John Curry the highest marks. His name never again appeared among international judges.

CHAPTER VI
TELEVISION RULES

Historically skiers competing in international races owed allegiance to the Federation International de Ski. But in 1993 the ski manufacturers set up the International Racing Team. Having the greater financial clout, international skiers naturally transferred their allegiance. Then the manufacturers entered into an unholy alliance with television companies. The FIS was left standing on the sideline.

The price television was prepared to spend on racing turned ski-ing into an industry. It was set through the Olympics. Back in 1956 Peter Cushing had jokingly entered his "fouled up swamp" of a ski resort as a contestant for the Winter Olympics. He was merely being factitious over what he considered the pretentious entry made by neighbouring Reno. To his utter amazement, not only did Reno loose but Squaw Valley won. He hastily borrowed two million dollars from his friend Laurence Rockefeller. He genuinely believed it was enough to cover all the costs. Though the sum may seem ridiculous, the total expenditure was, in the event, still well under eight million.

By 1968 outside television equipment was both unfettered by furlongs of cable and unphased by freezing conditions. Even more significantly, it showed that Olympic ski races could draw an estimated hundred million viewers. The TV rights were valued at $2m. By 1988 this figure was adjusted to £350 m.

With good reason it was assumed that such an astronomical price included soul as well as body. From then on the cameras had precedence over competitors, spectators and even snow conditions. At Innsbruck the events were scattered far apart. Officially this was to "suit technological advances". But it was generally acceded the arrangement was to suit the cameras. Events were scheduled to coincide with peak viewing times in those countries, notably the U.S.A, where advertising had the greatest spending power. By afternoon the snow is usually too heavy for ideal cross country ski-ing. No matter. Cross country events were held in the afternoon. Competition skating rinks were normally stained blue to make it easier for judges to see the tracings. But TV cameras were myopic over blue. The rinks were frozen white. There was only one instance where the Olympic Committee made a stand. For several years they resisted all demands to include ice dancing as an event. But the broadcasting executives were so insistent that in 1976 the committee capitulated this final point.

Perhaps their most unkind cut came in the ski-jumping . The only British entrant, Eddie (the Eagle) Edwards, had tailed in 56th place in the Calgary Olympics. As he so cogently pointed out, this was only because the Dutch, the Danes, Belgians and a dozen other lowland countries had not made any entry at all. In any case, his jump of 70 m. put him on a par with the early Olympic winners. His ready humour, courage and genuinely amateur enthusiasm won him world wide popularity. He even gained a degree of respect among his deadly serious professional peers. However the gently humorous publicity he occasioned wherever he went did not suit officialdom. The British Ski Federation preferred to become as drab and conventional as the Dutch, the Danes and the Belgians and refused him a place in the 1992 British Olympic team. Unfortunately the International Committee shared the British fear of becoming a laughing stock. So they passed "The Eddy Law". It banned all amateurs who did not come up to "professional" standards. And thus fell the last vestige of Baron de Coubertin's vision of the true Olympic spirit.

The degree to which the Olympic movement had become a travesty was made clear in December 1998.

Actually a foretaste of this state of affairs had occurred in the run up to the Olympics in 1994. As the time approached, one of the American hopes, Tonya Harding became convinced that nothing lay between her and a gold medal other than her rival Nancy Kerrigan. So her boyfriend obligingly hired a bruiser to break Nancy's knees. He failed and so did Tonya since she came eighth against Nancy's silver medal. The trail was eventually traced back and Tonya was barred from ever again skating competitively.

By 1998 it had become clear that most members of the committee were taking bribes on a massive scale. They accounted for three quarters of the million dollar budget Salt Lake City had allocated towards canvassing. All the members enjoyed extravagant accommodation during and after their offcial visits. Most had also received cash, clothes and additional holidays. Some had their children's university fees paid for them. One had even invented a daughter so that he could claim more. Jean Claude Ganga linked with that well known winter sports resort in the Congo, acquired the nickname of "The Human Hoover". He made six visits of "inspection". But he not only sucked up gifts for himself but his wife had cosmetic surgery and his mother in law a knee replacement operation.

When exposed, the chairman Juan Antonio Samaranch made a grovelling public apology.

This was considered so cleansing that by the time the Olympics opened at Salt Lake City in 2002, all but those ten members supposed to be the worst offenders, were still successfully clinging to office. The vice-president, Kim Un-yong of South Korea hung on until 2004 when he was imprisoned for embezzling a million pounds and taking bribes for sporting favours.

Rather than properly rectifying their own shortcomings, the Committee became ruthless with the athletes - only to buckle immediately they came up against any serious opposition. The Russian Larissa Lazutina was disqualified from the 20 km cross country after failing a drug test. But the Russians raised their protests to Putin level. So she was allowed to keep the medals she had won earlier even though she must have already been under the influence of the drugs. Then one western judge joined the eastern block in voting the Canadian pair skaters into second place. Ferocious protests from the spectators persuaded the Committee to invent a "shared" gold medal. However their magnanimous gestures fell short of the British. Alain Baxter had lost any of their sympathy the moment he appeared in the Olympic village. Indeed it was his appearance that was the trouble. His crew cut hair was died a light blue with the white St.Andrew's cross painted on it. Officialdom decided it was "controversial". Efforts to wash out the die proved largely unsuccessful. So he started the slalom race with his hair a peculiar dark blue and with a cross of a slightly paler hue.

The course had been watered and frozen, and then nature had thawed and frozen it again producing a ripple effect. It suited Baxter admirably; "the sort of scraggy snow you get towards the end of the season at Aviemore". But few of the competitors skied at Aviemore and to everyone's surprise Baxter came third and thereby the first British skier to win an Olympic medal.

Then a drug test proved positive. The offending chemical was traced to his nose spray which contained L-methamphetamine But that L makes all the difference. It is only plain methamphetamine that is banned. However, it is very difcult to tell the difference, especially in a urine test and the laboratory had not taken this into account. No matter, the Committee had decided - and over this one genuine exception they remained inexorable.

It was not long before television was corrupting not only the Olympic but the whole field of competitive winter sports. Armchair viewers like to see fabulous prizes. So in contemptuous contrast to the resale price of a bale of cloth, the prize money was now set at a £35,000 minimum.

Today's viewers have normally forgotten yesterday's events. However they are avid followers of the soap opera serial format. So each sporting event must build up to the climax of a seasonal grand winner. Ski-ing must also have a World Cup.

Events were next unceremoniously telescoped so as not to clash with the start of the spring calendar.

But perhaps television's most insidious crime was to cause death through neglect. It poured its vast wealth into just the five major races in the international calendar. It ignored all other events such as national open championships. Without the extravagant prizes, these competitions were ignored by most of the stars. Matters were worse for the ladies' races since they lack the speed of the men competitors. One sad example is the Swiss ladies open championship. It has become little more than a Grindelwald local competition.

In both skating and ice hockey, television demanded all the elaborations of electronic light and sound. Only a city catchment area can attract sufficient gate money to finance it all; only an area under cover can provide climatic certainty to ensure programme schedules remain unphased. So village rinks, open to the mountains and forests were abandoned for cavernous halls with tinny music and artificially frozen ice.

Even the spectators have changed. The local villagers brought a casual, carefree attitude, and saw no reason against cheering good sportsmanship regardless of nationality. Spectators in city stadiums are largely made up of "barmy army" claques and phalanxes of team officials.

Television has also turned its baleful eye towards ski jumping. FIS controls insisted that jumps were constructed so as to allow a maximum distance of 90 m. This was altogether too tame for the cameras. So ski jumping in such villages as Arosa and Pontresina was abandoned in favour of ski flying. Only a handful of jumps, notably Planica, Obersdorf and Kulm, are built so that competitors can fly 150m. or more. The run-in has a vertical drop of 60m. to ensure the speed at take-off is in excess of 75 mph. So when a competitor shuffles on to that narrow white ribbon, steeper than a staircase, he must launch himself into space above pin sized spectators lining the outrun.

It is all a far cry from those bold efforts of Alex Keiller before the First World War. After a long decline, in 1950 a Norwegian team revived British interest in jumping when it challenged some British students. As ever, the British were game even if their experience was nil. A jump was constructed on Hampstead Heath. It required 45 tons of snow imported in insulated containers and supplemented by numerous bales of hay. Indeed the buffer hay was so deep competitors had to be dug out. Over 50,000 people paid to watch the fun and almost as many gate-crashed. It really looked as though British ski jumping might enjoy a revival.

Colonel Percy Legard, with the blessing of the Downhill Only Club, took to coaching the British over a baby jump just outside Mary's Cafe at Wengen. Anyone inclined could try for their bronze or silver Ski Club medals. In the evenings Percy would reappear, this time playing the drums in the pink-washed cellar bar at The Palace.

International jumping was revived again at Neustade. An all seasons ski jump had a surface of plastic strips set like thatch on a cottage roof. It instantly and universally became known as the spaghetti jump.

Unfortunately, unlike spaghetti, it was expensive; too expensive to cover areas large enough for downhill ski-ing. In due course, though, the plastic industry invented a more economic alternative. Strips of bristles, like oversize toothbrushes, were set out in a hexagonal network. This made it practical to cover an entire ski slope and, indeed, at Edinburgh the entire side of a hill.

Television did, though, benefit the amateur skier in one way. Once shown on the small screen and thousands of viewers were determined to try their skills. There were so many, in fact, that all the pistes in all the resorts could not have contained them. A few resorts had already broadened their scope through forging tenuous links with neighbours. For years Wengen had shared the cog railway with neighbouring Grindelwald, and similarly Davos with Klosters. Other major resorts had lifts which linked up with satellite villages: St.Moritz and Samaden, Kitzbühel with St.Jacob. Kitzbühel went on to extend its network using a further 10 long lifts to create the "Ski Safari". It stretches 18km along the Pass Thurn providing 35 km. of linking runs.

Inevitably some villages got left behind. The vital strip of land between Villars and Les Diablerets was owned by one farmer. He believed that fields were for cattle even when under snow. Pylons were de trop. Both resorts went into serious decline until the farmer died.

Mürren has no such opportunity. Left literally isolated on its mountain shelf it has no neighbour to snuggle up to. To hold the loyalty of its adherents it erected a cable car with such enhancements as an altimeter in the cabins and a top station furnished with a tower and rotating restaurant.

Perhaps it was symbolic that in 1960, after all the hurley burley of the Arlberg Kandahar race; after the spectators had departed and the pisteurs had dismantled the barriers, a few old friends traced the now deserted course to scatter Bill Bracken's ashes. For a moment they lay dark upon the snow before the wind caught them up and dispersed them to become one with the mountains he loved so well. A small quantity was however put into a casket and set in the cleft of a rock on the Schiltgrat just at the top of Martha's Meadow.

But it was not long before even those slopes shared between resorts became insufficient.

The lifts that linked Verbier with neighbouring Tsuma became merely the first in a chain leading over four valleys to Thyon 2000. Similarly the construction of Val Thorens in effect converted Trois into Quatres Valleés. Val d'Isére developed l'Espace Killy to encompass Le Fornet on one side and on the other Le Daille, Val Claret, Tignes and Tignes les Brevieres. Sestriere extended its link with Sauze d'Oulx across four municipalities, not to mention the French border, to create the Via Lattea.

All this became possible because technology was slashing labour costs. The T-bar spring housing unit became so subtle it virtually eliminated the initial spine-compacting jerk. So the constant relay of "ski bums" emerging from their fuggy roadmender-type huts to push skiers on their way were no longer required. Instead it was left to a lone man pushing buttons in a control room.

Next Von Roll, the Zurich engineers, found a way to use the weight of the bubble to fix it onto a moving cable. The salient factor is to have the bubble suspended by an asymmetric pole. Directly the full weight of the chair or cabin is placed upon the pole, the cantilever force closes a toggle clamp so that it grips the revolving cable. It is only released when an overhead line at the terminus relieves the clamp of the weight of the cabin. This secondary line also moves the chair slowly round providing ample time for skiers to gather their gear together and get out at leisure. As a result the cable can be run faster and passenger capacity is increased six fold.

In due course, the principle was adapted for chair lifts. And eventually, using a lavatory type chain and a boot-high sensor rod, self service was extended to Poma drag lifts.

Compared with the 'thirties, cable car construction had entered a realm of technological and engineering wizardry. The Trockner Steg cable car above Zermatt was opened in 1979. The top station is the highest in Europe. At 12,000 ft. above sea level, it is a political 40 ft. higher than the Mont Blanc system. The point is made grimly evident in the cable car cabins. Alongside the emergency handle is an oxygen cylinder with a notice pointing out it is for the convenience of any passengers who may suffer a heart attack.

At this height, helicopters lose two thirds of their capacity. This was a major handicap in constructing the Trockner Steg since the metalwork for the three pylons alone weighed 320 tons. Consequently much of the work had to be carried up by a specially erected "slave" cable car. Even this proved laborious work. First a helicopter carried up a "leader" rope a third of an inch thick. This was used to drag up successively graduated cables culminating with the actual track cables of one and a half inch diameter. All this was, though, a marked improvement on the Mont Blanc enterprise which started with a cord a tenth of an inch thick dragged all the way up by a guide.

The top station of the Trockner Steg is linked on the Italian side by another cable car arising from Cervinia. Building the stations, along with the linking tunnel, entailed blasting out 3,000 cu. m. of earth and rock which then had to be replaced by 2,000 cu. m. of cement and concrete.

The sheer cold presented formidable problems of its own. The concrete had to be mixed at the lower station. Not only was it mixed with hot water but also with antifreeze before being taken up in insulated containers. Even then the workmen had only three minutes in which to pour it into the moulds. Taking account of all this the cost was a cool 80 m. francs.

The proliferation and variety of lifts inevitably brought its disasters. It is surprisingly rare for the cable to snap, so rare in fact, that there have been more emergencies caused by dare-do pilots. In 1961, one of them tried to show off by flying under the lift on l'Aguille du Midi atop Mont Blanc. He clipped the supporting cable with his wing leaving the gondolas suspended solely by the traction cable. It took 24 hours to inch all the passengers to safety. Embarrassingly the pilot, who was killed, turned out to be the son of the Defence Minister.

A similar catastrophe occurred in 1998 at the Italian resort of Cavalese. The cable car cabin crashed 650 ft into the valley. Amazingly there was a survivor, a little girl whose fall was cushioned by the bodies of the 42 adults. This time the pilot was American and he survived. The plane's black box was found but was unaccountably "damaged". The altimeter was said to have been malfunctioning, but there was nothing to substantiate the claim. Even so, people were astounded and the villagers of Cavalese furious when the pilot was exonerated by a court martial sitting far away in the United States.

One potential disaster was averted when a suicidal extrovert thoughtfully gave warning that he was going to crash his plane into the Zugspitze. The cable car was hastily halted while, true to his word, he smashed his Piper PA 28 into the rockface.

The enormous amounts of money now generated by the ski industry made it economic to introduce a phenomenally expensive hybrid lift: a funicular enclosed in a tunnel.

The first to be constructed for the ski industry was the Sunnegga at Zermatt. It was on the cutting edge of technology. When rising diagonally, a tunnel tends to pierce more strata than is encountered in conventional horizontal working. The Sunnegga found its first problem in a field of chloritec schist. The density ranged from mere soft to actual sloppiness. While it enabled drilling to progress much faster it also meant the roof had to be shored up with hundreds of additional supports and anchors. In complete contrast, other sections passed through granite which reduced progress to 1 cm. a minute. Working at a gradient, sometimes as steep as 63 deg., presented another formidable problem. Had even a small piece of rock broken free or a piece of equipment worked loose, it would have crashed the length of the tunnel wreaking death and injury among those working lower down.

Like most tunnels the final cost was more than double the original estimate of 6.5 m francs. The actual tunnelling was to have taken up 30 per cent of the total. However with all the unexpected problems, it in fact took up 50 per cent.

The tunnel up La Grande Motte from Val Claret is the longest of all. It was designed to serve the Olympic crowds. But the inevitable problems caused the opening to be postponed until the year after.

A train in a tunnel requires a lot of special measures. The noise in such a confined place would normally be deafening. So the rails in the Sunnegga Express had to be hermit welded and mounted on special sound absorbing blocks. Air pressure was another concern. The gap between rail and tunnel wall is little more than in the London tube and the train has a specially designed snub nose. Even so it requires two sets of doors in the valley station to contain the excessive draught.

The nearest comparable form of lift is the cable car which is considerably cheaper to construct. However, because there are no pylons to negotiate, the funicular can be run much faster at up to 80 km an hour. Since much of the weight is borne by the rail, it can carry two or more railway carriage loads at a time which amounts to more than 2,500 skiers an hour. A cable car with a capacity of 120 cannot transport more than 750 an hour. Then there are advantages through having the rail run through a tunnel. The service can be continued regardless of weather conditions. Protection from the elements reduces maintenance costs by about a half.

Val d'Isére chose a hybrid funicular for the bottom section of the Funival is on concrete stilts. The same composite was built at Kaprun. In such situations, however, there are no bottom doors. So when in the year 2000 fire broke out in the Kaprun tunnel, the flow of air up the semi-vertical chimney created a super blow torch. It turned what had been assumed to be a fireproof metal box into a red hot tomb for 180 skiers.

The sheer quantity of ski traffic was at last forcing the abandonment of the books of tickets. It cut out the hassle of counting and tearing out coupons according to the length of the lift. Instead there were week-end or one or two week abonnements. These were, in due course, replaced by plastic cards which could be sucked in and spewed out by an electronic scanner. Unfortunately progress in the development of these marvels of modern science were initially stymied by an old and apparently insoluble problem. The village fathers refused even to consider the idea of sharing their slopes and lifts with their traditional enemies in the next valley. At La Plagne the animosity raged even between villages set on the same mountain face. No. On no account were those animosities, so lovingly nurtured down the centuries, to be put aside so easily.

Courchevel's founding fathers had anticipated this snag back in 1947. They had hoped that in time the lure of money would overcome such traditional prejudices. It did eventually, but they could hardly have imagined that it would take quarter of a century.

The inter-village spats stayed on merely taking a more subtle form.

When the brash young Avoriaz was brought into the Portes du Soleil complex, sedate old Morzine just down the valley, viewed it with such disdain it refused to include a picture in its brochure. If Tignes could possibly claim there was too little snow, it would refuse to run the interlinking lift thereby excluding Val d'Isére skiers from the higher slopes. It would then add insult to injury by charging abonnement holders a further but "reduced" rate.

But ticket scanners are costly and no one these days feels the urge to climb a mountain just to avoid paying. So it made sense for tickets to be shown only at the valley station. A few roving inspectors with authority to collect hefty on-the-spot fines deterred any would-be gatecrashers.

Whereas conventional turnstiles cannot be twiddled more than about 500 times an hour the new system could cope with 143,000 skiers a day. The full value was analysed by Verbier accountants. Back in 1970 a staff of 200 oversaw the transport of 750,000 visitors up almost a million ft. of ski lift. Ten years later and seven million skiers were being transported over 1,360,000 ft., yet there were only 30 additional staff.

So instead of too many people queuing for too few lifts, too many lifts were soon delivering too many people. The Tommeuse was fed by an eight person gondelhahn from Tignes, a double three-seater chair lift from Val d'Isére and a single three-seater chairlift from Val Claret. Altogether almost a hundred people per minute were being decanted on to the one spot. With just the two trajectories down, there was a severe shortage of snow slope.

The Tyrol has quantified their maximum density at 300 sq. m. of piste per skier. Resorts in the United States have set the acceptable densities at between 150 and 390 sq m. France, Italy and Switzerland no longer dare publish such details.

Unfortunately not everyone can be like Lee Kun-hee, owner of Samsung Electronics. He took over three runs at Courchevel for two hours each day for three weeks. It cost him £40,000 - not much when one is a £2.2 billionaire. He was hardly a bashful beginner for he had an entourage of 80 - plus two ski instructors. He was more concerned over avoiding injury and, presumably, he counted on deference to ensure his employees kept at a safe distance.

Actually his gesture had a precedent. During the early days of Sun Valley Gary Cooper and Clark Gable rented the Ruud lift for one entire day.

Altogether it was hardly surprising that skiers all over the Alps sought an alternative to being part of the herd. Several of the options, however, require extended training and a degree of fitness far beyond the ordinary holiday skier. They include freestyle, mogul racing and the flying kilometre.

As early as 1913 Axel Henriksen had been giving exhibitions throughout the United States, somersaulting on skis. The stunt was more recently popularised through a postcard showing an

The first somersault on skis was demonstrated by Axel Henrichsen in the United States in 1913

airborne Stein Eriksen upside down.

Following another trail during the mid 'twenties, the Americans Bruce Bleakney and Ab Chilcott were experimenting with double tipped skis and making 360 deg. turns. But it was not until 1971 that it all came together as freestyle and was accepted in competition. By this time there were defined figures such as "the helicopter" and "front flip twist". The somersaulters had discarded the conventional slightly downward inclined take-off platform in favour of a snow structure with a vicious upward hook. This opened up high diving techniques. Somersaults were now doubled and could incorporate tucks, twists. and jack knifes.

The first races down a mogul field were held in 1971 at Waterville and Aspen.

The first straight line "flying kilometre" was held at St.Moritz in 1930. The Austrian Gustav Lantschner won it at 65 mph. After the Second World War the event was transferred to Cervinia where records were constantly being broken and speeds duly reached 100 mph. Today it means accelerating faster than most cars to reach 125 mph within seven seconds.

At such speeds, the skis barely touch the surface and, indeed, sometimes skim above it.

The aerodynamic position is a low crouch, hands together and forwards to help spear the airstream over the specially curved helmet. All clothing overlaps, such as the top of the boots, are masked with tape. Even so wind resistance is so strong the skier has a struggle not to be blown backwards and the slightest shift in position is enough to swerve off the track.

The ideal wind tunnel position has the head between the knees. The only problem is it prevents the skier from seeing. When the Italian Walter Mussner tried it he skied straight into one of the timing devices and was killed. Another death occurred at Les Arcs during trials when the flying kilometre was being introduced as a demonstration event in the 1992 Olympics.

At one point hang gliding on skis became a popular alternative. Much enthusiasm, though, can be dampened by such irksome matters as threading the 20 ft poles through the cable car window.

In contrast, the croissant shaped canopy for paragliding folds into a normal rucksack. It is also claimed to be a much safer sport. The canopy automatically reflates after freefall of 300 ft. But 299 ft. falls have not proved as fatal as unexpected downdraughts which slam helpless paragliders against rock faces.

A far more congenial alternative for the ordinary holiday skier is snowboarding.

Snowboarders, as against surfers, set their feet sideways so that they have to look over one shoulder. It was first practised in the United States by ocean surfing enthusiasts Jack Barford and Tom Sims. Control is almost entirely dependent on using the edges. It calls for the pronounced and energetic use of the upper body. So it appeals mainly to the younger generation. Perhaps its greatest asset is the ability to rip through deep snow which is too heavy to appeal to the ordinary skier. The proficient snowboarder has a penchant for banks. The ideal is to have the feet above the head. The nomenclature is no less individual with such phrases as "upside downers" and "off the lips". Snowboarding quickly crossed the Atlantic and found formidable practitioners in Austria and Switzerland. In France, however, development was initially retarded as a petulant ski school insisted that instruction could only be through their monitors. The problem was the monitors were ignorant of the niceties.

Indeed for a ridiculously long time both the skill and popularity of snowboarding were refused proper recognition. Skiers were haughty over such a nouveau sport. They looked upon it as an inferior appendage to ski-ing. Occasional bad manners were seized upon to give the entire concept a bad name. But it was wrong and snowboarding quickly acquired a life of its own. Certainly board construction and particularly the surface of the sole were directly derived from ski manufacture. So the sport never underwent all the years of experiment and development, not to mention fashion, which has contributed so much to ski-ing tradition. Nor has its quick development thrown up generations of eccentrics.

Other conventional skiers who have become fed up with rattling down the piste have discovered the lure of deep snow. A variation is to ski among the trees. It is reputed that a private, being taught winter combat during the First World War, found himself ignominiously head in the snow; skis in the branches of a fir. On being disentangled he coined the numiculture "Do you call this ski-ing? I call it bird nesting". An even more dangerous variation is to play off piste catch ball. Just how dangerous was illustrated when one of the American Kennedy tribe momentarily focussed more on the ball than the tree trunks and was killed.

More conventional off piste excursions have led to a major increase in avalanche casualties. A large avalanche can incorporate 12,000 tons of snow shooting down the mountainside at 180 mph.

One of the earliest recorded avalanches wiped out the village of Les Hameaux in 1767. Today a few piled stones and a plaque set in a rock between Val d'Isére and Le Fornet mark where it roared down from the Roche Blanche. It obliterated 12 stone hovels smothering all the inhabitants.

The full horror of a lethal avalanche has been recorded on film. It was above St.Moritz when a group of international racers had been working on an advertisement for Bognor stretch pants. As they cross the lower slopes the snow can be seen starting to break up "flowing like thick soup over the rocks". Willi Bognor skied down and turned left to find protection behind a rock. Barbi Henneberger started to follow but fell. Konrad Bartelski skied straight down, out distanced the avalanche and shot up a bank opposite. He and Bognor survived. The others are seen being caught up and swept along so that eventually all 12, including the cameraman, were smothered in the all enveloping snow.

Perhaps the most famous avalanche involved Prince Charles and his party at Klosters in 1998. In his official statement, the Prince wrote:

"The avalanche started with a tremendous roaring. Bruno Sprecher, Charles Palmer-Tomkinson, the Swiss policeman and myself all managed with great good fortune to ski to one side. To my horror, Major Lindsay and Mrs. Palmer-Tomkinson were swept away in a whirling maelstrom as the whole mountainside seemed to hurtle past us into the valley below. It was all over in a terrifying matter of seconds. Herr. Sprecher acted with incredible speed and total professionalism. He skied down as fast as possible having told the Swiss policeman to radio for assistance. Having reached the bottom of the avalanche, he found Mrs. Palmer-Tomkinson, using the audio phone radio and detection device. Mr. Palmer-Tomkinson and I skied down and just arrived as Herr. Sprecher had reached Mrs. Palmer-Tomkinson. He gave her mouth to mouth resuscitation and revived her. He gave me the shovel to dig her out and I tried using my hands as well. At this point I sat with Mrs. Palmer-Tomkinson while he quickly went to try and locate Major Lindsay. He found him about 15 yards above but tragically he had been killed outright from the fall despite Herr. Sprecher's valiant attempts to revive him."

James Riddell has also written a horrifyingly graphic description:

"At this point, with the Col less than an hour's climb ahead, there came the terrible crack and thunder of an avalanche from in front and above the climbers. The party came to an abrupt standstill as one thousand feet of ice and snow broke away from the west wall of the Lyskamm high up above and began its downward plunge straight in their direction. My first reaction, after the missed heart-beat that the sound of an avalanche always brings, was to stare in astonishment at the majesty of the spectacle before one. I realised that I was witnessing, this time from a ringside seat, a sight that I had often seen from afar - a large scale avalanche in the Alps - and the sight of this vast white turbulence was so breathtakingly beautiful that for a moment one stood in a condition of amazement and admiration. Although the impetus of this tremendous downrush of huge quantities of ice and snow was very considerable, things seemed to be happening very slowly. One was aware of the noise, but only vaguely - in the first moment it was only the majesty of the spectacle that mattered...then quite suddenly came the realisation that there was nothing to prevent this beautiful but terribly lethal instrument from sweeping down on top of us and engulfing our entire party."

It was only due to a concealed crevasse further up the mountain, which absorbed most of the moving snow, that James Riddell lived to recount this experience.

Professor Roget has defined a slope as dangerous if it looks too steep for a cow to graze on it. Then there are the exceptional situations which really do involve animals. Chamois at the top of a couloir have been known to scrabble to bring down an avalanche on a skier they consider to be trespassing on their territory.

The several ways devised by man to precipitate a controlled avalanche are not much different. Troops fighting on the Austrian Italian border during the First World War adopted similar tactics. It has been estimated that the two nations between them smothered 2,000 troops solely through man induced avalanches.

At one time Kitzbühel ski instructors were expected to rope together in groups of five. One would jump up and down on the crucial spot. The other stalwarts took the strain and hopefully prevented him from being carried away. Another hair raising procedure was for the instructor to ski across the top. It was to be fervently hoped the snow would not start sliding prematurely while he was still crossing. If it did not start at all he had the infinitely more perilous job of making the return trip.

Rather more scientific methods use a rocket or an air gun. These can be traced back to the start of the century when a cannon was positioned in the middle of Grindelwald. Visitors could at any time pay a franc to fire a shell in the hope of setting off an avalanche. The roar of the occasional success, would bring people to their windows and drinkers out of the bars clutching their glasses. Occasionally there was double value as the sheer sound triggered a subsidiary avalanche.

Today cannons are used with more logic. The shells have minimal loading so that they do not compound the risk should they fail to explode. An unexploded shell smothered in soft snow becomes infinitely more dangerous. Alternatively detonators with a timing device are lowered from helicopters. Areas which are particularly prone to avalanche, such as the Valluga above St. Anton, have the entire shoulder crowned by a cable loop mounted on pylons. The charge is carried round until it reaches the required spot where it is lowered to the ideal height of 80 cm. above the snow before being detonated.

With thousands of skiers rattling down the runs there can be serious financial loss should their pleasure be interrupted. Piste up-keep became a major concern. The ingenuous rollers designed by Allais at Courchevel and Payert at St. Anton were hopelessly inadequate. Instead there was the Swiss Ratrac. It is, in effect, a small tank and the caterpillar tracks enable it to ascend slopes so steep it raises fears it may overturn. It weighs over a ton and can pound its way through a spent avalanche piled 20 ft. high. So it easily compresses snow into a compacted iced piste capable of withstanding pounding by 10,000 skis a day. A plough harrow is tacked on behind to give the surface a cosmetic ruffle.

Although they travel at no more than six mph, Courchevel invested in so many that within a season they clock up 11,000 miles - the distance to Tokyo and back.

The cost is in a completely different category from Allais and Payert's humble rollers. At more than £100,000 apiece, many of the smaller resorts, particularly in Switzerland, have formed co-operatives in the style of farmers and combine harvesters. None the less it is an economic investment. Having strong headlights and a heated cab, work can be carried on throughout the night. It makes good use of those hours when the runs are clear of skiers.

When skiers fell in olden days they made holes in the snow. Today they hit solid ice. It has resulted in a major increase in shoulder injuries.

This factor is compounded by snow cannon. Although artificial snow should not be in a ratio above one of refrigerant to five water, The high moisture content in effect produces ice.

Snow cannon were initially installed to allow ski-ing right down to the village even late in the season. Like so many developments in ski-ing, they were invented in gloriously amateur fashion. The 1959 snow season in Connecticut was so sparse that Wayne Pierce started experimenting with different types of nozzle on his garden hose. He succeeded in producing snow but there was an accompanying high pitched whistle which dogs in particular found disagreeable. However by the next season the nozzle proved sufficiently reliable and quiet to be tested in two local resorts.

These early commercial cannon could produce snow only while the temperature was close to freezing. By incorporating computers it became possible to regulate the vital proportions of air, water and refrigerant into a more reliable freeze mix. However the refrigerant was polluting the earth. The solution was to pulverise just air and water so as to produce a mist rather than droplets. When this is discharged over distances between 10 and 20 m. it forms snow at any temperature below zero.

During the night 20 guns can nicely cover one km. of piste with 50,000 cu.m. of snow. Courchevel went on to install sufficient guns to keep entire runs in a good state even in the meanest snow conditions. No less impressive was the installation of 850 guns over the entire Via Lattea covering its international stretch between Sestriere and Montgenèvre.

Each gun processes 170 cu. m. of water an hour. To meet this almost insatiable demand, Courchevel has a 45 m. cubic metre reservoir. It has been ingeniously landscaped as a lake set just above the village. But in many resorts the demand and displacement is upsetting the water tables.

Indeed the piste has become the enemy of the environment. Most are sited close to the tree line at around 6,000 ft. At this height it is difficult even under natural conditions for vegetation to thrive. Erecting just one ski lift with its attendant runs entails heavy tree felling, earth moving and rock blasting. In many places the subsequent soil erosion has caused landslides which easily end up in a river bed. In 1957 unusually heavy rain caused mud and rocks to slip into the Isere. It created a terrifying wall of water seven metres high which rolled down the village street, floating cars and tearing the fronts off shops and houses.

Global warning is an additional and often unrecognised threat. The Belveda Glacier in Italy had melted to form a 900 m gallon lake. It was only by chance that it was discovered. Had it burst it would have swept away the little ski village of Macugnaga. The danger was averted by flying up three gigantic pumps to reduce the water level.

It has been calculated that global warning will have increased temperatures by four deg. by 2080. This will raise the snow line from 400 m. up to between 1,500 and 1750 m. above sea level. The trend has been proved in Scotland. Persistent lack of snow in the Cairngorms has made ski-ing so unreliable that now Aviemore opens largely in the summer. It threatens, too, the long term prospect for several major resorts such as Kitzbühel, St.Gervais and Gstaad. Andermatt has even conducted experiments with sheets of pvc to insulate the Stockli glacier from the summer sun.

The greens, particularly in Austria, have brought considerable pressure to bear. One of the most vigilant is Alp Alert, largely sponsored by the Aga Kahn, himself a keen skier.

They have had major successes. The construction of ski runs in the upper reaches above Nagano in Japan had already forced monkeys to move lower and occupy man inhabited areas. However the animals were in luck for they found some natural hot springs. But their migration had sounded the alarm. When the start of the downhill run for the Nagano Olympics threatened the lairs of bears, the Greens succeeded in having the course lowered.

In Switzerland, regulations have become so stringent it is almost impossible to construct a new cable car.

The major enlargement of resorts is another contribution to pollution. The French instituted a five year ban on all ski station development. However village mayors have a way of getting round such legislation.

Controversy over such major development is by no means new. But initially the protests were for humanitarian rather than environmental reasons. During the Second World War the French Government decided to construct a reservoir as part of a major Tarantaise hydro-electric scheme. Initially the threat of submersion hung equally over Tignes and Val d'Isére. Tignes claimed to be a ski resort. Indeed they had a dozen pensions and a hotel, a ski school with eight instructors and a ski lift. Desperate for self preservation, Val d'Isére had to do better. As it happened construction had already been started on a cable car up the Solaise. The project had, though, been halted on the outbreak of war. So the inhabitants surreptitiously re-started the work. Cable, however, was a vital commodity in the war effort and its use was strictly controlled. None the less some was found at Bourg en Bresse. Normally about one and a half hours by car, this journey was somewhat different. It meant transporting a load of 24 tons along winding and often ill kept roads which included four hairpin bends. And it all had to be done without raising the suspicions of the ever vigilant Gestapo. By November 1942 it was all in place and ready to go. Tignes had no hope.

After an appeal to Marshal Petain had failed, the 400 villagers offered every sort of resistance. They lay down in the path of the bulldozers. There was outrage when graves in the churchyard were removed to Les Boisses. Even after the water had started to flow several householders refused to move until their groundfloor was under water. One man appeared on the balcony of his doomed house brandishing a gun and threatening to shoot anyone who tried to rescue him. It required two policemen and considerable guile to get him to safety.

Construction of the dam was both formidable and dramatic. It is 180 ft. high and has a rim thick enough to carry a dual carriageway. There had to be accommodation for 5,000 men working in three reliefs around the clock. The building still exists in the form of barrack-like holiday apartments at Les Boisses. The twisting approach road proved quite inadequate for bringing up all the necessary materials. So a temporary 15 km. telepherique was successfully built from the lowland town of Bourg St.Maurice.

Almost like a legend, people still claim that when conditions are right, they can see the shade of the church tower beneath the water. It is fantasy for the tower was demolished along with the rest of the buildings.

The villagers moved into new and much superior homes up the mountain. It became the highest ski resort in Europe, and proved so popular Val Claret was built as a satellite even further up the valley.

A major ecological disaster occurred at Zermatt. This one, though, was precipitated through human greed. The outlay for increasing the number of ski lifts was proving alarmingly heavy. So the fatal decision was made to postpone modernising the village sewerage system. The fruits of this parsimony burst upon the village in the winter of 1963. A faulty pipe allowed sewage from military barracks higher up the mountain to contaminate the drinking water. There was an outbreak of typhoid. The first cases occurred three or four weeks before the Gornergrat Derby which always brought a profitable number of visitors. The village authorities did all in their power to hush up the danger. Patients were surreptitiously moved into isolation in the village school. Though normally there was little traffic on the line, the special trains taking them to hospital were scheduled for four and five in the morning.

The number of cases rose. But even after they had reached 400 the authorities still refused to take any precautions that might reveal the true situation. Eventually the Swiss Hotelkeepers Association had to intervene and order all hotels and restaurants to be closed. But good fortune, no matter how little deserved, attended their efforts and the next winter there was a positive increase in the number of visitors.

Ski-ing had become a major industry. Not only was it affecting the very fabric of village community but it brought some villages close to extinction.

Even after the Second World War the traditional resorts still received the greater part of their income from summer visitors. But gentians and distant snow capped peaks were rapidly losing their attraction. Increasing affluence and the development of charter air lines were encouraging holiday makers to look further afield for novelty and for sunshine that is reliable.

At the same time enormous investments were tilting village economics further askew towards a greater winter income. In 1984 Zermatt was at heart still a small village, yet it totted up a turnover of £65m. Almost all of this was generated during the winter. When Albertville won the bid for the 1992 Winter Olympics it was financed by some £625m; £100m. of it was provided by the Government. Most of it was spent enhancing the winter attractions.

Old Tignes before it was submerged by the hydro electric barrage

Those villagers who have retained their property have often invested savings in other hotels, shops and restaurants. So it is in their interest to attract ever more visitors. They also usually hold important places on the council. As a result the resorts have become too large for their natural environment.

Commercialisation has indeed changed the peasant outlook. Having acquired a thirst for gold, the Zermatt bourgeoisie noted with envy how often pictures of the Matterhorn, particularly as seen from their side, appeared in reproductions. So they bethought themselves to claim a royalty. The court rejected their application; hardly surprising since the creator's 70 year copyright had run out some thousand millenniums before.

The loss of summer tourists affected the hotels in particular. Traditionally their economy depended on spreading overheads across two seasons. Now they have barely half the time. Unlike ski lifts, hotels have not been able to shed their intensive labour costs. On the contrary, they find themselves between the proverbial sheer rock of legislation and the precipice of union demands. Staff had to be increased and there were dramatic wage increases. The Palace Hotel at St.Moritz has long held it a matter of pride that a bell rung in a bedroom is answered within 30 seconds. To maintain this sort of standard now requires 400 employees - more than one to each guest. Combine these staff levels with the high maintenance necessary for old premises and the costs become enormous.

So hotels have largely been overtaken by visitors leasing privately owned flats in apartment blocks. Also travel agents started renting chalets and bringing their own staff with them. Pioneer of this movement was Colin Murison-Small. He started his business in the ample spare time accorded to civil servants. He would make surreptitious trips to the barrier, number one platform, Victoria Station to bid his clients bon voyage. He instituted the chalet girl who duly acquired the title of Muribird. His idea was quickly adopted by others all dipping into a large source of debs who had attended expensive cooking classes. The debs were prepared to work like skivvies and had indulgent parents prepared to underwrite their pittance of a wage all so that they could ski every afternoon. One such distinguished chalet belonged to the racing driver Paddy McNally. His guests included the Marquess of Blandford, Michael Pearson of the Financial Times publishing conglomerate and Hugo Ferranti of the electronics company. The chalet girl looking after them all was Sarah Ferguson, later to become Duchess of York..

By 1993 the call for chalet girls had outgrown the deb circle and there were 6,000 girls playing an essential part for such major agents as Supertravel and John Morgan. The older and more experienced would gravitate to Klosters, Chamonix and Courchevel. The trendier ones seemed to favour Val d'Isére, Tignes and Verbier.

Then there was the army of ski bums. After electronic wizardry rendered them redundant they undertook any maintenance work so long as it kept them in cash for the season.

Unfortunately they sometimes rather lowered the ton of the British. There was the occasion at St.Anton when a group ascended the Rendl ski lift. At the top they took off all their clothes, excepting their ski boots and their ski passes which they hung strategically in place of a fig leaf. While a fellow conspirator took their clothes to a place among the trees close to the bottom, the group yodelled their starkers way down. Unfortunately they were photographed, recognised, and were duly arrested and fned.

Curling in the shadow of the Matterhorn

The stomach churning view from the start into the Planica ski jump

Initially the locals tried to counter this invasion of foreign labour. If any chalet staff were overheard giving advice to skiers they were in serious trouble with the local ski school. So as not to undermine local bars, chalets were were refused licenses. One agency tried to circumvent the problem by having all drinks on the slate, payment to be made at the end of the holiday, theoretically when back in Britain. Unfortunately an innocent invited some young men back for a drink and they turned out to be the local police. The chalet girl together with the agent's area representative spent the night in the St.Anton police cells.

But the threat to local employment became just as much a national problem. Previously visitors had eaten almost exclusively in their hotel or pension restaurants. But chalet girls want one night off each week and tenants in apartments want occasional relief from self catering. So restaurants proliferated and chain caterers were soon appearing, Macdonalds at Kitzbühel and Movenpick at St. Anton. There was, too, the demand for ingredients and dry goods. Soon Migros and Unita became as much household names as Tesco and Sainsbury.

However while business increased enormously, it was concentrated within the few months of the winter season. The big shops found it uneconomic to stay open throughout the rest of the year. Consequently they failed to provide employment for the locals. In the larger resorts even the police require seasonal recruitment from lowland cities to help control the Christmas, New Year and Easter traffic jams.

A few villages can provide summer labour. Maintenance on the Wengen and Grindelwald rack and pinion railway keep instructors employed during the summer. Not that they like it. As Gods of the Snow, they turn away should they think a summer visitor might recognise them.

Emile Allais was also careful to provide summer piste maintenance for his ski instructors. He was prompted to do this when he learnt that skiers prefer their instructors to be locals rather than from the lowlands or students brought up from a nearby university. As a result, four out of every ten instructors in the Courchevel ski school actually live in the village throughout the year while a further 50 per cent live within the region. So only 20 out of the total 200 can be considered outsiders.

The trend away from hotels to chalets and apartment blocks has destroyed village life in yet another way. Most mountain land is too stony to sustain crops and can only be used for grazing. So when the area suddenly becomes ripe for building development, prices rise dramatically. At Chamonix the ground was at one time priced at one or two francs a square metre. Come fashion and within a few years the price shot up to between 70 and 100 francs. If a resort is chosen for the Olympics, prices may easily double. The hitherto unknown satellite resorts around Grenoble tripled in value.

At Val d'Isére the mayor issued building permits in wild profusion and increased the number of beds from 15,000 to 25,000. Prices declined and even four years later, notices of bargain offers were still appearing in curtainless windows. Some of the farming families could not cope with such turbulence, sold their inheritance and became the victim of the nouveaux riches, such as alcoholism.

Those who did not own property also had their tribulations. Increased values put rented premises way beyond what they could reasonably afford. After 35 years, only one of the inhabitants of the old village was still living in the modern Tignes.

How amazingly the face of ski-ing has changed over a century. From the time when Christopher Iselin could only escape ridicule by ski-ing after dark to when a hundred million viewers watch the Olympics; from entire mornings spent wearily climbing just to snatch a few minutes winging down the slope to now when lifts and cable cars whisk skiers up the mountain and " Everests" are performed each day. Only a fool would predict what ski-ing will be like at the end of this twenty first century. One thing, however, is certain: so long as there is little more than boot sole thickness between the human frame and a fleeting glittering frozen surface, joy will fill the human heart.

BIBLIOGRAPHY

Arosa by J.B.Casti. Verlag und Verkehrseverein
Aspects of Arosa by Gunnar Johnston. F.Junginger-Hefti

British Ski Yearbook

Courchevel a Vingt Ans

Crans - Montana by M. Bagnoud & A.F.Barras. CRA Editions

Cresta Run 1885-1985 by Roger Gibbs. Henry Melland

D H O Journal

Engadine Year Book, 1908

From Skisport to Ski-ing by E.John B.Allen. University of Massachusetts Press

History of Ski-ing by Arnold Lunn. Eyre & Spottiswoode

Ice Skating, a History by Nigel Brown. Nicholas Kaye International Encyclopaedia of Winter
    Sports by Howard Bass. Pelham Books

Kandahar Review

Modernising Switzerland's Funiculars. Brown Boverie Neige Automatiq. York S.A.

New Offcial Austrian Ski System. The Association of Professional Ski Teachers

Our Skating Heritage by Dennis L. Bird. National Skating Association of Great Britain

Palace Hotel by Raymond Flower. Debrett

Planica by Drago Ulaga, Stane Urek & Marko Rozman. Mladinska Knjiga

Present Indicative by Noël Coward. Heinemann

Ringside Seat,JamesAllason.TimewellPress

St.Anton Ski Museum. Erwin Cimarolli

Short Guide of Davos. Davos Tourist Offce.

The Skaters Cavalcade by Arthur C Wade. Olympic Publications Ski Notes & Queries

Ski Runs of Austria by James Riddell. Michael Joseph

Ski Runs of Switzerland by James Riddell. Michael Joseph

Ski Survey

Ski-ing Heritage. Vol. 18 no 1 and others. International Skiing History Association, New Hartford.

Ski-ing Monthly

Snow Business by Emmanuel Carcano. Tetras Editions

Snow Crazy by Arnie Wilson. Metro Publishing.

Story of Ski-ing by Arnold Lunn. Eyre & Spottiswoode

Story of Ski-ing and Other Sports by Raymond Flower

Switzerland. Swiss National Tourist Office

Taki Theodoracopulos, "Spectator" articles

Tramway Guide. Von Roll.

Where the World Ends by A.A.H. Junginger-Hefti

Winter Sports in Switzerland. Swiss National Tourist Office Zermatt Saga by Cicely Williams. Rotten-Ve

INDEX

A

Abbonements 124
ABS Royalite 114
Abyssinia 47
Adalbert of Prussia, Prince 23
Adams, Bernard 75
Adelboden 43
Aga Khan 82, 85, 129
Agnelli, Giovanni 47, 103
Aguille du Midi, Mont Blanc 122
Ailsa Craig 17
Air Canada 30, 115
Albertville 130
Allais, Emile 63, 92, 93, 98, 99, 100, 128, 135
Allmendhubel, Mürren 51
Allmen, Heinz & Otto von 54
Allues, Les 104
Alp Alert 129
Alpbach 79
Alpina Hotel, Mürren 52
Alpina, Ski Club, St.Moritz 27
"Alpine Ski Guide to the Bernese Oberland" 27
Alt Post Hotel, St.Anton 63, 81, 83
Altwegg, Jeannette 91
American International Underwriters 102
Amstutz, Max 52
Amstutz spring 63
Amstutz, Walter 89
Andermatt 54, 62, 129
Andrew, Grand Duke 23
Andrew, Prince 83
Andrews, Julie 103
Angas, L.L.B. 57
Anglo-Swiss Parliamentary Ski Meeting 86
Annemarie of Greece, Queen 82
Anschluss 78, 79, 86
Anstey, Colonel 38
Apres ski 40
Arcs, Les 103, 106, 108, 111, 125

Argentine Tango 76
Arlberg crouch 60, 61, 63
Arlberg Kandahar race 79, 116, 121
Arosa 1, 2, 3, 4, 5, 6, 7, 9, 10, 12, 13, 14, 15, 16, 17, 22, 23, 25, 27, 30, 31, 33, 40, 42, 43, 44, 45, 53, 60, 68, 77, 96, 112, 120, 121, 127, 135, 137
Aspen, U.S.A. 88, 125
Astor, John Jacob 33, 36
Attenhoffer 27, 94, 95
Austro-Hungarian Empire 66
Aviemore 120, 129
Avoriaz 103, 111, 124

B

Badrutt, Caspar 24, 33
Badrutt, Johannes 10, 13, 24
Bainter, T.C. 48
Bandy 18, 19, 30, 33, 77, 82
Barclay, Florence 21, 36
Bardot, Brigitte 89
Barford, Jack 125
Bartelski, Konrad 126
Bartock, Eva 86
Basualdo, Luis 102
Baudouin, King of the Belgians 84, 103
Baxter, Alain 119, 120
Bear Hotel, Grindelwald 6, 38
Beau Rivage Hotel, St.Moritz 24
Bedford, Duchess of 38
Bedford, Duke of 104
Bees, Baron 66
Beetle Club, Mürren 48
Belgians, Queen of the 60
Bellevue Hotel, Grindelwald 43
Belvedere Hotel, Davos 11
Benaschak, Brent 88
Benatsky, Ralph 63
Benson, E.F. 76

Berlin 18, 29
Bibbia, Nino 89
Billiard Table, Pontresina 25
Biner Family 4
Blanc, Jean 98, 105
Blandford, Marquess of 132
Bleakney, Bruce 125
Bledisloe, Lord 35
Bobsleigh 31, 36, 45, 73, 74, 87, 89, 90
Bogner, Willie 126
Bon, Anton 25
Bond, James 109
Bosch 6, 16, 38
Bott, J.A. 18, 33, 35, 43
Boughton-Leigh, Edgie 49, 50
Bourbon Parma, Prince of 82
Bourg en Bresse 129
Bourget, Le 108
Bourg St.Maurice 106, 130
Brabazon of Tara, Lord 89
Bracken, Bill 50, 55, 56, 59, 114, 121
Bradl, Josef 78
Bristol Hotel, Grindelwald 44
British Alpine Ski Championships 55
Brooklands, Wengen 52
Buhlmann, Christian 31
Bulgaria, Queen of 82
Bulpett, Major W.H. 33, 34, 35
Bumps, Wengen 45, 53
Bundage, Avery 116
Bunny Hug, The 68
Burberry 72
Burroughs & Watts 25
Bury, Viscount 28
Butlins Holiday Camp 18
Button, Dick 90
Byblos Hotel, Courchevel 83
Bylandt, Jules de 35
"Bystander, the" 69

C

Cable cars 47, 48, 97, 135
Caledonian Club 17
California 27, 95, 98
Callaway, Betty 92
Carlos, King Juan 83
Carlton Hotel, St.Moritz 25, 72
Casalta, Arlette 106
Caulfeild, Barry 114
Caulfeild, Vivian 26, 114
Cavalese 122, 123
Celerina 30, 32, 33, 34
Cervie Hotel, Zermatt 3

Cervinia 90, 107, 122, 125
Chair lifts 122
Chamonix 3, 59, 73, 74, 75, 80, 82, 132, 135
Chanel, Coco 86
Chantarella, St.Moritz 25, 45, 73, 102
Chapis, Laurent 106
Charles, Prince 83, 126
Charpentier, Georges 69
"Chatanooga Choo Choo" 75
Chesa Grischuna 83
Chibuhel, Marguard of 65
Christiania 27, 55
Chur 12, 15, 23, 24, 37
Churchill Junior, Winston 89
Cinerama 90
Circus, Kitzbühel 98
Citroen, Andre, 24, 107
Cobb, Humphrey 31
Colbert, Claudette 104
Colledge, Cecilia 75, 90
Collins, Joan 103
Combined Services Ski Club 85
"Complete Ski Runner, The" 59
Connecticut 128
Constantine, Eddie 89, 99
Constantine of Greece, King 82, 83
Cooper, Garry 104, 124
Cooper, Lady Diana 72
Corbier, Le 111
Cordle, John 87
Cornish 33
Cortina 42, 112, 117
Corviglia Club 85
Corviglia, Pitz, St.Moritz 45, 73, 85
Coubertin, Baron Pierre de 74, 119
Courchevel v, 83, 89, 93, 98, 104, 105, 106, 108,
        109, 111, 124, 128, 132, 135, 137
Courmayeur 88, 102
Courtauld, Stephen 38
Cousins, Robin 91
Coward, Noël v, 9, 27, 38, 48, 79, 85, 115, 137
Crans 13, 30, 137
Cresta v, 21, 34, 35, 36, 37, 40, 43, 73, 80, 89, 108,
        137
Crewdson, Di 50
Cross country ski-ing 113, 118
Crystal Hotel, St.Moritz 25
Cubberly, Mitch 115
Curling
        clubs 17
        rinks 30, 74
Curry, John 91, 117
Curzon, Hon F.N. 18, 33, 35
Cushing, Peter 118

D

Daille, La 107
Dalrymple, Donald 53
Davos 1, 2, 3, 9, 10, 11, 13, 14, 15, 17, 18, 23, 27, 30, 31, 43, 44, 46, 54, 75, 86, 96, 101, 121, 137
Davos Skating Club 17
Davos Ski Club 27, 54
Davos Toboggan Club 14
Dean, Christopher 92
Defsots family 63
d'Egville, Alan i, 51, 52, 59, 69, 116
DeHavilland Aircraft Company 94
Delasevers family 63
Denman Cup, Lady 54
Denny, Doreen 91
d'Estain, Giscard 86
Diana, Princess 83
Dibhah, Farah 82
Dixon, Robin 90
Dobbs, Leonard 55
Dod, Lottie 18
Dolly Sisters 44
Dom 7
Douglas, Lord Francis 4
Dowding, Air Marshal Lord 52, 90
Downhill Only Club 52, 121
Doyle, Sir Arthur Conan 2, 3, 20, 77
Drag lifts 97, 98, 122
Durrand, Miss 7
Durrell, Mavis 50

E

Eagle Club, Gstaad 85
Edinburgh, Duke of 86
Edlin, Freddy 58, 99
Edward, Prince 83
Edward, Prince of Wales 31, 67, 103
Edwards, Eddie the Eagle 119
Eggevert Cafe, Kitzbühel 67
Egypt 9, 102
Eiger 3, 4, 44
Elliot, Julius 5
Elliott, Doreen 50, 56, 73
Emmanuell, Prince & Princess Victor 82
Engadine 11, 12, 137
Engelberg 43, 61
Engelhard, Captain 108
"Englishman in the Alps" 59
Eriksen, Stein 82, 125
Evans, James 45

F

Falch, Robert 93
Fanck, Dr. Arnold 64
Farner, Sepp 93, 94
Farnham, Lord 103
Farouk, King 102
Fath, Jacques 106
Faulhorn Hotel, Grindelwald 7
Fearon, Robert & Henri 5
Federation International de Ski 55, 118
Fenns, the 14, 15
Ferdinand, Archduke Franz 18, 30
Ferguson, Sarah 132
Ferranti, Hugo 132
Ferranti, Lady 87; *See* Laing, Hilary
Festetics, Count Tassilo 29
Fiat 47
Fiske, Billy 80
Flaine 103, 107
Flims 101
Fluela Hotel, Davos 27
Flynn, Errol 89
Forarorri, Itio 47
Ford, Bernard 91
Ford, Henry 86
Fornet, Le 121, 126
"Forty Years On" 49
Foster, Ken v, 46, 53, 62
Fowler, Raymond 24' 68
"Fox Chase" 64, 65
Fox, Gerald 1
Fox, Tom 53
Franz-Joseph Tunnel, St.Anton 63
Funival Lift, Val d'Isére 123, 124
Furka Pass 2
Furse, Dame Katherine 26

G

Gallico, Paul v, 34
Galzigbahn, St.Anton 47
Gamage, Professor John 37
Ganga, Jean Claude 119
Garbo, Greta 83
Gardner, Charles 54
Garmisch, Partenkirchen 74, 75, 79
Gaulle, General Charles de 103
Geiger, Hermann 5
Geneva 5, 24, 92, 104
George VI, King 82
George V, King 31, 75
Gerschweiler, Arnold, 28, 75, 90
Gertsch, Oscar 53, 54
Gibson, Harvey 79

Glanner Head Waiter, Mürren Palace 51
Glarus 1
Glasgow Ice Rink 30
Gloucester, Duke of 75
Golden Greif, Kitzbühel 66
Goldsmith, Sir James 85
Gomme, Donald 94, 95
Gomperz 78
Gontrie, Pierre de la 105
Gornergrat Derby Race 130
Gornergrat Railway, Zermatt 64
Gossage Mirror 77
Goulandris, Aleco 102
Gower, David 89
Grafton, Duke of 103
Grande Motte, Val Claret 123
Grand Hotel, Adelboden 43
Grand Hotel, Kitzbühel 66
Grand Hotel, Morgins 31
Gredig brothers 24
Greenall, Peter 83
Greensmith & Downes 21
Greig, J. Keiller 38
Gremon, Lake 30
Grenandier, H. 38
Grenoble 90, 135
Griggs, W. 28
Grindelwald, 4, 5, 6, 13, 16, 31, 45, 53, 77, 120, 127,
    135, 138
Grisons 18, 23
Grove, General Sir Coleridge 18
Gruber, Peter 58
Gstaad 40, 43, 85, 101, 103, 129
Guerin, Christian 111
Guinness, Lady Evelyn 28
Guinness, Loel 102
Guler, Ruth 83
Gustav, King of Sweden 83

H

Hackett, General Sir John 89
Hahnenkamm, 46, 47, 59, 66' 98
Hahnenkamm, Kitzbühel 46, 47, 59, 66, 67, 98, 113
Hall, Henry 68
Hallyday, Johnny 111
Hampstead Heath 121
Hanselmann Cafe, St. Moritz 40
Harald, Burgomaster 66
Harding, Tonya 119
Harmsworth, Lady 28
Harriman, Averell 97, 103, 104
Harrods 63, 70, 71, 73, 95
Haute Savoie 104

Hawthorn, Gina 59
Head, Howard 95
"Hearts in the Snow" 63
Heimele, Baron 81
Helmsley, Lord 18
Henie, Sonja 73, 74, 75, 77, 91, 92, 116
Henneberger, Barbi 126
Henriksen, Axel 124
Henry of Reuss, Prince 23, 33
Hepburn, Katherine 83, 104
Hereford, Bishop of 43
Herwig, Otto 1, 9, 10
"High Speed Ski-ing" 59
Hill, Virginia 86
"Hindenberg Line," Mürren 54
Hinterseer, Ernst 112, 113
Hinterstadt, Kitzbühel 65
"History of Ski-ing" 59, 137
Hitchcock, Alfred 101
Hitler 74, 75, 78, 79
Hockey League, The International 31
Hogg, Gladys 91
Hogg, Quentin 44
"Hogg's Back", Mürren 48
Holkar of Indore, Maharanee 23
Holland, A. 18
Holland, Dr. 16
Hong Kong 102
Horstmann Band 88
"How To Ski" 26
Huber, Fritz 112
Hudson, Charles 4
Hudson Cup 30
Huitfeldt binding 62
Hunt, Sir John 87
Hutton, Barbara 69
Hutton, Miss 28

I

IBM 117
Ice Martins Club 90
Ice skating 92, 137
    Continental 37, 38, 39, 90
    dancing 38, 75, 76, 91, 119
    English 72, 76
    fashions 73
    hockey 19, 30, 31, 77, 82, 120
    rinks 30, 96, 118
Igls 32, 90
Imboden 107
Inferno Bar, Mürren 52
Inferno race, Mürren 89
Ingham Brothers 84

Innsbruck 18, 57, 86, 91, 94, 118
International Journalists Ski Club 87
International Police Federation Ski Meetings 88
International Racing Team 118
Iran, Shah & Empress of 82
Irvine, A.C. 49
Iselin, Christopher 1, 135
"Isle of Capri" 68

J

Jackson Cup 30
Jackson, L.F.W. 53
Jakobsenki 26
Jakobshorn, Davos 2
Jamieson, Bland 38
Jaun, Fritz 5
Joannides, J.A. 55
Johnson, J.H. 38
Jones, Aubrey 87
Jones, Courtney 91
Jordan Family 72
Juliana, Queen of Holland 83, 86, 103
Julier Pass 11, 107
Julier Ski Jump, St.Moritz 73
Jungfrau 4, 44, 45, 52, 54
Jungfraujoch 5

K

Kandahar Club, Mürren 53, 54
Kandersteg 30
Kaprun, 123
Kaps, Schloss, Kitzbühel 66
Karajan, Herbert von 102
Kaufmann, Peter 5
Keiller, Alex 28, 121
Kent, Duchess of 83
Kent, Prince Michael of 90
Kerrigan, Nancy 119
Kessler, Duncan 54
Kessler, Jeanette 56
Khashoggi, Adnan 85
Killy, Jean Claude 113
Kingsmill, Lady Diana 73
Kirchberg 48
"Kitchener's Crash", Mürren 54
Kitzbühel v, 18, 26, 27, 28, 30, 31, 32, 33, 46, 50, 59,
    65, 66, 67, 72, 78, 84, 85, 86, 92, 94, 98, 101,
    109, 112, 113, 121, 127, 129, 134
Kitzbühelerhorn 66
Klosters 10, 54, 83, 86, 121, 126, 132
Knappentanz Dance 68
Knebworth, Tony Viscount 54
Koflak Ski Sole 114

Krazy Kangaroo, St.Anton 88
Krobberger, Lilly 37
Kronenhof Hotel, Pontresina 24
Krukenhauser, Professor 100
Küblis 27, 58
Kulm Hotel, St.Mortiz 11, 18, 23, 39
Kun-hee, Lee 124

L

Ladies Open Championship, Ski 56
Lagazuoi Cable Car 42
Laing, Hilary 87
Lake Placid 74, 75, 91
Lamb, Allan 89
Lamberg, Countess Paula 28, 66, 76
Lamberg Family 28, 66, 76
"Lambeth Walk" 68, 88
Landeck 57, 79
Landquart 23
Lantschner, Gustav 125
Lauterbrunnen 23, 37, 46, 52, 56, 109
Lazenby, George 109
Lazutina, Larissa 119
Lebenberg Schloss, Kitzbühel 78
Lebenberg, Schloss, Kitzbühel 78
Lech 2, 59, 103
Legard, Percy 121
Legoux, Robert 111
Leigh, Edgie Broughton, 49
Leigh, Pennington 18
Leipzig 18
Leitner, Hias 112
Lenzerheide 41, 43
Lettner 61
Lever, Lord Harold 85
Leysin 3, 10
Lifted Stem Turn 60
Lilenfeld Pole 61
Lillywhites 61, 72
Lindsay, C. Scott 13
Lindsay, Major Hugh 126, 127
Lindsay, Peter 104
Lindsey, Jimmy 60
Linlithgow, Lady 25
Locharno Dance Chain 68
Lone Tree Club, Mürren 48
Longhi, Stefano 5
Longines 59
Lowe, Frank 85
Low, Erna 84
Loze, La, Courchevel 105
Lubomirsky, Prince 29
Lucan, Lord 85

Luges 13, 31, 37, 101
Lunn, Peter v, 57, 59
Lunn, Sir Arnold 20, 26, 50, 51, 54, 55, 56, 57, 69, 79, 80, 104, 105, 116, 137, 138
Lunn, Sir Henry 23, 30, 42, 43, 48, 52, 53, 68, 69, 84
Lytton, Earl of 39

M

Mackinnon, Esme 56
MacKintosh, Chris 49, 50, 52, 54, 55, 57
Macmillan, Harold 86
"Mac's Leap" 54, 154
Mainwaring, Martha 54
Mais, S.B. 52
Major, Olga 54, 55
Manchester Ice Rink 75
Manfried 45
Manufacturers Trust of America 79
Marden Club 58
Marden, Jock 54
Mariners of England 71
Mari Pia of Savoy, Princess 82
Markham, June 91
Marlbrough Cigarettes 117
Marples, Ernest 86
Marshall Aid 96
Martha's Meadow, Mürren 54, 56, 121
Martineau, Hubert 89
Mary's Cafe, Wengen 121
"Ma's Hell", Villars 54
Matterhorn 4, 7, 9, 48, 132
Matt, Rudi 93
Mavrogordato, E.E. 39
Maximilian of Furstenberg, Prince 23
Maxwell, Elsa 24
McNally, Paddy 132
Mechanised Transport Corps 90
Megève 103, 105
Menhuin, Sir Yehudi 103
Menshenger, Baron Carl 66
Menuires, Les 105
Méribel 95, 104, 105
Mersheng, Baron 109
Metzenthin 16
Meyer, Bror 75
Michael of Rumania, King 82
Migros 134
Milford Haven, Marquess of 86
Milne, A.A. 77
Mitchell, Harold 59
Mittersill, Schloss 86
"Modern Ski-ing" 59
Molitor, Karl 54

Molterer, Anderl 112, 114
Monch, Wengen 44
Montana 10, 13, 30, 31, 37, 43, 101, 137
Mont Blanc 3, 102, 103, 122
Monte Rosa 2, 4, 8, 13
Montgenèvre 42, 128
Montgomery, Field Marshal Lord Bernard 84, 89
Monti, Eugenio 90
Montreux 31
Moore, Roger 85
Moredy, W.W. 94
Morgan, John 132
Morgins 16, 30, 31, 72, 76
Moriond 105, 106
Morton, George 96
Morzine 103, 124
Moser 79, 91
Moutier 108
Movenpick 134
Mueller, Gerhard 96
Mugnier, Francis 105
Munich 18, 79
Munro, Hector 40
Murison-Small, Colin 132
Mürren, 33, 42, 44, 48, 49, 50, 54, 56, 64, 68, 69, 80, 84' 107, 109, 121
Murrs family 63
Museum of Antiquities, Zurich 31
Mussner, Walter 125

N

Nagano 115, 129
Napier, Colonel 1
NASA 90
Nash, Tony 32, 90
NATO Forces 89
Neiges Hotel, Des, Courchevel 83
New Hampshire 79
Niarchos, Stavros 102
Niven, David 103
Northesk, Lord 35, 73
Northland, Lord 35
Norwegian American Society 116
Nottingham Council 92
Nylon 95

O

Ogilvy, Sir Angus 89
"Oh God!" Scheidegg 54
"Olga's Wood", Mürren 54
Olympic Games 16, 31
        1908 London 16
        1924 Chamonix 73, 78

1928 St.Moritz 45, 73, 80
1932 Lake Placid 74, 75, 77, 80
1936 Garmisch Partenkirchen 58, 77
1948 St.Moritz 90
1952 Oslo 82, 89
1956 Cortina 114
1960 Squaw Valley 95
1964 Innsbruck 32, 90
1968 Grenoble 59
1976 Innsbruck 91
1984 Sarajevo 92
1992 Albertville 119, 125
1994 Lillehammer 119
1998 Nagano 92
2002 Salt Lake City 115
Onassis, Aristotle 102
Onassis, Christina 102
"On Her Majesty's Service" 109
Ordt Cup, Auffm 33
Orly Airport 108
Ossulston, Lord 41
"Over Greenland by Ski" 2

P

Palace Hotel 29, 50, 83, 132, 137
    St.Moritz 29, 132
Palais Glide 68, 88
Palmer-Tomkinson, Charles 126
Palmer-Tomkinson, Pati 127
Paris 12, 111, 112
Parsennbahn 97
Parsenn Derby Race 27
PAS 96
Paso Doble 76
Pass Thurn 121
Paula, Queen of the Belgians 84
Paul Jones Dance 68
Payert, Andree 99
Pearson, Michael 132
Pecar, Marjam 78
Penhall, William 5
Pennell, H 35
Pepys, Samuel 37
Perrens Family 8
Pestalozzi Village 91
Petain, Marshal 129
Philadelphia 31
Pierce, Wayne 128
Pinching, Eve 56
Pissaillas Glacier, Val d'Isére 81
Piz Corvatsch, St.Moritz 102
Plagne, La 111, 124
Plague Chapel 65

Planica Ski Jump 134
"Plum Pudding Hill", Wengen 54
Poiret, Paul 21, 22
Polytechnic, The 44
Pomagalski 96
Pontresina 24, 77, 84, 120
"Poor Little Angeline" 68
Pope Leo 63
Portes du Soleil 124
Post Hotel, St.Anton 43, 59, 63, 93
Post Hotel, St.Moritz 28
Prariond Refuge, Val d'Isére 81
Pravda, Christian 94, 112, 117
Praxmair's Cafe, Kitzbühel 65, 67
Praz, Hubert 86
Premier Neige Race 59
Propagation of the Gospel, Society for the 25
Public Schools Alpine Sports Club 43
Putin, President 119

R

R.A.F. 52, 80, 85
Railways 23, 37, 44, 45, 46, 57
Rainier, Prince 103
Reckitt Bobsleigh Challenge Cup 33
Red Devils, Kitzbühel 94
Reeb, Vicountess de 86
Regent's Park 16
Regina Hotel, Grindelwald 44
Regular's Ramble, Mürren 54
Reich Hotel, Kitzbühel 68
Reinalter, Edi, 112
Reisch, Burgomaster Franz 66
Reiss, Carol 117
Renault 117
Rendl, St.Anton 101, 132
Rhiner, Raymond 94
Rhodes, Daniel P. 7
Ribblesdale, Lady 36
Richardson, E.C. 26, 27
Richardson, Mrs T.G, 74
Richmond Ice Rink 90
Rickmers, W.R. 26
Riddell, James v, 52, 127, 137
Riefenstahl, Leni 78
Riffelalp Hotel, Zermatt 7, 8, 45, 64
Riffelberg Hotel, Zermatt 8, 59
Rifugio Averau 42
Rigg, Diana 109
Ritz, Caesar 13
Roberts of Kandahar, Lord 49
Robertson, Ronnie 90
Roche Blanche, Val d'Isére 126

Rockefeller 118
Rocque, Gilles de La 87
Roget, Professor 127
Rominger, Rudolph 112
Rosen, Dr. 79
Rossi, Count Theo 102
Rossignol Skis 106
Rothschild, Baron de 103
Rowley, Monica 21
Royal, Princess 75
Rubi, Christian 54
Ruti 14, 15

S

Saas Fee 107
Sachs, Gunter 82, 85
Sailer, Rudi 112
Sailer, Toni 112, 113, 114
Sainsbury 134
Salcher, Dr. 82
Sale-Barker, Audrey 50, 56, 87
Salt Lake City 115, 119
Salzburg 26, 61, 109
Samaranch, Juan Antonio 119
San Francisco 94
Sauze d'Oulx 122
Sawtooth Mountain 103, 104
Schaeuble, Dr. 10
Schagotsch, Frederich & Felix 103
Scheidegg 44, 45, 55, 69
Schilthorn, Mürren 50, 56
Schindlerkar, The, St.Anton 93
Schlick, Count 78
Schlumninger 51
Schneider, Hannes 59, 61, 63, 57, 59, 60, 61, 63, 64,
      79, 82, 93, 109, 116
Schneider Trophy, The 53
Schonegg Cafe, Wengen 40
Schranz, Karl 112, 113
Schuler, Karl 43, 57, 59, 64, 78, 79, 93, 109
Schuschnigg, Chancellor 60
Schuster, Betty 54
Schuster, Professor Oscar 2
Scone Palace 17
Scott, Barbara Ann 90, 116
Seden, "Mongoose" 52
Seehof Hotel, Arosa 10
Seelos, Toni 49, 55, 61
Seiler, Alexander 4, 7, 8, 9, 13, 64
Selfridge, Gordon 44
Seligman, Richard 1
Selkirk, Countess of 87; See also Sale-Barker, Audrey
Serpentine 16

Sestriere 47, 101, 103, 121, 128
Shaftesbury, Lord 11
Sharem, Princess 82
Sharp, Graham 90
Shuttlecock Club 34
Shylock 72
Siegel, Buggsy 86
Silvaplana 102
Silver Broom Trophy 30, 115
Silvester, Victor 68
Simeon of Bulgaria, King 82
Simpson, Mrs. Wallis 67
Sims, Tom 125
Skating Association of Great Britain, The National
      137
"Sketch, The" 69
Ski
      binding 63
      boots 114, 132
      downhill 28
      fashions 73, 95
      -joring 28, 29, 67
      jumping 78
      racing 44, 48, 56
      school 50, 59, 62, 63, 65, 78, 81, 82, 92, 93, 94,
            95, 100, 105, 112, 113, 116, 126, 129,
            134, 135
      slalom 52, 55, 56, 57, 58, 59, 61, 82, 88, 109,
            112, 114, 120
      wax 113
Ski Club of Great Britain, 38, 48, 85, 115
"Ski-ing for Beginners and Mountaineers" 26
"Ski-ing in a Fortnight" 59
"Ski-ing Technique" 59
Ski Jumping 78, 120
Ski Jumping Club, St.Moritz 28
"Ski Runner, The" 26, 59
"Ski Running" 26
Ski Safari, Kitzbühel 121
"Slip Cartilage Corner", Wengen 54
Smith, Harald 28
Soldenella Hotel, Wengen 25
Somerville, Crichton 26
"Sound of Music" 109
Southport Ice Rink 30
Spengler, Dr. Alexander 1
Sprecher, Bruno 126
Squaw Valley 59, 113, 118
St.Anton v, 43, 47, 57, 59, 63, 64, 73, 78, 79, 81, 82,
      83, 85, 86, 88, 93, 95, 99, 100, 101, 102, 108,
      109, 112, 128, 132, 134, 137
St.Bon 104, 105, 106
St.Christoph 94
St.Germain des Pres 111

St.Gervais 129
St.Jacob 121
St.Moritz v, 1, 3, 10, 12, 14, 16, 17, 18, 21, 23, 24,
    25, 27, 28, 29, 30, 32, 38, 39, 40, 41, 42, 43,
    44, 45, 54, 69, 72, 73, 75, 81, 82, 83, 84, 85,
    89, 90, 101, 102, 107, 108, 109, 112, 121, 125,
    126, 132
St.Moritz Bandy Club 18
St.Moritz Skating Association 16
St.Nicholas Bar, Courchevel 89
St.Peters 12
Starr, Cornelius 102
Steele 27
Steffani's Hotel, St.Moritz 28
Stem turn 2, 26, 60
Stephanie of Belgium, Princess 23
Stevens, Jocelyn 85
Stevenson, Robert Louis 37
Stick Riding 26
Stockli Glacier 129
"Story of Ski-ing, The" 59, 138
Stowe, U.S.A. 102
Strand Magazine 20
Strasser, Father 13
Stroltz Family 63
Strutt, Col. E.L. 18
Stuck, Hans von 81
Sturges, Hubert 87
Sunnegga Railway, Zermatt 123
Sun Valley 75, 97, 104, 124
"Sun Valley Serenade" 75
Supertravel 132
Suvretta House Hotel, St.Moritz 25, 41, 69, 75
Swan, Sir Kenneth 38
Swiss Ladies Open Ski Championship 56, 120
Syers, Edgar 27, 39
Syers, Madge 16
Symonds, John 13, 14

T

Tams, Jakob 73
Tarantaise Hydro-Electric Scheme 129
"Tatler, The" 46
Taylor, Elizabeth 103
Tcherkasova, Marina 117
Telemark Turn 2, 26, 27, 50, 60, 62
Tennerhof Hotel, Kitzbühel 67
Tennyson, Alfred Lord 23
Tesco 134
Tessier 104
Thams, Thullin 78
Thomas, E.M. 26
Thun, Lake of 44

Thyon 2000 121
Tignes 101, 121, 124, 129, 131, 132, 135
Tignes les Brevieres 121
Toboggan 14, 37, 48, 99
Tomlins, Freddie 74, 90
Torvill, Jayne 92
Towler, Diane 91
Tracy, Spencer 104
Trans-Andean Railway 46
Trefor 17
Trockner Steg, Zermatt 122
Trois Valleés, Les 106
Trotsburg, Count Anton 66
Tschols Family 63
Tsuma 121
Twentieth Century Fox 75
Tyrol 93, 124

U

Ulmer Hutt, St.Anton 83
Union Pacific Railway 104
Unita 134
Unter See Lake 33
Un-Yong, Kim 119

V

Val Claret 107, 121, 123, 124, 130
Val d'Isére v, 59, 65, 107, 113, 121, 123, 124, 126,
    129, 132, 135
Valluga, St.Anton 83, 102, 128
Val Thorens 103, 106, 121
Vandervell, H.E. 15
Venice 65, 113
Verbier 104, 108, 112, 121, 124, 132
Vermont 96
Via Lattea 122, 128
Victoria Hotel, Davos 13
Victoria, Queen 17
Vienna 29, 37, 66, 79, 81, 93, 101, 112
Villa Gentiana, Arosa 10
Villars 17, 44, 54, 76, 121
Visitors Club, Villars 54
Visp 64
Vives, Boix 106
Von Roll 122, 138
Vulture Perch, Cresta Run 34

W

Waghorn, Dick 53
Wakefield, Bishop of 43
Waldteufel 41
"Walk in the Black Forest" 88
Walser, Andrew 52, 53

Walter Restaurant, Grindlewald 40
Wartsaal, Wengen 46
Warwick, Earl of 85
Wasserngrat 85
Waterville, U.S.A. 125
Wedeln style 114
Wembley Lions 77
Wembley Stadium 77
Wengen 23, 25, 33, 40, 41, 42, 43, 44, 45, 48, 49, 50,
        52, 53, 54, 55, 56, 57, 62, 64, 68, 69, 72, 77,
        79, 95, 107, 121, 135
Wengen Ski Club 53
Wengernalp 45, 46
Westminster Ice Rink 30
Wetterhorn, Grindelwald 7
Wheble, Ursula 36
Whistler Gay Ski Week 88
White, C.J. 53, 62
"White Dream of Arlberg" 64
White, Graham 35, 108
White Hare Club, Andermatt 54
"White Horse Inn" 63
White Rose Club, Kitzbühel 86
Whitney, Stephen 31
Whymper, Edward 4
Wickham, Sir Henry 77
Wilkie, Reginald 76
William, German Crown Prince 25, 33
Wilson Bobsleigh Cub, The Fleetwood 33
World Cup 120
Wynyard, Capt. E.G. 18

Y

York, Duchess of 83, 132

Z

Zanuck, Darryl F. 104
Zdarski, Mathias 59
Zeller, Adolph 44
Zermatt v, 2, 3, 4, 5, 7, 8, 9, 13, 25, 44, 45, 47, 48,
        59, 64, 85, 94, 101, 107, 122, 123, 130, 132,
        133, 138
Zermatterhof Hotel, Zermatt 8, 9
Ziegler, Michael 108
Zogg, David 49, 112
"Zorba the Greek" 92
Zugspitze 123
Zurich 18, 24, 29, 31, 66, 122
Zurich Grasshopper Football Club 18